The Dilemma of Reform in the Soviet Union

The Dilemma of Reform in the Soviet Union

Timothy J. Colton

COUNCIL ON FOREIGN RELATIONS BOOKS

The Council on Foreign Relations, Inc., is a nonprofit and nonpartisan organization devoted to promoting improved understanding of international affairs through the free exchange of ideas. The Council does not take any position on questions of foreign policy and has no affiliation with, and receives no funding from, the United States government.

From time to time, books and monographs written by members of the Council's research staff or visiting fellows, or commissioned by the Council, or written by an independent author with critical review contributed by a Council study or working group are published with the designation "Council on Foreign Relations Book." Any book or monograph bearing that designation is, in the judgment of the Committee on Studies of the Council's board of directors, a responsible treatment of a significant international topic worthy of presentation to the public. All statements of fact and expressions of opinion contained in Council books are, however, the sole responsibility of the author.

Printed in the United States of America.

Library of Congress Cataloging-in Publication Data

Colton, Timothy J., 1947–
The dilemma of reform in the Soviet Union

Includes index.
1. Heads of state—Soviet Union—Succession.
2. Soviet Union—Politics and government—1953–1982.
3. Soviet Union—Politics and government—1982–
I. Council on Foreign Relations. II. Title.
JN6540.C64 1986 947.085'3 86-19744
ISBN 0-87609-014-5
ISBN 0-87609-013-7 (pbk.)

Contents

Acknowledgments

I am pleased to record not a few debts incurred in the preparation of this study. The first is to Robert Legvold, then of the Council on Foreign Relations and now of Columbia University, who first enlisted me in the project and contributed enormously as sounding board, critic, and editor to the writing of the first edition. Paul Kreisberg, Director of Studies of the Council, suggested that I revise the original monograph and provided useful suggestions on how to do so. Also of great help to me in thinking through the book's main outline were the array of experts who made presentations about a wide range of issues at a 1982–83 Council study group on Soviet internal affairs. The group was led by Professor Samuel P. Huntington, and the speakers included Jeremy Azrael, Seweryn Bialer, George Breslauer, Zbigniew Brzezinski, Gail Warshofsky Lapidus, Herbert Levine, William Odom, Richard Pipes, Dimitri Simes, and Douglas Whitehouse.

A number of colleagues were generous with reading of drafts of chapters in the original or the revised edition, access to unpublished research and data, and more generally with ideas. I have found ongoing dialogues with Thane Gustafson and Jerry Hough to be especially stimulating. I am deeply grateful as well for the assistance and encouragement of Professors Bialer, Breslauer, and Lapidus, all of them involved in the original Council study group, and of Lawrence Caldwell, John Campbell, Barbara Chotiner, Alexander Dallin, Paul Goble, Franklyn Griffiths, Werner Hahn, Ellen Jones, Robbin Laird, Dawn Mann, Michael Mandelbaum, T. H. Rigby, Blair Ruble, Marshall Shulman, Brian Silver, Strobe Talbott, Robert C. Tucker, and Alexander Yanov. David Kellogg, Jana Oldfield, Robert Valkenier, and Andrea Zwiebel gave excellent technical support, and Patricia J. Colton support of every kind. Finally, the Kennan Institute for Advanced Russian Studies of the Woodrow Wilson International Center for Scholars in Washington, D.C., provided a hospitable setting for completing the original draft.

—T.J.C., August 1986

Introduction

A famous Sovietologist of the senior generation used to tell his students that his textbook was so influential that every time an edition was published the leader of the Soviet Union either died or was overthrown. Inasmuch as the editions of his book came out in 1953, the year of Stalin's death, and 1963, shortly before the ouster of Khrushchev, some of us thought he had a point and wondered whether the textbook theory was not as sound as some of the others we were reading about. Our professor went on to explain that influence did not come without a price: the disappearances of the leader made half of what he had written in the respective versions of the textbook obsolete!

I have thought of my former teacher more than once during the several rounds of writing and rewriting this far more modest book. While I will not claim even in jest to have influenced anything, I now know at first hand the frustration of writing about events in motion and the worry that tomorrow's newspaper headlines will supersede what was written yesterday.

The initial outline of this essay was sketched in October 1982, before the opening of a series of Council on Foreign Relations seminars on the prospects for change in the Soviet system. The plan was to survey Soviet economic and social difficulties, do some background analysis on the Soviet political elite, and write a precis of the several paths that the Soviets might conceivably pursue after Leonid Brezhnev was gone. The series was barely under way, and the first chapter outlines barely on paper, when Brezhnev died on November 10, 1982.

Brezhnev's death closed a chapter of Soviet history exceptional for its stability and predictability. Now unpredictability seemed better to characterize the Soviet scene. Speculation immediately shifted to Yuri Andropov, the new General Secretary, who, it was thought, would have no more than five or six years to leave his mark on the Soviet Union. I joined my fellow Sovietologists in poring over Andropov's speeches, and the monograph was now designed as an introduction to the Andropov era in Soviet affairs. A draft along these lines was completed in the late spring of 1983. It would have appeared that autumn had my confidence, and that of the editors, not been shaken by the rumors that Andropov was seriously ill and by his strange disappearance from public view in August. In January 1984, assured by Soviet spokesmen and Western armchair analysts that Andropov would soon resume his duties, we sent a revised version to production. It was being set in type when Andropov died of kidney disease on February 9, 1984.

There was all too little time to fit Konstantin Chernenko into the picture before the monograph was finally published in the summer of 1984. Undeterred by the unmistakable signs that Chernenko would be a lame duck, and fastening more on underlying trends, the first edition argued that the internal course most likely to be taken as new leaders took charge was one of moderate reform. This was portrayed as a strategy to which the Soviet rulers would be turning with great reluctance, and which was fraught with difficulties and contradictions of its own, but which would be their way of responding to economic and social difficulties without losing political control.

Chernenko, of course, held office for a still shorter time than Andropov did. The accession on March 11, 1985, of Mikhail Gorbachev, at long last a representative of the emerging political generation about which so much had been speculated, altered the situation yet again, only this time much more decisively. Gorbachev promptly set about shaking up the higher echelons of the Communist Party and Soviet state as they had not been shaken in decades. Grigori Romanov, Nikolai Tikhonov, Viktor Grishin, Boris Ponomarev, and untold hundreds of lesser figures have been pushed out of the limelight. New names, hitherto known only to a few specialists in the West, have come to the fore: Nikolai Ryzhkov, Yegor Ligachev, Lev Zaikov, Eduard Shevardnadze, and Boris Yel'tsin, to mention only a few.

General Secretary Gorbachev, beginning with his first address as leader, has called for frank debate about Soviet problems, hailing the principle of *glasnost'* or publicity. In speech after speech he has demanded dynamism, decisiveness, socioeconomic "acceleration," "reconstruction" of economic management, and the like—

while often declining to give specifics of how he would improve the situation. At the Twenty-seventh Party Congress in early 1986 Gorbachev accused Leonid Brezhnev of letting the country down by "trying to improve matters without changing anything," and insisted that he, Gorbachev, favored "radical reform" in the economy.

This revised edition of *The Dilemma of Reform in the Soviet Union* aims to make these and other developments within the Soviet Union intelligible to the lay reader and student. It looks both backward and forward. In doing the latter, its time horizon is roughly ten years. The revision is necessitated chiefly by the Gorbachev phenomenon and by the challenge of accounting for what has happened, and what has not happened, since March 1985. Although Gorbachev has built on the initiatives begun by Andropov, he has also differed from him in some interesting ways, in domestic and in foreign policy. The second edition is expanded and not merely updated because, as the post-Brezhnev period unfolds and nagging problems begin at least to be examined more openly, the need for contextual information about them has increased. This modified version is still short as books go, but it is not as short as the original was because there is now more to explain, refute, and wonder about than there was originally.

Gorbachev's first months in office, in my view, validate the essential thesis put forward in 1984. They verify that the regime has little if any urge at this juncture to democratize the Soviet Union or embark on truly fundamental reforms of the political system, although considerably more willingness has been displayed than under Andropov to ease controls over the media and Soviet culture. Developments both in the social and economic environment of Soviet politics, and within the political and administrative stratum, have been further shown to be conducive to the bundle of limited but nonetheless significant innovations that I have labeled "moderate reform." In words if not yet nearly so clearly in deeds, Gorbachev and his colleagues have begun to depart from the plodding style and the pattern of consensual, status-quo-oriented decisions characteristic of the preceding two decades. Real progress, to repeat, has been modest, and even that has been controversial. There is considerable evidence to indicate that, although Gorbachev and his allies have had no small impact, they are not a monolithic group and theirs is not the only point of view within the wider elite. The possibility exists, therefore, of substantial resistance being directed against the proposed innovations and even of open discord erupting.

The structure of the book is similar to that of the first edition. Chapter 1 summarizes the ambiguous record of Brezhnev's eighteen years in power. Chapter 2 takes stock of the main problems, chief among them economic problems, now on the agenda of an evolving leadership. Chapter 3 treats the succession struggle and the larger trends within the Soviet elite, including the transition of generations and some important changes in personnel policy. The heart of the book is Chapter 4, which scans the Soviet system's several options and presents the case for moderate reform as the most tenable. It also suggests what kinds of concrete changes moderate reform would call for. Chapter 5 broadens the discussion to consider the links between Soviet domestic events and the world outside and the implications of change within the Soviet Union for Western policy.

It is important to nail down key terms at the outset. Politicians do not always display the consistency that the authors of definitions do. The Brezhnev leadership, though predominantly conservative, amalgamated elements of several different strategies, and some degree of mixing can safely be predicted for the future. It is useful, nonetheless, to start with the main choices as they look in their pure form, as it were, leaving the blending to the more detailed description. The Soviet Union's political choices in the 1980s and 1990s can be placed on a left-right spectrum corresponding roughly to the alternatives facing any contemporary society. At the left-hand pole is *revolution,* which brings about fundamental, rapid, and violent change. *Reform* involves improvement and change, but promoted by gradual and peaceful means. *Conservatism,* the main philosophy of the Brezhnev leadership, preserves the status quo and keeps change in abeyance. And *reaction,* at the right end of the spectrum, embodies backward change, a restoration of some previously superseded state of affairs.

Reform, the option most central to this study, bands together a wide range of actions and styles. It is useful, therefore, to differentiate among three types of reform. *Radical reform* is the closest to revolution: all-encompassing change containing as an essential component the restructuring of the country's political institutions and central, legitimating beliefs and myths. Radical reform is not at all likely to be carried out in the Soviet Union in the near future. *Minimal reform,* at the cautious extreme, entails relatively minor adjustments of policy and practice designed to cause the least possible disruption and conflict. Minimal reforms are often spliced onto a core conservatism, as happened in the USSR under Brezhnev. *Moderate reform,* the most likely course for the years immediately ahead, takes in the middle zone between radical and minimal reform. The moderate reformer, as distinct from the radical reformer, does not set out to remake his society's basic political structures and traditions. His targets are the more modest ones of government personnel, policy, and implementing machinery. But, in contrast to the minimal reformer, the changes he effects here are recognized as significant departures, not marginal ones. Working selectively within the existing institutional framework, the purveyor of moderate reform self-consciously alters the way rewards, privileges, and punishments are allocated in society. He accepts that one price of doing so will be overt and covert conflict over his program.

To see why moderate reform became a plausible avenue for the Soviet leadership to follow, it is necessary to begin with the record under Leonid Brezhnev and with the problems that ripened during his lengthy reign.

1
Brezhnev's Ambiguous Legacy

If durability alone constituted a claim to greatness, Leonid Il'ich Brezhnev would rank with the twentieth century's outstanding politicians. Already a fixture of the Soviet elite since the 1940s, he held one of the most powerful offices in the world, General Secretary of the Communist Party of the Soviet Union, for the eighteen years and twenty-seven days up to his death on November 10, 1982. Longer than that of any Soviet leader except Stalin, his reign stretched over more than one-quarter of the history of the Soviet system to date. Be that as it may, it was apparent before he died, and brought out into the open by his immediate successor, Yuri Andropov, that the political ledger of the Brezhnev years contained minuses as well as pluses. Against the accomplishments of Brezhnev and his associates in the regime's old guard, which cannot be denied, have to be set disappointments and looming problems. With the swift passing of the interim rule of Andropov and Konstantin Chernenko, Mikhail Gorbachev and younger politicians are now stepping into the shoes of the party elders and sorting out a decidedly ambiguous inheritance.

The Brezhnev Leadership Style

Brezhnev's legacy defies easy analysis. Although some in high places, Chernenko included, referred fondly after his death to a distinctively "Brezhnevite" (*brezhnevskii*) approach to governing, the attempt was short-lived and seemingly half-hearted.[1] Admirers and detractors alike have found less to say about Brezhnev the leader than about the era over which he presided. His rule, by the lights of the Soviet past, was oddly impersonal. Lenin was a revolutionary, Stalin a despot, and Khrushchev a flawed reformer, to follow the chapter headings of Western textbooks. But what was Brezhnev? What did he stand for, and what did he leave behind?

Part of the puzzle arises from the character of Brezhnev himself. The Brezhnev family name was derived from the Russian adjective for careful (*berezhnyi),* and the fit with the man seemed as apt as Stalin's surname having been drawn from the word for steel (*stal'*). In social situations, Brezhnev may have been, as he was with foreign statesmen in the 1970s, the soul of bonhomie. When it came to business, he was reticent and self-reliant, qualities that had stood him in good stead during his methodical climb up the Soviet political ladder. Before snatching the highest rung, Brezhnev did long tours of duty in the industrial Dnepropetrovsk area of the southern Ukraine, where he had been born in 1906, but he also served elsewhere in the Ukraine, in Belorussia, the Urals, Moldavia, the Virgin Lands of Kazakhstan, and Moscow, as well as on several fronts of World War II. He had been everything from farm laborer to agricultural administrator, metallurgical engineer, and municipal official, and eventually to military commissar, regional party viceroy, coordinator of Soviet defense and space programs, titular head of the Soviet state, and national party secretary sharing responsibility for organization and personnel. Throughout, he had been the consummate tactician, wedded to no particular strategy and a master at landing on his feet after setbacks. October 1964 found him in the inner circle of his old friend and patron from the Ukrainian party apparatus, Nikita Khrushchev, ideally situated to spearhead and exploit the first and only successful conspiracy against an entrenched Soviet leader.

As head of the party from 1964 to 1982, Brezhnev remained in many respects an elusive and enigmatic figure. His quirks and endearing gestures, few in number, were better known outside the country than inside. He did have his own policy priorities—such as building Soviet military might and modernizing the country's agriculture—but even these he touted in the manner of someone reeling off the minutes of a committee meeting. Given the chance in his ghost-written memoirs to show the Soviet public what made him tick, Brezhnev could think of nothing better to relate than how he had inherited his parents' proletarian rectitude. From his father, he confided, he had gained "stubbornness, patience, and the habit, once having started something, of without fail carrying it through to its conclusion," and from his mother "amiability, interest in people, and the knack of meeting trouble with a smile or joke."[2] Soviets who had known the rule of his predecessors were comforted and a touch amused by such blandness and by the sight of Brezhnev in his square-cut suits and oversized neckties, laboriously reciting speeches from note cards on the evening televison news. In most, Brezhnev evoked neither strong affection nor strong antipathy. Foreigners who tried to lure Soviet acquaintances into conversation about him more often than not drew only a shrug of indifference.

The murky nature of the Brezhnev era owed as much to the politics that carried him to power as it did to his unprepossessing personality. The 1964 palace revolt against Khrushchev was at its most basic a repudiation of Khrushchev's idiosyncratic operating mode. After denouncing Stalin and routing his Kremlin foes in 1956–57, Khrushchev had installed his own leadership team and pursued an ambitious but rowdy reform program. Ambivalent about how far change should be pushed, handicapped by his own prejudices and dreams of personal grandeur, and inhibited by more conservative colleagues, Khrushchev ended up lurching from one policy and fancy to another. In the process he often rode roughshod over the opinions and interests of his fellow leaders and of key sections of the Soviet establishment. If a Stalin, morally unconstrained and armed with more potent weapons of tyranny, could have gotten away with this, Khrushchev could not. He discovered too late, now that the Gulag labor camps had been largely emptied, mass terror had been foresworn, and the myth of the infallible leader had been exploded, that he was dictator enough to alienate the members of the power elite but not enough to cow them.

The new leaders, once Khrushchev had been safely relegated to his *dacha* and his name expunged from the public record, drew up what has been called a "charter of oligarchy" for the Soviet system.[3] They agreed to breathe life into the formula of "collective leadership," adopted after Stalin's death in 1953 but mocked by Khrushchev's push toward one-man rule. To underscore the commitment, the Central Committee passed a resolution that henceforth no single person would combine, as Stalin and Khrushchev each had done, the supreme positions in both the Communist Party and the Soviet government. Brezhnev ran the party machine only, while a second power in the Politburo, Aleksei Kosygin, became head of government, or Chairman of the Council of Ministers. For a time, in fact, Premier Kosygin was treated almost as General Secretary Brezhnev's co-equal.

Brezhnev step by step amended this understanding in his favor. Capitalizing on his powers of appointment, he implanted cronies from Brezhnev redoubts like Dnepropetrovsk and Moldavia in sensitive party and state posts and put together a strong personal secretariat. He cajoled and maneuvered to advance policies he favored and block those he opposed. By the early 1970s Brezhnev had asserted his primacy over Kosygin. Later in the decade he sent into early retirement Aleksandr Shelepin and Nikolai Podgornyi, the two most independent-minded of the authors of the 1964 coup. Beginning in 1976, an expansive leadership cult, though also a stilted one, took shape around Brezhnev—a personality cult without a personality, Soviet wags called it. Brezhnev birthdays became media events at which Soviet and foreign dignitaries weighed down his lapels with medals and ribbons. His memoirs were printed in huge editions, awarded a Lenin Prize, and made required reading in political education classes. His patchy war record was extolled, his hitherto unannounced position as Chairman of the Defense Council (the top-secret arbiter of Soviet national security) was given emphasis, and he was granted the military rank of full marshal. In June 1977 Brezhnev displaced Podgornyi as ceremonial head of state, or Chairman of the Presidium of the Supreme Soviet, a position he had gladly relinquished on a previous occasion (in July 1964) but which now seemed to gratify his growing ego.

Nevertheless, even as Brezhnev's power increased, the essentials of the 1964 charter of oligarchy remained in effect. Major members of the original anti-Khrushchev coalition, the likes of Mikhail Suslov, the party's chief ideologist, and Andrei Kirilenko, the national party secretary supervising economic coordination and many personnel decisions, retained their positions and spheres of influence. Even Kosygin, whose chilly relations with Brezhnev were one of the worst-kept secrets in Moscow, carried on as premier until shortly before his death in 1980. The ruling group was augmented by others, like Foreign Minister Andrei Gromyko, who wielded great authority in specific bailiwicks. It was revealing that, when the Brezhnev cult blossomed, his associates' praise fastened not on his brilliance in deciding things on his own (as was said of Stalin and Khrushchev), but on his success in fostering team decision-making. "One of the best qualities of Leonid Il'ich," stated the then first secretary of the Georgian party committee, Eduard Shevardnadze, in 1976, "lies in the fact that he does not don the mantle of a superman, that he does not think and work for everyone but, while making his own outstanding contributions to the common cause, creates the conditions under which all can think creatively."

This and other tributes were inspired most by the things Brezhnev did not do. He did not affect omniscience, he did not push others around, he did not sow "blind fear, egoism, envy, or suspicion."[4] Brezhnev himself, though far from bashful about his own exploits, was careful to save some credit for the other oligarchs. Replying to the toasts at a mawkish seventy-fifth birthday party (his last) in December 1981, the General Secretary returned to the theme of collaborative leadership. The strides made since 1964 were not his alone, he allowed, but the product of "true mutual understanding in the leadership . . . the practice of joint investigation and serious discussion . . . and the joint taking of decisions."[5]

If Brezhnevism resists pigeonholing, therefore, this reflects the political settlement around which it was fashioned. Power at the apex of the system was divided and shared, notwithstanding Brezhnev's symbolic mastery and the humbling of some of his early allies. As for the kingpin of the regime, he was temperamentally suited to its colorless image and far less gripped than previous bosses by strong ideas that he wished to impose on those around him.

The Three Faces of Brezhnevism

A more fundamental factor obstructs a smooth assessment of the Brezhnev period. Whatever is said about power relations and personalities, we are left with a chronicle of action that is complex and less than fully consistent. The leadership followed not one but three main lines of domestic policy—conservative, reactionary, and timidly reformist—and among these there were both overlap and contradiction.

It was far from clear at the outset which way the Brezhnev Politburo would lean. A gut conservatism was evident in their early statements, yet there were other straws in the wind as well. Khrushchev's removal cheered neo-Stalinists in the establishment, owing to whom Moscow in the winter of 1964–65 was abuzz with rumors of an impending rehabilitation of Stalin and roundup of thousands of politically unreliable citizens.[6] From a different angle entirely, an opening was also seen in the early months by partisans of concerted economic and social reforms, changes that would have outdone Khrushchev's and built on some of the ideas floated in the comparatively open political climate of the late Khrushchev period. One group of economic advisers, at work since 1962 on a study of Western economic systems, reported in 1965 that capitalism had features that could be selectively adopted in the Soviet Union. A number of Soviet economists and managers "clearly favored a basic change in the balance between markets and central planning," and Aleksei Kosygin, in particular, indicated sympathy with this point of view.[7] An ambitious plan to enlarge the autonomy of enterprise managers and lessen the powers of central planners to meddle in plant operations was proclaimed, though already in compromise form, in September 1965.

By this time, there was little doubt that conservatism was to be the foremost of the several strands of policy. The oligarchs under Brezhnev wanted nothing more than to give the USSR, and themselves, a chance at stability and equilibrium after the turbulence of the Khrushchev years. Their conservative bent was best exemplified in the area of personnel. Most members of the Soviet elite, first achieving prominence after the terrible purges of the 1930s, had lived with the constant threat of disgrace or oblivion during Stalin's lifetime. The lifting of this cloud after the death of Stalin had only whetted their appetite for greater security and dignity, but these were denied them by Khrushchev, who hired and fired freely on the basis of policy and whim and in 1961 had the party rules revised to require regular rotation of the membership of party committees. To the thousands of office-holders who make up the Soviet political machine, Brezhnevism translated above all into the novel notion that they had the right to retain their positions indefinitely, barring gross incompetence or physical incapacity. Turnover at all levels was unhurried: changes within the Politburo proceeded at a third of the rate of the Khrushchev period, and membership in the Central Committee "almost took on the appearance of a life peerage."[8] The 1961 rule on the turnover of party committees was rescinded. Staffing was put on a more orderly footing, as promotees now came chiefly from within the given agency or territory. When demotion from a major post occurred, it was done quietly and the pill was often sweetened by appointment to a sinecure in Moscow or an ambassadorship abroad.

This convention of "respect for cadres," as it came to be known, had a corollary: "trust in cadres," which signified the enlarging of officials' authority and of their leeway in carrying out their functions. Brezhnev rationalized the resultant diffusion of power on good conservative grounds as an overdue expression of faith in the human products of the Soviet system: "It has been a long time since there grew up in our midst qualified cadres, able to resolve correctly all the questions falling within their competence. We must trust them more and accordingly make them responsible for more."[9] There was to be for the first time a presumption of the proficiency of the administrator, be he government minister, party secretary, factory or farm director, army general, or city mayor. It was implied if not stated that, so long as public duties were discharged passably well, the leadership would not poke into the functionary's private affairs.

A pro-establishment conservatism was no less apparent when it came to institutions and ideology. Khrushchev had treated the units of the party and state apparatus like building blocks that he could stack at will to suit the slogans and enthusiasms of the hour. Ill-considered changes—for example, the 1957 abolition of most of the industrial ministries in favor of regional economic councils, the 1962 bifurcation of the local organs of the party into separate urban and rural branches, and the heaping on of coordinating bureaus and committees—had antagonized the bureaucracy without contributing to efficiency. Within months of his fall, most of his restructurings were erased and an indefinite moratorium was declared on big reorganizations. Also frowned on was Khrushchev's populist incitement of amateur and public interference in administrative decisions.

Similarly, after an initial period of hesitation, the Brezhnev Politburo decided to choke the flow of doctrinal invention to a trickle and to limit formal Marxist ideology mainly to legitimation of the status quo. The new catchphrases for Soviet reality, "developed socialism" and "real socialism," exuded self-satisfaction, and the major programmatic declaration of the Brezhnev era, the 1977 Soviet Constitution, presented little more than "a generally pragmatic statement of already existing practice and principle."[10] Brezhnevite propaganda gave pride of place to the symbols of continuity and stability beloved of conservative regimes everywhere: patriotism, duty, army, the feats of the elder generation, the benevolent state. Particularly after détente brought closer dealings with the West in the early 1970s, incantation of tired jargon was justified by a purportedly intensifying "ideological struggle" with capitalism.

Beginning with the trial of the nonconformist writers Andrei Sinyavskii and Yuli Daniel in February 1966, active measures were taken to combat ideological deviance, especially by individuals and groups wanting a more permissive stance toward intellectual and cultural self-expression. When tighter editorial controls were clamped on the literary magazine *Novyi mir* (New World) and other previously outspoken publications, this as much as anything drove a troubled minority of intellectuals to profess open dissent against the regime. Although mass arrests and show trials were avoided, and opposition persisted in muted form, almost all the leading dissidents were eventually silenced by police checks, character assassination, incarceration (for a relative few, confinement in psychiatric hospitals), and internal and foreign exile. In the same key, Soviet tanks were used in August 1968 to smother the radical reforms begun by Alexander Dubček's government in allied Czechoslovakia. Thirteen years later, the threat of another invasion helped bring about the crushing of the Solidarity movement by the Polish armed forces.

A prime beneficiary of the leadership's aversion to risk was the Soviet military establishment, the ultimate guarantor of the security of the regime and its foreign clients. Notwithstanding the tendency toward improvement in East-West relations and in the country's strategic position generally, the defense effort was given as large a bite of national resources as in more parlous times. Military spending, which Brezhnev liked to pose as a "sacred duty" of the party, grew in step with the Soviet economy, that is, by 4 to 5 percent a year until the mid-1970s and at maybe half that rate afterward. These outlays financed an expansion and upgrading of both nuclear and conventional forces, including the building of a blue-water fleet and of other forces for projecting military power to areas remote from Soviet frontiers. Military manpower drifted up to almost the level it had been at when Khrushchev started his troop cuts in the mid-1950s. The Brezhnev regime also extended the civil defense program, allowed retired and reserve army officers into the secondary schools to conduct pre-draft military training and war games, and imposed a regimen of "military-patriotic education" on the mass media, youth, and sports organizations. Beginning in 1973, a seat in the party Politburo was reserved for the Minister of Defense: Marshal Andrei Grechko until his death in 1976, and Dmitri Ustinov after that.

Conservatism and circumspection also infused the Brezhnev leadership's approach toward making public policies. From the beginning, its professed orientation was "scientific" and "objective." Grand policy problems were to be factored into digestible subproblems, and remedies set only after planning and empirical testing in conformity with clear procedures—the antithesis of Khrushchev's "voluntaristic" brainstorms and crusades. Consultation was to be close with the established authorities in the area, among whom the regime numbered not only officials in the government, party, and military hierarchies but scientifically and technically trained specialists at a remove from the administrative machinery. Specialists were to be valuable lightning rods for criticism and insurance against policy mistakes. Brezhnev thought enough of their role to endorse it in his first major speech as head of the party, saying that the regime should "treasure" them and "rely on their knowledge and experience."[11] As in other countries, deference to bureaucrats and specialists tended to produce narrowly focused decisions and, at most, gradual modifications of established policy, not bold departures from it. Unless the Politburo had strong preconceptions about a problem, experts and what the Soviet lexicon calls "the interested agencies" (*zainteresovannye organizatsii*) were left to themselves to thrash out disputes through analysis and bargaining, with a minimum of intrusion from on high.

If conservatism was the foundation of Brezhnevism, it by no means made up the complete structure. Some of the regime's actions went beyond preservation of the status quo to outright reaction, working to turn back the clock rather than glue its hands in place. One reactionary policy of great moment was the cutting-short of the de-Stalinization pressed in fits and starts by Khrushchev.[12] Sensational disclosures about Stalin's misdeeds ceased to be made after the Twenty-third Party Congress in 1966. The brutal and irrational features of the Stalin era were largely glossed over in party texts, while Stalin's reputation as leader of the Soviet industrialization drive and wartime commander-in-chief was restored, especially in works for mass consumption. Returned to grace in much the same way was the KGB, the security police force, which had perpetrated many of Stalin's worst atrocities and was still generally feared and resented for its snooping and arbitrary powers. Especially after the appointment of Yuri Andropov as its chief in 1967, the KGB's image was burnished, the scope of its domestic and foreign activity widened, and its representation in decision organs of the party increased.[13] Without this rehabilitation—capped by the elevation of Andropov to full Politburo membership in 1973, the first time a head of the secret police had sat in that body since the death of Stalin—Andropov's coming to power after Brezhnev's death would have been unthinkable.

The relentless campaign to glorify the epic victory in the "Great Patriotic War," World War II, was another backward-looking policy, disseminated through traditional propaganda channels, the best-selling memoirs of Soviet generals, and the television sets now found in most Soviet living rooms. Leonid Brezhnev, its most ardent champion, seemed at some moments almost to want to bring bygone days back to life: "The war ended long ago, but in our memory there still sound the voices of our fallen dear ones, our friends, our brother soldiers. We see their faces, our hands feel their firm handshakes, we remember what they talked about and what we dreamed of together."[14] More broadly, official interest in Russian history, folklore, and art reached a new crescendo during Brezhnev's term of office. The bulldozing of historical buildings to make way for new construction was slowed in Moscow and many provincial towns, and millions of rubles were spent restoring run-down landmarks, among them Russian Orthodox churches. A year never went by without the extravagant observance of at least one big political or institutional anniversary. A similar upsurge of government interest in historical roots occurred in most of the non-Russian republics. The regnant mood was often one of nostalgia, of a quest, as one aged army marshal termed it in 1981, for bridges "to connect the past with the present, yesterday with tomorrow."[15]

It would be wrong to make too much of this backpedaling. The reinstatement of Stalin, as an example, was incomplete in that it sidestepped his crimes and purges, the victims of which continued one by one to be exonerated. In 1969 the Politburo expressly rejected a bid by pro-Stalin forces in the party and the arts to whitewash his entire career.[16] Suspicions ten years later that the hundredth anniversary of Stalin's birth would bring his total exoneration came to naught. The KGB, although also boosted in status, remained under tight party control, never approaching its place under Stalin as a predatory state within a state. Repugnant though its dealings were, they were a far cry from the horrors of the earlier era, when the political police had their own kangaroo courts, used physical torture, and murdered their countrymen and banished them to Siberia almost as a normal constabulary hands out traffic tickets. Likewise with the veneration of the Russian heritage: by the early 1970s, censors and editors were instructed to tone down extreme versions, such as had been associated with the youth magazine *Molodaya gvardiya* (Young Guard) and with religious groups, and Russian nationalists in the party were warned to square their views with Marxism-Leninism.[17]

By and large, the reactionary side of Brezhnevism dovetailed with its core conservatism. But how did these two qualities fit with a third, namely, Brezhnev's circumscribed reformism? There is no denying that the Brezhnev leadership turned up its nose at radical reform, regarding democratization of the brand advocated by Dubček in Czechoslovakia as heresy and shunning the freewheeling if less systematic changes attempted by Khrushchev. Nevertheless, Brezhnev and his colleagues did originate or tolerate a great many minimal reforms—piecemeal policy changes intended to ease specific problems or allay the frustrations of particular groups in the establishment or the population without seriously altering the system. Some were motivated by the desire to stave off more far-reaching reforms, but this did not obviate the fact that they occurred and that they made a perceptible difference at the time.

The at-heart conservative instincts of Brezhnev's coalition coexisted uneasily with this third tendency. Even so, Brezhnev's stabilizing policies, and also a few of his reactionary ones, at times tallied surprisingly well with the spirit of minimal reform. Thus, certain backward-looking developments in the cultural realm—the attention to old buildings, the authorization of movies and books casting traditional village life in a positive light, and the boom in patriotic and World War II lore, to name several—were welcomed by many and perhaps most Soviets. Though past-oriented, to the average person these adjustments amounted to a kind of reform. Conservation of prerevolutionary historical sites and buildings, ridiculed by Khrushchev, became a truly mass cause during the Brezhnev years, pursued in the Russian Republic by a semi-independent voluntary association, the All-Russian Society for the Preservation of Historical and Cultural Landmarks, founded in 1965 and soon signing up more than 10 million dues-paying members. Writers affiliated with the "ruralist" school, like Fedor Abramov, Vladimir Soloukhin, and Valentin Rasputin, reached huge and willing audiences with their novels and essays lamenting the negative effects of industrialization and romanticizing the threatened Russian village. On issues such as these, regime policies probably responded to public opinion as much as they did shape it.

A similar intertwining of ostensibly opposing tendencies could be found in the regime's more reassuring personnel policy. It was the very conservative and security-oriented mentality of the new leaders that led them to break with the peremptory ways of treating officials common in the Soviet past. As one Western scholar has observed, to the extent that Brezhnev scrapped the essentially Stalinist practices of arbitrary dismissal of officials and capricious redefinition of their duties, he in his own fashion "pushed the reform of Stalinism further than Khrushchev did."[18]

The same can be said of the oligarchy's conservative partiality toward businesslike determination of social and economic objectives and scientific choice of policy instruments. This position, and the mobilization of think-tanks and experts accompanying it, had a settling effect on government policy, averting the gyrations and "harebrained schemes" over which Khrushchev came to grief. By the same token, the new-found preoccupation with knowledge, rationality, and the "scientific-technological revolution" made the authorities more amenable to temperate, problem-solving change within the confines of the existing order.

One of the regime's very first acts was to disavow Trofim Lysenko, the vicious charlatan who, with backing in the Kremlin, had warped Soviet biology and agricultural science since the late 1940s and on whose behalf Khrushchev had blustered about disbanding the revered Academy of Sciences. It was as strong a gesture as could be given to the intelligentsia that ham-handed political meddling in the work of competent and loyal specialists was to be curtailed.[19] This and other new guidelines had the potent side-effect of accelerating the movement begun in Khrushchev's time toward fuller public airing of policy questions. Whereas ideology at the highest level stagnated after 1964, the elbowroom of the professional or adviser interested in middle-level questions was expanded in nearly every field of policy. Avoidance of grand theory, state secrecy, and the immunity of senior officials from personal criticism meant that policy debates tended to be compartmentalized and on the bookish side. Participants were expected to make their suggestions in an upbeat tone and not to dwell on past mistakes. And, since political taboos and the ultimate power of the party remained, an indiscreet editor or institute director could still be called on the carpet. Yet, the richer coverage and discussion of policy questions should impress anyone delving into Soviet publications of the day.[20] Discussants became defter at finding loopholes in formal doctrine and at selectively using it to their advantage. Social scientists and even officers of the party were permitted and urged to do public opinion polls and incorporate the results into their recommendations.

In the economic sphere, the contested issues included decentralization of socialist planning and management, investment strategy, the country's worsening energy problem, the USSR's relation to the world economy, the reasons for the slow progress of Soviet technology, wages and incomes policy, and the role of the peasants' private plots in agriculture. Soviet jurists and administrative experts differed openly on the division of labor between prosecutors and defense lawyers, the handling of citizens' complaints, the possibility of running more than one party-approved candidate in Soviet elections, the place of the trade unions, juvenile delinquency, the relative powers of central and local agencies, and the best means of countering the increase in official corruption. Among the social controversies of the Brezhnev period were those over pollution, income equality, affirmative action for disadvantaged ethnic groups, demographic trends, nature versus nurture as determinants of human behavior, urban and regional planning, the decay of village life, women's rights, the needs of the elderly, alcoholism, and the effects of television. Culture and the arts, though subject to more stifling party scrutiny, also spawned controversy over issues of style and substance running from the future of the burlesque theater to the merits of post-modernist architecture. In short, the same regime that locked dissidents in psychiatric clinics and outlawed proposals for radical change also countenanced the most candid debate seen in Soviet Russia since the 1920s on all manner of within-system issues.[21]

Many Western readers will have to be reminded that the oligarchy's actual policy choices under Brezhnev, in the early years in particular, also embodied a good deal of pragmatic adaptation. They involved "marginal adjustments, evolving experiments, and creeping innovations within the system," not abrupt divergence from precedent, but their cumulative significance cannot be denied.[22] In the crucial field of economic management, the Kosygin reform of 1965 was conceived as a move toward "intensification" of economic growth, to be followed up by further changes as needed. Emphasizing price and profit incentives, managerial autonomy, and product innovation, it was a major concession to decentralization.[23] Unfortunately for the decentralizers, the reform was closely identified with Kosygin and never had Leonid Brezhnev's full support. When Kosygin's star waned in the late 1960s and the decentralization was obstructed by the reinstated industrial ministries, Brezhnev had it rolled back in favor of strengthened central planning. The merger of individual factories into large "production associations," beginning in 1973, further downgraded enterprise management.

This reversal did not bring an end to all economic innovation. Central decision-making itself was improved by more sophisticated data collection and the adoption of mathematical forecasting techniques. Gosplan, the State Planning Committee, instituted automated systems for numerous functions, and computers began to be introduced in the planning and ministerial establishments. Soviet ideas on management science and related questions were tugged into the international mainstream, despite "bureaucratic lethargy and even fierce resistance from conservative forces in the Soviet establishment."[24]

The Brezhnev leadership also remained receptive to economic innovation in the form of experiments, small-scale field trials of new ideas at the level of the individual plant or locality. Dozens of such experiments were run, most of them at local initiative and most aimed at increasing productivity. The odd experiment, such as the effort (originating under Khrushchev) to introduce small "link" work teams into the collectivized farm system, foundered when its patrons ran afoul of well-placed conservative opponents.[25] More commonly, the Politburo's attitude was benign, though it rarely imposed the experiments across the board. It recommended general adoption, for instance, of one of the earliest and most famous experiments, that directed against industrial overmanning at the Shchekino Chemical Combine near Tula in 1967. New techniques of "social planning" were put to the test in other large enterprises and urban areas, tying productivity to improvements in working conditions and social services; job placement bureaus, based on a critique of Soviet manpower policy, were pioneered in the cities of Ufa and Kaluga; some local governments, beginning with the city of Orel, asserted greater control of the construction of housing and urban amenities and pooled ministerial resources for municipal purposes; experiments in worker participation, including the election of shop foremen, were given a try at a series of Soviet factories.[26]

In the area of popular welfare, the Brezhnev regime implemented low-key reforms that went beyond experimentation. Brezhnev personally was most interested in food production and improvements in the Soviet diet. From his first months in office, he threw his political weight behind an unprecedented drive to build up the neglected farm economy. Agriculture's share of total investment in the economy marched from 20 to 27 percent (it is about 5 percent in the United States), as the better part of one trillion rubles was lavished on irrigation and land reclamation projects, rural electrification, farm machinery, and the like. So deep was Brezhnev's belief in this spending that he doggedly persevered with it even when evidence mounted that it was being inefficiently used. The bulk of the hard-won increment to grain production was used to feed livestock and fowl and thereby put more meat, dairy goods, and eggs on the Soviet family's table.

Provision of consumer goods and services also benefited from greater Kremlin attention. Compared to Khrushchev (to say nothing of the abysmal conditions under Stalin), the Brezhnev administration "demonstrated greater pragmatism in confronting the consumer sector [and] greater willingness to disregard the ideological implications of consumerism."[27] In the second half of the 1960s, spurred by budgetary reallocations and pressure on heavy industry to manufacture more consumer goods, per capita consumption surged by over 5 percent a year, a postwar zenith for the Soviet Union. The 1971–75 five-year plan was the first in Soviet history to peg the rate of growth of light industry and consumer goods higher than that of heavy industry. That result was not in fact achieved, but in 1981 the leadership wrote a similar dictate into its final five-year plan. Between 1970 and 1980, although rates of growth of consumption tapered off from the late 1960s, they sufficed to raise the percentage of Soviet families owning refrigerators from 32 to 86, television sets from 51 to 83, washing machines from 52 to 70, and cars from 2 to 9.[28]

In social policy, the Brezhnev Politburo is best known in the West for its inegalitarian expansion of the network of closed clinics, stores, dining rooms, and like facilities. Catering only to senior officials and other favored groups, who together constituted at most several percent of the population, they gained importance in the elite's eyes as economic conditions worsened in the second half of the Brezhnev period. For Soviet citizens below this thin crust, however, the regime's policy was broadly egalitarian, persevering with the leveling trend begun under Khrushchev, away from the wide social disparities common in Stalin's Russia. The spread in earnings was shrunk further, as wages were hiked at the bottom of the scale and virtually frozen at the upper end.[29] The prices of most foodstuffs, consumer staples, housing, and transportation were held constant, a practice that favored the more poorly paid.

Meanwhile, farm incomes, traditionally much inferior to urban incomes, were raised more rapidly than the average. Soviet peasants were brought fully into the social security web, given pension and other benefits previously unavailable to them, and they were also issued internal passports that added to their mobility and marked the final elimination of the serf-like status to which they had been reduced by Stalin's collectivization of agriculture. Construction of rural housing, roads, and schools was much better funded than before 1964. A special program was started in 1974 to improve life in the non-black-earth zone of central Russia, one of the most impoverished parts of the country.

Ecological concerns, to take another area of incremental reform under Brezhnev, aroused far greater notice than ever before. The emotional fight to protect Lake Baikal in eastern Siberia from pulp and paper mills and other polluters, joined under Khrushchev and waged openly in the Soviet media in the late 1960s, marked a turning point. Pro-growth forces in the industrial and hydropower bureaucracies fought back, but "official receptiveness was sufficiently strong and consistent to enable environmental advocates to [develop] an institutional and professional base, from which they now participate regularly . . . in the mechanism of policy formation."[30] The government in 1973 quintupled annual investment in water quality, and over the course of the 1970s more than fifty pieces of national legislation on pollution control were put on the books and a host of new enforcement agencies set up. In the cities, planning and construction were made more responsive to local climate, topography, and architectural tradition.

Another cautious innovation of the Brezhnev period was the move toward greater openness to, and interaction with, the outside world. Economic intercourse with the capitalist countries, given respectability by Khrushchev in the 1950s after years of Stalinist autarchy, continued and deepened. In the wake of the poor 1972 harvest, the regime for the first time committed itself to routine purchases of immense quantities of foreign-grown grain, both to make up for shortfalls in bad crop years and to allow quicker startup of the livestock-raising program. In the period 1976–81 alone, Soviet longshoremen unloaded 69 million tons of corn and 64 million tons of wheat bought on the world market, about 40 percent of it from the United States.[31] Just as massive grain purchases were used to offset the weakness of domestic agriculture, so imports of high-technology goods and know-how were employed to assist Soviet industry. Shelving some early reservations, Brezhnev was converted to this policy by 1970, when the Soviets with a new urgency entered the market for Western licenses, advanced machinery, and even whole factories—such as the Kama Automotive Works, supplied by Ford, which now makes the best trucks in the Soviet Union.[32] Overall, bolstered by détente and the windfall profits from Moscow's oil and gold sales in the 1970s, trade with the United States, Western Europe, and Japan reached over one-third of the Soviet total in the latter half of the decade, up from one-fifth in 1965. Soviet professionals and managers were given greater opportunities to travel and study abroad, read European and North American publications, and discuss foreign concepts and practices without at first ritually condemning them. As direct and mediated contacts with foreign, especially Western, ideas and personnel were destigmatized, a large domestic constituency with a thirst for more contact was created.

Stereotypes to the contrary, there were also ginger reforms in the area of individual liberties. The rough and systematic (though almost never lethal) stamping out of cultural and political dissent was one side to regime policy, producing martyrs known the world over. Conversely, as is often omitted from Western accounts, the Brezhnev regime relaxed controls over not a few other facets of Soviet life.[33] It greatly moderated the Khrushchev-era persecution of religion, the harassment of private production and sale of food, and the pressure for conformity in matters such as dress and hair style. The five-day work week, instituted in the late 1960s, freed up leisure time for the industrial work force. In a move predicted by almost no one, some 400,000 Soviet citizens, mostly of Jewish, German, and Armenian descent, were permitted to emigrate, numbers unheard of since shortly after the Russian Revolution. Communication with relatives and friends outside the Soviet bloc was much eased, and there was a letup in the jamming of foreign radio broadcasts. Censorship in literature remained oppressive, though even here there was a proliferation of less restricted journals serving the needs of specialized groups of readers.[34] Meanwhile, state fetters were perceptibly loosened in some of the other arts, including cinema, music (especially popular music, where Western jazz and rock made big inroads), and architecture. Grudgingly, Brezhnev's Politburo made its peace with movie anti-heroes, the boogie-woogie, and, where they could be afforded, buildings that would not look out of place in Munich or St. Louis. It seemed to accept that it was "compelled to deal with the public's actual cultural preferences, rather than considering them putty from which a New Soviet Man would be formed," and, when it reconciled itself to this, "it did so without bothering to justify itself ideologically."[35]

The Loss of Vigor and Direction

Brezhnev's policies were an alloy of conservatism, reaction, and muted reformism. His Politburo was neither a collection of cardboard villains nor, as it was lampooned by some in the West, a "regime of clerks."[36] As originally conceived, Brezhnev's conservatism was flexible and adaptive. What is more, for a time it worked tolerably well. At home, Brezhnev could with some credibility talk on the occasion of his seventieth birthday in December 1976—the high-water mark of the regime's declared optimism—of "great things accomplished . . . under the leadership of the party" since his accession. Communist rule seemed more unassailable than ever The regime's blend of policies was widely accepted among the population and strategic elites. Brezhnev personally was spared the ignominy that befell his predecessor. In foreign policy, Brezhnev could trumpet that "never before over the length of its entire history has our country enjoyed such authority and influence in the world."[37] The Soviet Union had attained nuclear parity with the United States and détente with the Western alliance, contained the Chinese threat, maintained its imperial holdings in Eastern Europe, and acquired new beachheads in the Third World.

It is fair to say that the euphoria voiced by Brezhnev in 1976 died before he did. The closing years of his administration were marked by reverses and self-doubts at sharp odds with the smugness of his birthday speech. The 1972 corruption scandal in the Georgian republic and the bad harvest of the same year, an early warning on the economic front, were thought by most Soviets to have been isolated occurrences, and many took a similar view of 1975's crop shortfall and, in foreign relations, the skirmish with the United States over Angola. In fact, these events foretold a more general onset of difficulties as the decade wore on. Some could be written off to bad luck. For example, annual increases to the work force, the product of fertility and mortality rates beyond the Kremlin's immediate control, began to decline in the mid-1970s. There was an inexplicable onset of foul weather in many parts of the country in the winter of 1978–79, which snarled railroad transport and helped send agricultural output tumbling for four straight years. Petroleum exploration in the rich west Siberian fields turned up smaller reserves than previously thought. The value of Soviet natural resources, which dominate its export trade, dropped sharply due to trends in world commodity prices after 1980, and this cost the Soviets billions in foreign exchange.

What is most striking about the troubles of the late Brezhnev years, however, is how wide-ranging they were. There was ample evidence that there was more to the regime's problems than mishap, that some quite basic formulas were no longer working as expected. The Brezhnev leadership stumbled badly in several foreign-policy arenas: witness the demise of U.S.-Soviet détente and the stalemate in arms control talks, the bogging down of the Soviet Army in Afghanistan after the December 1979 invasion, the peaceful revolt against Moscow's client regime by the Polish working class the following year.

More noticeable yet were the storm flags in domestic affairs, and especially in the economy. Worries about sagging growth rates and productivity, and about demographic and other trends that might exacerbate matters, were being voiced in the early 1970s. But they prepared Soviet planners poorly for the harrowing experience of drafting and executing the Tenth Five-Year Plan, covering the years 1976–80. Struggling to cushion the defense budget and social programs, and banking on the soundness of Brezhnev's conservative management policy, the Politburo pared growth and investment targets. Instead of the hoped-for intensification, or efficiency-driven growth, it got the opposite: shortages of key raw materials, among them iron ore and coking coal, which contributed in a major way to shortages in rolled steel products and important chemicals; a slump in oil production, necessitating in 1977 a crash program to bring on stream Siberian oil and natural gas reserves; a massive underfulfillment of the plan in agriculture; near gridlock in parts of the transportation system; a higher mountain of unfinished construction projects; and pressure on both the military budget and consumer welfare. Overall industrial growth slid by 2.6 percent in 1976, the largest drop in any single year since 1950. In sector after sector throughout the late 1970s and early 1980s, "once the break in trend occurred, performance continued to deteriorate erratically along the new, steeply declining trend line."[38] As imbalances multiplied, "plan discipline" was undermined, midyear revisions in production plans being made in each year from 1979 on.

Had Brezhnev left the scene in the mid-1970s, he would have been remembered by most Soviets for piloting their country through a decade of comparative prosperity and tranquility. As it was, he overstayed his time, augmenting and enjoying his personal power but making no real effort to use it to address emerging problems. The wind had shifted and previously uncharted reefs had come into view, but the ravages of old age, if nothing else, made it increasingly unlikely that Brezhnev would be the one to change compass. Following a bad heart attack in 1975, Brezhnev alternated between illness and semi-recuperation—aided toward the end by a pacemaker, round-the-clock nursing care, and, according to the Moscow diplomatic grapevine, the ministrations of a Georgian faith healer. He finished his rule a semi-invalid who had difficulty remembering, hearing, and speaking clearly and who, some of the Soviet foreign policy establishment claim, was given to emotional breakdowns, with outbursts of weeping, in the course of ordinary Politburo sessions. Though he was reported to be considering voluntary retirement in 1982, he had groomed no obvious heir and made no provision for an orderly power transition. More and more of his time seemed wasted on the trappings of office and reverie about the past.

On matters of political staffing, the main prerogative of a Soviet General Secretary, the aging Brezhnev showed increasingly unsound judgment. The strongest sign of this was his winking at behavior by high officials that brazenly flouted regime mores. He stood by a national police chief, Interior Minister Nikolai Shchelokov, who, it was alleged later, connived in widespread influence-peddling in his organization and lined his own pockets in the process. Shchelokov, who had served with Brezhnev in both Dnepropetrovsk and Moldavia and was known to be his hunting and drinking companion, would be dismissed five weeks after Brezhnev's death and expelled from the party in 1983.

The nepotism that surfaced in the late Brezhnev era was another mark of growing indiscretion, conveying to the population that crass personal gain was being put ahead of public service. Khrushchev had drawn fire for making his son-in-law the editor of *Izvestiya*, but in 1979 Brezhnev had his own son Yuri named First Deputy Minister of Foreign Trade, and the next year his daughter Galina's husband, Yuri Churbanov, became Shchelokov's first deputy in the Interior Ministry; both were appointed candidate members of the 1981 Central Committee.[39] A whispering campaign about the Brezhnev family and coterie in the winter of 1981–82—centering on a police probe into Galina's black market activities which, it was claimed, provoked the suicide of the number two man in the KGB, Semen Tsvigun, and the death from stress of Politburo member Mikhail Suslov—was a sure sign that Brezhnev's authority was dimming and that he was vulnerable on the corruption issue.

Seemingly worried less about administrative competence than about preventing challenges to himself—such as the one that had unseated his predecessor in 1964—Brezhnev brought few fresh faces into the Soviet elite. Hence the entire oligarchy, not just the General Secretary, grew elderly and infirm in office. The average age of the full members of the Politburo in 1966, after the Twenty-third Party Congress, was fifty-eight. It was sixty-one in 1971, sixty-six in 1976, and seventy in 1981 (it would have been seventy-two were it not for the atypical decision to include the then forty-nine-year-old Mikhail Gorbachev in 1980). The Twenty-sixth Party Congress in 1981 was the first such gathering in fifty-four years at which the leadership made not a single change in Politburo or Secretariat membership. Repeatedly after the mid-1970s, Brezhnev replaced middle-aged men with old men and old men with individuals who were older still or were from the same age bracket but had some personal connection to him. Konstantin Chernenko, a Brezhnev crony since 1950 and for a long interval his personal aide, was brought into the party Secretariat in 1976 and into the Politburo in 1978, at age sixty-seven. In 1977 the second youngest of the senior Soviet leaders, the fifty-year-old Konstantin Katushev, was replaced as national secretary for intra-bloc relations by a sixty-eight-year-old, Konstantin Rusakov, directly out of Brezhnev's office. The only member of the party high command younger than Katushev in 1977, Yakov Ryabov, was dropped from the Secretariat in 1979 after less than three years on the job.[40] When a dying Kosygin retired in 1980, his replacement as Chairman of the Council of Ministers, an illustrious position once held by Lenin and Stalin, was Nikolai Tikhonov, a nondescript, pension-age functionary (at seventy-five, only one year younger than Kosygin). Tikhonov's one distinguishing feature was his having worked with Brezhnev in Dnepropetrovsk three decades earlier.[41]

The leadership was no more vigorous politically than it was physically. From the mid-1970s forward, the balance among the three basic tendencies of policy tilted perceptibly in favor of plain conservatism. A popular joke of the time, playing on Brezhnev's slurred speech, said that the injunction to work *po-Brezhnevu* (as Brezhnev worked) was really a mispronunciation of doing things *po-prezhnemu* (as they have always been done). Reforms, even minimal reforms, presuppose an openness to alternative courses of action and energy in their execution. At the pinnacle of the Soviet system, and indeed throughout high officialdom, curiosity and drive became increasingly scarce commodities. While straightforward redirections of capital could still be accomplished—the oil drilling program and the campaign to develop Siberian natural gas for export to Western Europe in the early 1980s were proof of that—decisions breaking new ground were a rarity. More and more, the leadership scurried from one political brushfire to another, warding off decline in one sector by exploiting one-time gains.[42]

There was to be no repetition of Kosygin's 1965 attempt to shake up the economic bureaucracy. The best the late Brezhnev Politburo could offer by way of management reform in industry, a toying with planning indicators in July 1979, was ineffectual; minor changes in agricultural administration, mostly at the local level, were enacted in May 1982. Rather than re-examine institutions and key behavior patterns, the leadership grafted onto the existing system "targeted programs" for specific problems—the 1982 "Food Program" for agriculture, less costly projects for economy-wide problems and trouble sectors, and others for geographic areas—and then created special monitoring and troubleshooting commissions to force interagency coordination. The targeted programs, most of which were just getting off the ground when Brezhnev died, tended to "reinforce the system's traditional bureaucratic features by increasing centralization and control."[43] At the same time, major Brezhnev policy commitments of the early years that were not producing benefits commensurate with cost—mammoth irrigation and land reclamation expenditures and egalitarian social policy being the best examples—were debated by experts but obstinately adhered to by the leadership. Not a few of the worthwhile initiatives launched in the late 1960s and early 1970s in domains such as consumer welfare and pollution control ran out of steam later for want of resources or follow-through. Auspicious pilot projects tried out at the base of the administrative hierarchy, the Shchekino experiment and others, languished in various provincial backwaters, their authors learning the hard way that a stray kind word in a *Pravda* editorial or a Brezhnev speech was not enough. Without active top-level support, each challenge to bureaucratic inertia "had to be guided through so great a volume of paperwork as to drive out the taste for changes of even the most optimistically inclined executives. . . . The enthusiasm of many supporters was extinguished by the wave of paper."[44]

There is much to indicate that apprehensiveness over the country's loss of direction and momentum was building in the late Brezhnev era. Indeed, anxiety over this was not absent from the public remarks of Brezhnev himself, who as early as 1976 was noting the regime's failure to implement well thought-out decisions. Many sound measures, he stated, "are on account of weak control either not carried out or are carried out imprecisely or incompletely." Second or third resolutions were sometimes merely tacked onto the first, he added, and all of them left unfulfilled. In later addresses, Brezhnev imparted increasing exasperation: "Comrades, I am probably telling you things you already know, but [here Brezhnev resorted to an expression used by teachers to scold their pupils] repetition is the mother of learning (*povtoreniye—mat' ucheniya*)."[45]

Brezhnev gave signs of developing second thoughts about certain of his commitments, though not of having acquired the stomach for changing them. Some of his most agitated comments were directed at the very compact underpinning his regime: the vow to "respect" and "trust" its servants. In November 1979, in the gruffest Brezhnev speech ever made public, he lashed out at do-nothing officials who would never improve, "no matter how much you speak to them, how much you appeal to their conscience or sense of duty." The time had now come "to replace those who cannot cope with their assigned work," and "more freely to promote energetic and creatively thinking comrades, [people] with initiative." Eleven members of the Council of Ministers were named in the kind of tirade not heard since Khrushchev's day.[46]

From time to time Brezhnev's rhetoric betrayed a fear of political calamity lest the situation, especially in the economy, not be turned around. Failure to make good on promises of material progress, he said in 1978, was not just an economic matter but "a major political question," one that "exerts a direct influence on the mood and the will to work of the Soviet people." In February 1981—with the regime in Poland running scared from Solidarity, a situation surely not far from his mind—he told delegates to the party congress that it was largely on mundane economic matters that the public gauged the party. "They judge strictly, exactingly. And this, comrades, we must remember." In his next-to-last public appearance, an extraordinary audience with the military high command two weeks before his death, Brezhnev intimated that Soviet economic woes, coinciding with the political and military offensive of the new Reagan administration, were posing a threat to national security. While defending his spending priorities, he in effect implored the generals to be patient and patriotic, assuring them that efforts at economic efficiency would be redoubled and that he and his Politburo colleague, Defense Minister Ustinov, were paying full heed to their complaints.[47]

The problem with these pronouncements was that, when all was said and done, they were not backed up with action. More damning than the Brezhnev regime's inability to devise a strong tonic for ever more evident Soviet ills was that it did not obey even its own mild prescriptions. The General Secretary paid lip service to purging inept administrators, but few officials (and none of the eleven ministers lambasted in November 1979) were cashiered. Little was done to rescue the partial reforms and experiments of previous years, to reassess one-time successes gone sour, or to consider more radical solutions. For the impasse to be broken, the oligarchs would have had to rethink their basic approach, and they obviously preferred the costs of inaction to this. Vested interests would have had to be confronted. The implicit "social contract" with the population, with its understandings about issues like income equality and working-class job security, would have had to be reconsidered.[48] Changes in policy would inevitably have been accompanied by renewal of personnel. At intermediate levels, this would have meant tampering with the post-1964 pledge of semi-permanent job rights for bureaucrats. At the top, few in Brezhnev's geriatric Politburo could have doubted that their own positions would be on the line. It was far more natural, operating with so short a time horizon, to make room for the Tikhonovs and Chernenkos. "Energetic and creatively thinking comrades," desirable though they sounded in pep talks, could strike out in unwanted ways.

Brezhnevism began as an equivocal working philosophy, combining as it did conservative, reactionary, and reformist tenets. The more its core conservatism prevailed, the more inconsistent it seemed with the imperatives facing Soviet society. The analysis of the new edition of the party program, adopted by the Twenty-seventh Party Congress in March 1986, serves to summarize Brezhnev's ambiguous legacy as many Soviets now see it: "In the 1970s and early 1980s, along with the incontestable successes achieved in the development of the country, definitely unfavorable tendencies and difficulties manifested themselves. To a significant degree they were caused by the fact that timely and proper account was not taken of the changes in the economic situation, of the need for profound shifts in all spheres of [Soviet] life, and the required urgency was not displayed in pursuing them."[49] By settling for stultification when imagination was needed, Brezhnev and his cohorts made it harder for those who came after to perpetuate the policies to which they had clung. A leadership that enshrined certainty and stability as its highest values handed its successors uncertainty and, some thought, maybe even potential instability.

2
What Ails the Soviet System?

As the post-Brezhnev era takes shape, the survival of the Soviet system is not in question, but the utility of many of its policies is. The regime's estimate of the severity of Soviet problems finds expression in the wooly language of official ideology. It shows substantial rethinking of how far the USSR has progressed from socialism, the transitional state ushered in by the Russian Revolution, toward communism, the Marxist nirvana of affluence and equality. The 1961 Communist Party Program, adopted in Nikita Khrushchev's heyday, maintained that the Soviet Union was in the thick of the "full-scale construction of communism," which would be attained in its essentials by the early 1980s. By contrast, Leonid Brezhnev's precept of "developed socialism" bespoke less optimism about the future but more contentment with the present. Representing the USSR's socialism as developed connoted that its condition was acceptable and stable, if not ideal.

As the Brezhnev period wound down, greater pessimism crept into Soviet doctrine. In a major speech in 1982, seven months before succeeding Brezhnev as General Secretary, Yuri Andropov declared that the USSR was merely engaged in "perfecting" developed socialism, and was at an early stage at that. He argued that the full realization of socialist ideals, let alone communism, "will be a most complicated process, inevitably connected with the overcoming of contradictions and difficulties," certain of them more intractable than others. "In some areas we will be able to move more quickly, in others more slowly. This is what the real map of social progress is like. It cannot be smoothed out into a straight line."[1] Words to this effect were woven into the revised party program ratified at the 1986 party congress. General Secretary Mikhail Gorbachev disclosed there that, during the internal debate over the program, some party members had proposed excision of all references to "developed socialism," a recipe which, he conceded, had "often . . . been reduced to a mere recitation of successes." Gorbachev announced that the label would be retained, but with an accent on "the problems embedded in the legacy from previous stages," which together could not be solved until some undefined point in the twenty-first century.[2]

Contradictions and Difficulties

What are these "contradictions and difficulties" that have so set back the Soviet regime's timetable? Some, especially at the level of the individual and social group, do not lend themselves to exact measurement. Personal conduct and morality make up one such problem area, the subject recently of frequent and caustic comment in the official media. One *Pravda* homily on "the struggle with various kinds of negative phenomena in the life of our society" cites "violations of labor discipline, embezzlement and bribe-taking, profiteering and sponging, drunkenness and hooliganism, displays of a private-property and money-grubbing psychology, toadyism and servility." All had become more prevalent of late, and all "significantly damage socialist society, the state, and hence the personality."[3] Tensions between the Russian majority and the dozens of smaller Soviet nationalities, also said to be on the rise, are not much easier to calculate with precision. Andropov, however, found it necessary shortly after taking power to decry "national conceit . . . the tendency toward isolation . . . the disrespectful attitude toward other nations and peoples" finding increasing currency among Soviet ethnic groups.[4]

Many of the adverse tendencies in Soviet life can be pinpointed with considerably more rigor than this. Demographic trends provide telling examples. Aggregate growth of the Soviet population dropped 50 percent between 1960 and 1980. The current rate of 0.8 percent a year disturbs a regime that has customarily identified national power with population size. It also has economic repercussions, for it cramps the growth of the work force and inflates the population share of the retired, who must be supported by those who work; 16 percent of all Soviet citizens are now pensioners, and they will make up 20 percent by the year 2000. Perhaps the most unnerving demographic data relate to death rates and life expectancy. The Soviet crude death rate, which bottomed out at 6.9 per 1,000 in 1964, jumped by 50 percent to 10.3 in 1980—a turn of events said by a leading U.S. expert to be "unique in the history of developed countries."[5] Deaths among middle-aged men shot up particularly quickly, in the process pulling down the life expectancy for Soviet males at age zero from 67 years in 1964 to an estimated 62 years in 1980; female life expectancy was lowered during the same period from 76 to 73 years. The causes encompass factors as diverse as alcohol abuse, higher stress levels, worsened hygiene, and overloaded hospitals. The rise in mortality has not been confined to the adult population but extended to young children in the early 1970s. According to official Soviet statistics, the infant mortality rate, after declining from 80.7 per 1,000 live births in 1950 to a low of 22.9 in 1971, increased to 27.9 in 1974 and 30.8 in 1975. While as much as half of the observed increase in infant deaths may have been due to improved methods of statistical reporting, the trend was still highly disturbing to the Soviet authorities.[6]

Most graphically conveyed in numbers, and of the greatest moment to politics, are the Soviet Union's economic problems. Although Soviet and Western indices differ on minor points, there is unanimity over one essential thing: the Soviet economy has been in a protracted growth slump, and the regime and the population are smarting from the effects. The annual rate of expansion of the Soviet GNP, 4.9 percent in the 1966–70 planning period, dipped to 3.1 percent in 1971–75, 2.3 percent in 1976–80, and 2.2 percent in 1981–85. Growth of 3.5 percent in 1983, the first year after Brezhnev's death, was taken by some as a rebound of lasting significance, but the figure then subsided to 1.5 percent in 1984 and 1.6 percent in 1985, leaving the summary picture unchanged.[7]

The sharp downward break in industry in 1975–76 was followed by stagnation in some long-time showcase branches, including steel and coal production. Energy has become a major economic headache. Titanic efforts in the west Siberian fields after 1977 were not enough to keep oil production from standing nearly still in 1980–83 and then sliding by 1.4 percent in 1984–85, and power outages and brownouts have grown in frequency. Agriculture remains a weak and volatile sector despite abnormally high farm employment and voluminous infusions of capital under Brezhnev. Net agricultural output, which advanced by 3.7 percent a year in 1961–70, was up by an anemic 0.9 percent a year in 1971–79 and declined far below planned levels in 1979–82. The Soviets have published no proper statistics on grain production since 1980, but early U.S. government estimates indicate perhaps 1.8 percent annual growth in agricultural output in 1981–85.

Personal consumption, gauging the goods and services the Soviet household gets from the economy, has been under similar pressure. Growth in per capita consumption slipped to 2.2 percent a year in 1976–80 (as opposed to 5.1 percent ten years before), with food, housing, recreation, and educational and health services faring the worst. It appears to have inched up at only about 1 percent a year in 1981–85, and most Western specialists have been predicting no greater growth in the second half of the 1980s. Food supply, though apparently holding its own in terms of caloric intake, has in many parts of the country worsened for items over and above the staples of bread and potatoes. Some Soviet reports now attest no improvement at all in the provision of food over the last two decades: "It has become especially evident how the food problem has worsened in comparison with the mid-1960s."[8] Lineups outside shops for food and consumer goods seem to have become more prevalent in the late 1970s and early 1980s, and rationing of key foods (such as butter, sugar, and milk for children) was reintroduced in some Soviet cities at this time.

Not only has Soviet economic performance ebbed, it has also lagged significantly in relation to other countries. Since growth rates normally subside as economies develop, one would expect the Soviet Union's growth to be outpacing the more advanced capitalist economies. Yet, a comparison with the sixteen OECD countries shows the reverse. Soviet growth rates, which had outstripped the OECD by 0.4 percent a year in 1966–70, fell 1 percent behind in the late 1970s. In per capita consumption, the USSR trailed OECD annual growth by 1.4 percent, inverting an earlier Soviet advantage of

0.6 percent. After closing the chasm some between Soviet and Western standards of living, the Soviets have watched it open up again since the mid-1970s, especially in housing, recreation, health, and education.[9]

Explaining the Soviet Union's Problems

What lies behind these untoward trends? The underlying difficulties with which the Soviet state must grapple can be divided into six categories: the congestion of the policy agenda by perennial, new, and resurgent problems; the obsolescence of old policy formulas, especially in the economy; new doubts about ethnic identity; the widening split between popular expectations and Soviet reality; the turn toward a self-centered morality; and the mixed benefits of the regime's minimal reforms.

A crowded political agenda. When Gorbachev expounded in 1986 on how, during the Brezhnev years, "Problems in the country's development accumulated faster than they were resolved," he was not adverting to any single type of problem.[10] Many of the issues before the Politburo today are perennial ones, passed on without final resolution from decade to decade. In the economic realm, the Hungarian scholar Janos Kornai has depicted the Soviet system as a "chronic-shortage economy," in which planners, firms, and households constantly feel deprived of material resources. In the absence of markets through which needed inputs can reliably be secured, Soviet decision makers habitually engage in strategic behavior—in particular, hoarding of resources and attempts to shift the burden of uncertainty onto the shoulders of others—and this perpetuates shortages and the psychology feeding them.[11] Soviet leaders have been struggling to manage endemic shortage ever since the Soviet command economy was set up under Joseph Stalin in the early 1930s. They have also encountered over the years, in one guise or another, many of the other issues on Gorbachev's priority list—corruption, ethnic tension, public hygiene and health problems, anomie among the young, and so forth.

What, then, is distinctive about the political agenda of the 1980s? The most obvious difference from ten or fifteen years ago is the widely shared belief that certain of the USSR's perennial difficulties have become more acute and pressing. Related to this is the perception, not without foundation, that the Soviet Union has in some fields of endeavor relapsed and, modern though it may be in other respects, once again has to give priority attention to tasks usually linked with economic and social backwardness. Problems the regime thought it had resolved, or at least held in check, have in recent years come back to haunt it. Exceptionally clumsy or ossified policies have helped reanimate some dormant difficulties, as have skimping on resources and the coming due of bills, as it were, for deferred social and economic maintenance. Well before Brezhnev's death, Soviet critics were wondering out loud whether failure to stop backsliding might some day force the regime "to rebuild, to unlearn our acquired habits, . . . in a certain sense to turn around and start over," at untold cost.[12]

Examples abound. The bulge in death rates in the late 1960s and 1970s pointed to a partial unwinding of previous accomplishments in medicine and health care. It is hard to avoid the conclusion that the mortality statistics, for adults as much as infants, mirrored a deterioration in the quality of Soviet life more broadly. The housing situation, the improvement of which was one of Khrushchev's great achievements, offers another illustration. Thanks to the poor showing of the housing lobby in the budget wars after Brezhnev's accession, the number of apartments completed by Soviet construction organizations since 1969 has failed to keep up with new families formed. Although new apartments are roomier and better designed, Soviet urbanologists and municipal executives are now writing about the quantitative shortage of housing with a plaintiveness not heard since the 1950s.

Agriculture and food supply are an additional sector in which evidence of decay was plentiful by the late Brezhnev period. Brezhnev boasted in the early 1970s that the regime had solved the food problem, but he had long stopped doing so by the end of the decade, when some foreign experts were going so far as to wonder if the Soviet farm system was not sliding into absolute decline. Certain of the regime's own actions lend credence to such a conclusion, notably its decision in early 1979—before the four-year string of disastrously bad grain harvests—to make compulsory what had been a spontaneous move toward re-establishing subsidiary plots and gardens at industrial plants and other non-farm enterprises. For the average Russian, once again seeing a cabbage patch or chicken coop in the courtyard of his factory or institute was a throwback to the lean 1930s and wartime years and a glum commentary on the collective and state farms.

What is fascinating about the present-day Soviet Union is the simultaneous eruption of these symptoms of regression and of afflictions of the opposite sort. As the leaders have known for some time, the very accomplishments of building a machine-based industrial economy and a modern, urban society have been bringing the country up against new and hitherto unanticipated problems—those of success. Economic planners who used to dictate with relative ease deliveries of pig iron and cement are now taxed to the limit by schemes for computerization and robotization, none of which could have been so much as discussed had previous economic successes not occurred. Some of the upsurge in infant mortality in the early 1970s is explained by analogous successes in health care. As births were shifted from small, ill-equipped delivery rooms in rural areas to larger urban hospitals with better equipment, more infants were saved from asphixia during childbirth. The revived infants, however, were particularly vulnerable to illness, and thousands of deaths that would earlier have been recorded as stillbirths (not affecting the infant mortality rate) now entered the statistics as infant deaths. "Paradoxically, . . . one reason for the increase in infant mortality rates in European Russia during the early years of the last decade [was] an improved medical care delivery system—an improvement that affected the system unevenly."[13]

Many of the emergent ills of progress in the Soviet Union are less economic and technical than social and cultural. So it is that environmental pollution, a consequence of rapid and unregulated industrialization long passed over by the government, became in the 1960s and 1970s a gripping issue for widening portions of the Soviet population, and it is bound to remain so. In natural science, Soviet breakthroughs in molecular biology and recombinant DNA research have raised the same questions of technique and conscience posed in other advanced countries. The foreign reader of Soviet debates on genetic engineering "is increasingly struck by the similarity of these discussions to the ones that have been occurring in the West."[14] Urbanization, while intensely desired by the regime, has also bred new issues. The Soviet Union, mostly rural in 1917, now has almost 300 cities with populations of over 100,000 and 20 larger than a million, all badly in need of integration and servicing. Traffic congestion and a shortage of parking, in their own way proof of economic advancement, have come to pose a serious concern. The profusion of huge tracts of high-rise housing, welcomed by all as a needed response to the apartment shortage, has created a faceless and monotonous milieu. Soviet musings about how to humanize their cities remind one of inquiries elsewhere in the developed world.[15]

The Soviet leaders' political agenda is crowded, then, by issues differing in point of origin, incubation period, tenacity, and seriousness. Along with many of the inveterate problems that puzzled their predecessors, they confront new problems of modernity and renascent problems of backwardness.

Old formulas lose their effectiveness. The Soviet Union, probably to a greater extent than most countries, lives by time-tested practice. It addresses its major problems with remarkably stable formulas and approaches. The catch is that sooner or later all old habits generate diminishing returns. This waning effectiveness of inherited solutions accounts for no small part of the load under which the regime now labors.

The main reason that familiar formulas misfire is that the conditions under which they were first defined evolve more quickly than the formula itself. This has happened in area after area as Soviet society has developed. The party's system of political education, for instance, was set up after the Revolution to carry its gospel, through personal agitation and simple texts, to an illiterate or semiliterate population. Although it did a serviceable job in the early years, it has a good deal less impact on today's better educated and more discriminating Soviet public, and it makes stunningly inept use of modern electronic technology. The Soviet hospital and clinic system, to take a different example, successfully introduced elementary health care and curbed epidemic disease in a largely agrarian country. Today it is less in tune with an urbanized and industrialized society with sedentary occupations, high tension levels, heavy air and water pollution, richer diets, and greater alcohol consumption. In the field of culture and entertainment, official taste typically lags behind the public's, and for this reason popular art forms that have atrophied in other modern countries—big bands, music hall ensembles, and circuses are some of them—linger on in the Soviet Union, bureaucratically run and subsidized by the state.[16]

The pattern of declining dividends bears particularly upon the Soviet economy. The USSR's traditional economic model was outfitted with, in Charles Lindblom's apt metaphor, strong thumbs but no fingers.[17] Potent indeed were the thumbs of government ownership of the means of production, highly centralized planning of inputs and outputs, direct administrative control over factories and farms, and periodic campaigns for implementing the latest political priorities. Beginning with Stalin's first five-year plans, they were used to propel the Soviet Union through the phase of "extensive" growth, as the Soviets (using the same terminology as Western economists) now call it. This was done primarily by vastly increasing the quantity of inputs into the economy—land, capital, raw materials, energy, and above all labor—through mobilization from above. The Soviet leaders got the high growth tempos they wanted, notwithstanding gross inefficiencies in the use of resources. The shortcomings tolerated for decades were many. Central planners, lacking scarcity prices to indicate social value and responsible for thousands of "material balances," as the resource transfers between firms and branches were labeled, faced a herculean task of coordination. This led to a concentration on quantity of production at the expense of quality and to frequent disequilibria and bottlenecks. Economic ministries and enterprise managers, for their part, perfected elaborate dodges, costly to the economy as a whole, for protecting themselves from the center and from other firms. Households and individual consumers had to make do with few and poor goods and services, by international standards, and employee motivation inevitably suffered.

One glaring weakness of the command economy has had to do with technological innovation. The Soviet economic mechanism may do quite well when assigned a mission of national importance by politicians, but without that impetus it has manifested a deep-seated bias against innovation. Not infrequently, as Mikhail Gorbachev has observed, "an enterprise puts out outmoded production of a low technological level, or consumer goods for which there is no demand, but lives normally and at times even flourishes."[18]

Cross-national studies show Soviet technological attainment to have worsened since the mid-1960s in relation to other countries. The comparison is particularly unflattering with Japan, which once operated on the same technical plane as the Soviets but is now duelling the United States for world leadership.[19]

Computerization of the economy, indispensable to late twentieth-century manufacturing and service industries, began under Brezhnev, but barely so. The USSR is thought to have in place at present about 100,000 mainframes and minicomputers, compared to the United States' 1.3 million, and only a few thousand microcomputers and personal computers, a tiny fraction of the Americans' 25 million.[20] It was estimated in 1985 that more than one-third of all Soviet industrial machinery and equipment "is simply worn out," exerting "a most unfavorable effect on productivity." The repair of outdated equipment absorbs the labor of 6 million workers, 35 billion rubles in annual expenditures, every sixth ton of iron and steel produced, and every fifth machine tool in the country.[21] The lack of competition between firms is an obvious reason for this failing, magnified by the protection of the Soviet economy from world market forces. Soviet managers are not rewarded for innovation. Nor are they often penalized for the lack of it. As Joseph Berliner puts it, the Soviet economy is missing not only the coordinating "invisible hand" of the marketplace but the "invisible foot applied vigorously to the backside" of unproductive enterprises under capitalism.[22]

Problems of coordination, quality, and innovation, which have always plagued the Soviet economy, have recently become more blatant—and the need for finer, suppler fingers of management more crying—because circumstances have changed. Slowly but surely, application of the coarse thumbs of the classic formula has brought into being a mature, albeit imbalanced, industrial economy that is many times larger and incomparably more complex—hence harder to direct from a single point—than the primitive economic machine of Stalin's day. Equally serious, the cheap resources around which the original Soviet blueprint for industrialization was drawn up have now been largely exhausted, as became increasingly apparent in the 1970s. Few opportunities exist any more to bring more land under the plow, other than by huge expenditures on irrigation and drainage. Investment needs have clashed directly with those of the military and the consumer sector, as became painfully evident in the 1976–80 and 1981–85 five-year plans. For the most part, raw materials and energy are still plentiful in absolute amount; but conveniently located stocks of both have been depleted, and the richest reserves are now found east of the Urals. Energy, in particular, has exacted a much heavier toll from the leadership since the 1977 near-panic over oil production, both in effort and in funds to pay for exploitation of new sources on the Siberian frontier, maintenance of old fields (including oil wells prematurely degraded by wasteful water-injection methods), and greatly heightened transportation costs.[23]

The tight supply of labor is the most worrisome resource constraint of all. The pools of underutilized labor tapped in the past, mainly in the villages and among women, have pretty well dried up. The interaction of lower birth rates and the aging of the population has in the most recent period wrenched back the rate of net increase in the labor force. Whereas the population of normal working age (aged 20 to 59) expanded by 8.5 million in 1971–75 and a very high 13.8 million in 1976–80, it was expected to grow by only 7.7 million in 1981–85. In 1986–90, with the entry of the small group born in the second half of the 1960s and the retirement of the large numbers of Soviets born in the second half of the 1920s, the able-bodied population will actually decline by 1.0 million. There will be some recovery in 1991–95, to an increase of 4.2 million workers, but the increment for 1996–2000 will be only 1.5 million.[24] New work hands, moreover, are unevenly distributed geographically and ethnically. The European part of the country, the location of most established industry, will lose manpower over the rest of the century, while all of the gains will be in Central Asia, Kazakhstan, and the Caucasus.

Although the Brezhnev leadership accepted in principle the need to adopt an "intensive" growth strategy, it made little headway in this direction. As Gorbachev observed later, "Due to inertia, the economy continued to be developed to a considerable degree on an extensive basis, oriented toward the drawing into production of extra labor and material resources."[25] Rather than making better use of dwindling resources, the only way growth rates could have been sustained, the Soviets used them less effectively than they had before. Total factor productivity in the Soviet economy (the increase in output per added unit of capital and labor input) is the best yardstick of this. After rising by 1.1 percent a year in the second half of the 1960s, it declined at an annual rate of 0.5 percent in the first half of the 1970s, about 1.2 percent in 1976–80, and about 0.9 percent in 1981–85. In industry, negative growth in total factor productivity commenced in the mid-1970s.[26]

New questions about ethnic identity. The changing relations among Soviet ethnic groups also impinge upon the regime's agenda. The Soviet Union, it should never be overlooked, is a multinational state, the most heterogeneous in ethnic makeup of any large industrial society. The 137 million Russians (the total as of the 1979 census) are by a big margin the largest single ethnic community, and they dominate Soviet institutions and political culture, but they constitute a bare majority (52 percent) of the total population. A hundred-odd other nationalities, living under Moscow's sway since before the Revolution though still concentrated in their ancestral territories, are arrayed in a great arc around the Russian heartland. The Russians' fellow Slavs (mostly Ukrainians and Belorussians) account for 20 percent of the population, with the other major European groups representing 8 percent. Of the remainder, the biggest bloc by far is the 17 percent of Moslem heritage, speaking languages akin to Turkish or Persian and based predominantly in Central Asia, Kazakhstan, and Azerbaidzhan in the Caucasus. Among the twenty-one non-Russian nationalities numbering more than a million, the majority of the members of all but two speak chiefly their mother tongue. Fourteen of the biggest non-Russian groups, ranging from the 42 million Ukrainians to the 1 million Estonians, have their own "union republics," national units which together with the RSFSR (Russian Republic) are the formal partners in the Soviet federation.

Stalin, though a Georgian by birth, ruled as one of the most fervent Russian nationalists in the country's history. The national minorities were kept in line by symbolic concessions, economic development programs, inculcation of the Russian language, administrative controls, and, of course, the brute force of purges and, for unlucky groups like the Crimean Tatars and the Volga Germans, mass deportations. Khrushchev abjured violence as part of his de-Stalinization drive, but otherwise acted inconsistently on the nationality question, putting greater emphasis on the legislative and economic rights of the union republics while at the same time pursuing cultural integration and insisting that ethnic divisions were on their way to being obliterated.

The leadership under Brezhnev took a less rosy view, replacing Khrushchev's theory of the imminent merger (*sliyaniye*) of the minorities into the Russian majority with the idea of rapprochement (*sblizheniye*) among the Soviet nationalities. Rising Kremlin concern about the ethnic issue was demonstrated by the revival in the late 1960s of the moribund discipline of ethnography and the creation of a new Scientific Council for Nationality Problems under the Academy of Sciences. The interest in research and soliciting expert advice was accompanied by a fuller recognition in official statements of the obstinacy of ethnic identities and the hazards of communal conflict. Concern about the ethnic balance (though not only this) prompted Brezhnev's call in 1976 for development of an "effective demographic policy." Greater heed was paid to language policy, and especially the systematic teaching of Russian. A detailed Council of Ministers resolution on Russian-language instruction outside the RSFSR appeared in 1978, and the first of several major conferences on implementation was held the following year in Tashkent.[27]

The post-Brezhnev leaders have continued this trend toward raising the profile of the nationality issue. In the most forthright acknowledgment of the problem to date, Yuri Andropov declared in December 1982 that the economic and social development of ethnic communities "is inevitably accompanied by the growth of their national self-consciousness," not by its decline. The ideal of melting the Soviet nationalities into one has not been discarded, but it has been relegated to the remote future, after a classless and fully communist society has been constructed. In the meantime, Andropov said, "problems in the relations among nationalities will not be crossed off our agenda." They would demand the "special concern and constant attention of the party," which had to be endowed with "a well-thought-out, scientifically based nationality policy."[28] Five months later, Andropov's Politburo announced that it would step up Russian-language training.[29]

What concrete signs, aside from the Soviet leaders' own expressions of foreboding, attest to growing ethnic friction? The most palpable is the greater openness with which the various nationalities' concerns and demands are being articulated. Non-Russians feel less inhibited than they did a generation ago about showing pride in their natural surroundings, literary traditions, crafts and music, and links to cultural communities (Islam, for example) that transcend state frontiers. Recognition of ethnic distinctiveness and of the individual group's contribution to the Soviet whole is being insisted upon by many officials, and more generally by the literate and urbanized middle classes that have emerged in the national republics.[30] Some local politicians have sympathized enough with national grievances to be charged with ethnic exclusivism—most prominently Petr Shelest, the party first secretary of the Ukraine, who was dismissed and condemned as a closet Ukrainian nationalist in 1972. Ethnic grievances became in the 1960s and 1970s a conspicuous theme in political dissent. The appeals of Soviet Jews for the right to emigrate, and of the Crimean Tatars for return of the homeland from which Stalin evicted them during World War II, were but the most vocal of many such demands. There have been mass public demonstrations against Moscow's cultural and linguistic policy in several areas, notably in the Lithuanian city of Kaunas in May 1972 (where paratroopers had to be called in to disperse crowds after a Lithuanian student, Romas Kalanta, committed self-immolation) and in Georgia in April 1978, during the discussion of the Georgian language's standing in the republic's constitution. A few nationality protests have taken a violent turn, the most serious incident being the bomb blast in the Moscow subway in January 1977, set off by a group seeking Armenian secession.

Strange though it may sound, even the Great Russians, or at least many intellectuals among them, are feeling a similar frustration and pent-up nationalism. Like Lithuanians, Georgians, or Uzbeks, "they too are concerned about the right to express their national identity [and] about the homogenization of their culture."[31] The government-approved movements to preserve historical buildings and the verdant beauty of the Russian countryside draw on a recrudescent Russian nationalism, as does the ideologically less acceptable interest in the Russian Orthodox Church.

Ethnic loyalties seem also to be intruding more into economic and socioeconomic policy areas. This is visibly so in the competition for investment resources, which has become keener as Soviet economic growth has tapered off. Partisans and opponents of regional mega-projects—like exploitation of Siberian oil and gas, rerouting of northern Russian rivers to parched Central Asia, and rehabilitation of the Ukraine's Donbass coal fields—have invoked national dignity and rights alongside narrowly utilitarian arguments. Similarly, rivalry between Russians and non-Russians over professional and administrative jobs has picked up in the minority areas, despite an affirmative action policy favoring native personnel for most positions. The economic slowdown of the 1970s shriveled career opportunities just as the expansion of higher education for late-modernizing groups, especially Moslems, produced larger graduating classes of native cadres. Crackdowns on local corruption rings have sparked further ethnic controversy, drawing "false lamentations that merciless criticism of negative phenomena somehow infringes upon national honor."[32] Attachments to a national style of life have stymied efforts by Soviet planners to get workers to relocate from labor-surplus areas, especially Central Asia, to construction sites and factories in Siberia and other regions where manpower is in short supply. Ethnic considerations also shaded the debate over demographic policy in the 1970s, as academics and officials tried in vain to devise a way to elicit higher fertility in the Slavic republics without simultaneously encouraging it among Moslem women. For this more than any other reason, the measures, when brought out in 1981, were mild and ineffective.

Looking ahead, the longest shadow is cast over the Soviet ethnic scene by demographic trends. The most alarming from the Russian vantage point is the enormous asymmetry in fertility between the European population, Russians included, and the other Soviet peoples. By far the swiftest natural increase is that of the Moslem nationalities, which suffered less from World War II and other earlier demographic catastrophes, which retain an age and sex structure conducive to high fertility, and among whom large families are sanctioned by religion and culture. In the 1970s, the total number of Soviet Moslems grew at an annual rate (2.5 percent) more than quadruple the rate of the Russians. The inescapable result is a heavier weight for non-Russians and non-Europeans in the Soviet population as a whole and, before too many years are out, the loss by the Russians of their majority position. Government demographic policy seems likely to have little or no effect on this outcome. Whereas the Russian population is expected to creep up by only 3 million between 1979 and 2000, and the number of other Slavs by another 3 million, the increase for Moslems will be, depending on the projection, 20 to 31 million. By the turn of the century, the Russian share of the total population will be down to 45 to 47 percent and the Moslem share up to roughly half of that.[33]

The growing expectations gap. Never is there a perfect match between what a government does and what its population expects it to do. What counts politically is the size of the gap and the direction in which it is moving. One element in the Soviet regime's present quandary is that a large and widening gulf has opened between performance and aspirations.

To the ultrarepressive Stalinist state of a generation ago, Soviet citizens did look for some irreducible benefits—a basic education, employment, shelter, free medical care, defense against foreign powers—as interviews with refugees after World War II established. Even during Stalin's lifetime, in the period of postwar reconstruction, the regime was reaching out to the Soviet middle class with a "Big Deal," predicated on material comfort in exchange for support for the regime.[34] In the wake of Stalin's death, aspirations escalated rapidly, and among all sections of the population. The regime's own rhetorical excesses were partly responsible for this. The bragging of the 1961 party program that the Soviet Union would eclipse the United States economically by 1980 (as it happened, Soviet GNP per capita was but one-third of the American by 1980) was only the most hyperbolic of a chain of such promises. Of more consequence was the tacit pact with society that, with the shedding of both the social utopianism of the revolutionary period and the indiscriminate political terror of the Stalin era, the regime was henceforth to be judged essentially by its ability to "deliver the goods" to the people.[35] Though the Brezhnev leadership muffled the Khrushchevian sloganeering, and harped more in its later years on the spiritual superiority of the "socialist way of life," it left the basic vow of material improvement intact. By continuing with Khrushchev's egalitarian wage policy and freezing most consumer prices, it also let it be known that it favored spreading the payoffs across all major social groups.

Mass aspirations have been further galvanized, as in so many other societies, by the rising educational profile of the population. Universal literacy has pumped up self-esteem and facilitated comparisons of social condition, and higher education, in particular, has stimulated young people to be critical of Soviet shortcomings and to covet respected and rewarding careers in which their knowledge can be used. Another accelerator has been the unlimbering of communication within Soviet society, both among specialists and at the level of the mass media—especially television, which came into general use only under Brezhnev. This has spotlighted the regime's specific failings and contributed to a broadly based yearning for the good things of life.[36] Enhanced contact with the outside world, direct and indirect, has also played a role. Accurate knowledge of the West is still largely the preserve of professional elites, who have substantial access to foreign publications, the language skills to read them, and some hope of foreign travel. But a diffuse (and sometimes exaggerated) awareness and envy of the West's wealth, and a concomitant interest in American and West European news and cultural fads, now exists among all strata of Soviet society. No less arousing has been the example of the communist states of Eastern Europe, to which Soviet citizens have had infinitely greater exposure through propaganda, military service, and tourism. Here, in some countries at least, consumers get a much better deal from institutions originally modeled on the USSR's.

The regime's performance since Stalin in meeting mass expectations has been satisfactory in a fundamental sense. But it is also true that the regime has been losing ground: the distance between its actions and popular aspirations has increased. On many issues, including consumer goods and food, the slide is associated with the later phases of Brezhnevism. On others, it began somewhat earlier. In either case, as Gorbachev said in 1986 of the economy in total, "a breach (*razryv*) was formed between society's demands and the achieved level of production."[37]

Possibly, defenders of the regime console themselves with the knowledge that some kinds of poor performance by Soviet institutions have acted to depress expectations. Consider one question well studied by Soviet social scientists: diminishing access by ambitious Soviet youth to high-status occupations. If in the early 1950s 77 percent of all daytime secondary-school graduates were being admitted to higher education, the stepping-stone to a professional or managerial career, and 57 percent as late as the early 1960s, by the early 1970s (as many more tenth-graders jostled for entrance and universities and institutes grew at a slower pace) only 22 percent were making it in. A scant 20 percent were admitted in 1977.[38] Following their initial disappointment, many young people in fact adapted to the new conditions by entering technical and vocational programs and lowering their sights. Once in the work force, they often "feel themselves in social terms to be no worse off than those who became [university] students and acquired a diploma . . . Youth is quite tactfully grasping the change in the real situation."[39]

This, however, does not mean the larger problem is self-correcting. For one thing, expectations thwarted in some areas are being diverted into others. As one sociologist wrote in 1975 about the young person barred entrance to the university, such an individual tends to seek out satisfactions "that would compensate for his loss," including higher pay and better leisure.[40] Nor have expectations been ebbing nearly as quickly as regime performance. Studies of Soviet buying habits observe that citizens now feel entitled to more and better goods than in the past, that "the demands of people have significantly grown, and industry trails along behind them."[41] Over the whole gamut of issues, particularly those touching on popular welfare, it is fair to say that the expectations gap has been stretched out during the last decade.

Another poignant fact about expectations is that under Soviet conditions the continued wilting of hope and belief in the future is apt to be extremely damaging to the regime itself. In a system where the state doubles as employer and provider of goods and services, popular despondency can feed back directly onto the state's ability to realize its own goals. While some puncturing of unrealistic expectations has been expedient, past a certain juncture it becomes counterproductive because it sullies people's willingness to work. There were many in the Soviet Union by the late Brezhnev period who thought that this divide had already been reached, that disaffected workers and managers were simply putting out less on the job. The "social factor" or "human factor," as it was often referred to, was presented as the final link in a vicious circle: society gets and expects less, so it gives less; the state promises and gives less, so it gets less. A prominent Soviet economist and sociologist, Academician Tat'yana Zaslavskaya, two years before Brezhnev's death placed the expectations gap and the motivation issue at the hub of the regime's predicament. Inducing the worker-consumer to produce in a low-growth economy with a flat earnings structure, she said, "now forms a unique 'solar plexus,' the center of all the socioeconomic problems of our society."[42]

The reach for private solutions. Because of the regime's faltering capacity to slake popular demands, Soviet citizens have increasingly sought gratification from other sources. This interest did not originate in the last ten or fifteen years, but it clearly gathered momentum during that interval. The partial withdrawal of citizens from public life, which takes a multitude of forms, compounds the Soviet system's many other difficulties.

Ordinary folk exhibit this spirit when, the blandishments of the regime to the contrary, they follow their own lights in making the key life-cycle decisions. Divorces, abortions, common-law marriages, and illegitimate births, all legal but disapproved, are more numerous. In the European regions, women have fewer children than the government wants, in Asia more. Choices about employment and location are weakly regulated and expensive to managers and planners, all owing to "the fact that migration depends on the personal element, on the taking by the individual of the voluntary decision to change his place of residence."[43]

A different and destructive avenue of escape is provided by vodka, the consumption of which has climbed at a speed disconcerting to the leaders, the medical profession, and many others. "The problem of drunkenness and alcoholism," to quote the 1985 party resolution that at long last tried to come to terms with it, "has been exacerbated in recent years."[44] Soviet per capita consumption of alcoholic beverages, rated in liters of pure alcohol, rose 50 percent between 1965 and 1979, one of the highest rates of increase anywhere. Purchases of state-produced alcohol (not counting moonshine) were thought by the early 1980s to soak up 15 percent of total disposable income. The bottle is implicated in job absenteeism, in the majority of violent crimes, in many degenerative diseases, in the decline in fertility, and (due to poor quality control and the Russian habit of binge drinking) in thousands of deaths every year directly from alcohol poisoning.[45]

It is in the Soviet economy that individualism thrives in the most exotic mixture of revived and new forms. "The person," as Zaslavskaya put it in a searching analysis in 1980, "is not at all a bolt that can be snapped into a machine and forced to work there. He does not simply adjust to the system of economic relations. He also actively studies it, finds if necessary its weak spots, and tries wherever possible to use them."[46]

One manifestation of this is the withholding of prodigious amounts of money from circulation. Insofar as nominal incomes have outrun the supply of desired goods and services, the prices of most commodities have been frozen, and opportunities for legal investment are foreclosed by government policy, many Soviet consumers have not had a great deal of choice in this matter. But what discretion they have had has been exercised in favor of rounding out savings bank deposits and cash hoards in preference to buying more low-quality products from state stores. Accumulated savings, which were 20 percent of the population's money income in 1960 and 40 percent in 1970, were by 1982 equivalent to 70 percent of annual income and nearly 90 percent of all retail sales.[47] This bloated reserve of currency is a lien on future production, a reminder of popular disenchantment, and a disincentive to hard work—why worry about pleasing your boss if you have eight months' income stashed away with nothing in particular to spend it on? The problem had become serious enough to warrant mention by Gorbachev and other speakers at the Twenty-seventh Party Congress.

A related phenomenon is the personal stockpiling of scarce or potentially scarce commodities, a habit slowly fading in the Soviet Union until it gained new life in the mid-1970s. The upshot is artificial shortages: "So much pressure has been created in demand for certain goods that the purchaser is starting to take for a reserve up to fifteen or twenty pairs of nylons or stockings, large amounts of cloth and thread, etc. In such a situation, the consumer himself worsens the shortage."[48]

In human terms, a shortage is a collection of frustrated buyers, and this in turn is an invitation to sellers to come forward to meet the compressed demand. This is precisely what has occurred in the Soviet Union, where "colored markets" of every tint—black, grey, pink, and others recognized in the argot of the street—have by innumerable accounts swelled in recent years. In the official economy, there is more barter outside the plan, merging often into what the Soviets term *protektsiya,* or networks for exchanging non-pecuniary favors. More and more of the able and restless members of society, bumping up against the low ceiling on earnings set by wage egalitarianism and bored by the regimented life of the enterprise and trade union, shunt their efforts into the illegal "second economy," as Western analysts now call it (Soviets prefer the phrase "shadow economy"). Particularly in construction and agriculture, more managers count on free-lance laborers and craftsmen (*chastniki*) and itinerant work gangs (*shabashniki*) to help them meet their end-of-month production quotas. Frustrated consumers buy or trade for more of what they need *nalevo* (on the side) from friends, small-time producers and middlemen, sales clerks, waiters, and so on, most of whom depend to a considerable extent on materials purloined from store shelves or state warehouses and even on state vehicles and tools. Stolen and privately fabricated goods find ready buyers at inflated prices because, by Andropov's admission in 1983, state production is often so bad "that people prefer to overpay the speculator for articles that are good and made with taste."[49] Many find themselves in the position of the farmers in the Kharkov region of the Ukraine who paid large sums to private entrepreneurs to hook up their homesteads to natural gas mains—at the rate the state construction trust in charge was going it would have taken it 100 years to finish!—and then told a reporter that "they do not consider the 'on the side' gas mechanics to be criminals, and, more than that, they are sincerely grateful to them."[50]

Behavior deviant by traditional Soviet standards has also been on the ascent among officials, as numerous sources of information tell us. The economic slowdown of the 1970s and the unremitting pressure to meet production quotas spawned not only efforts to have plans scaled down, but a greater incidence of phony and padded reporting (*pripiska*) of economic results by managers. When the Procuracy (public prosecutor's office) of the USSR did a random check of enterprises in three industrial ministries in 1985—two and a half years after Brezhnev's death—it found inflated production statistics in 50 to 85 percent of the plants checked. This kind of deception, a press report said, "inspires alarm . . . [for] it has, alas, come to be widely practiced."[51] Such conduct, it is often pointed out, has a demoralizing effect on the work force as a whole. "Where there is lack of correspondence between the visible, real results of production and the announced results, such as is completely obvious to the collective, this dispirits workers . . . negatively affects the attitude toward socialist property . . . stimulates the erosion of moral values."[52]

In as over-policed and bureaucratized a society as the Soviet Union, black market activity and fabrication of statistics could not exist without some connivance on the part of officials in law enforcement and general governmental roles. That cooperation surely was there, and was growing in scale, during the Brezhnev era. It was prevalent enough to have been described as the basis of a Brezhnev "Little Deal," tacitly accommodative of reciprocity systems as well as of petty private marketeering and corruption, equal to Stalin's "Big Deal" in importance.[53] Policemen, inspectors, procurators, the compilers of waiting lists for housing and consumer goods, party secretaries—many were willing, and some were downright eager, to look the other way in exchange for a bribe or the promise of future benevolence.

Members of the administrative elite had their own reasons under Brezhnev for bypassing official channels. They, too, had economic expectations that could not be met on the basis of salary and state stores alone, wives who bridled at standing in queues, sons and daughters wanting admission to the small number of university places. The expanding system of "special" or closed stores and service facilities helped plug the gap for many. Others crossed the boundary into personal and family enrichment through illegal means. They could only have been encouraged by Brezhnev's apparent nonchalance about the spread of corruption (symbolized for many by the preferential treatment afforded his own relatives), by the maxim of "respect for personnel," by lax policing, and by the Kremlin's reluctance to extend regional anti-corruption drives (such as the 1972 cleanup in Georgia) to the national level. They created a ready-made issue for Brezhnev's successors, who were able to proclaim, as Andropov did in 1983, that the bureaucrat or policeman on the take is striking "nothing less than a blow at the very essence of our system."[54]

Greater personal disengagement from common concerns is found in abundance in Soviet culture and the arts as well. Self-absorption, in distinct contrast to the socially engaged style of Khrushchev's time, became a compelling force in official culture in the 1970s. The most noticeable feature of Soviet literature, once devoted to preaching the virtues of collectivism, came to be "its preoccupation with private human concerns."[55] Novels, poetry, and plays dwelt on individual melancholy, fatigue, and solitude.

Parallel to the official culture, and communicating many of the same themes in less inhibited form, is the unofficial culture of the dissent movement. The sovereignty of the individual, expressed in the individual statement of moral opposition to the state, was a badge of most Soviet political dissent when it came of age under Brezhnev. Denied an open platform by party conservatives and the KGB, dissent went underground, finding outlets in such novel forms of expression as *samizdat* (private publication), *tamizdat* (publication of forbidden texts abroad), and, most recently, *magnitizdat* (tape recording of illicit material). Pulverized by the police, and subject to the same centrifugal tendencies found in Soviet society at large, dissent by the late Brezhnev period was more and more a disparate phenomenon, subject to "egoistic, chauvinistic, and xenophobic moods, . . . [to] a move away from concern about social problems . . . to a weariness and cynicism."[56]

The mixed blessings of minimal reforms. A final cause of the Soviet malady lies in the regime's preferred way of coping with its problems. The minimal reforms typical of the Brezhnev era, diffident and unhurried as they were, worked on balance to the benefit of the regime and the population. But they also engendered losses and irritations that new leaders are obliged to come to terms with one way or another.

Again it is the economy that drives the point home. Here the skin-deep revisions of structures and operating rules from the mid-1960s on were much less disruptive than the spasmodic renovations of the Khrushchev years. Yet, tinkering changes, followed by measures to fine-tune what were from the start inadequate measures, were by the late Brezhnev period "becoming a part of the problem, rather than contributing to its solution."[57] The leadership frequently resorted to local experiments, launched in one sector or place and then slowly extended elsewhere. While the pragmatic and consultative manner in which the pilot projects were formulated and executed was often preferred to past ways, the aggregate effect was to complicate the administration of the economy without much improving it. The experiments siphoned off time and energy into monitoring, reporting, and analysis. Most of them, after many dry runs, were not comprehensively introduced. The dozens of "targeted programs" added in the late 1970s and early 1980s aggravated the situation.

Many other of the creeping economic changes instituted under Brezhnev also had hidden costs, while at the same time falling short of the benefits they might have yielded had they been followed through more systematically. Transfer of foreign technology to Soviet industry is a case in point. It was shorn of much of its potential utility by self-imposed restrictions on "people transfer" and by an inability to forge incentives for Soviet industry to use imported equipment productively. Advanced Western machinery often clattered away in Soviet factories or field sites at one-third to one-half of its normal efficiency level. In the high-priority field of computers, Western export restrictions hurt Soviet interests, but equally damaging was the failure on the Soviet side to approximate the human and technical environment that enables effective use and continued development of computers in the West. Consequently, "The duplication of U.S. computer systems falls far short of ensuring the productive use of such systems."[58] Problems include political restrictions on information flow that preclude the emergence of a world-class user community and, on the mechanical side, the lack of proper ancillary equipment, storage media, electrical power, static-free communication lines, access to satellites, backup parts, servicing crews, and software.

The experience of the Soviet consumer sector sheds revealing light on the results of irresolute reforms. Agriculture excepted, the regime in the last two decades has attempted to satisfy popular demands for housing, soft and durable goods, and personal services without reallocating budgetary resources in any emphatic way. It has also shrunk from sanctioning private enterprise in the area or creating authoritative new state organizations able to do the job on their own. Instead, institutions with different missions entirely have been ordered to add consumer-directed work to their existing repertoires. Industrial construction trusts are obliged to build housing and kindergartens, truck factories and radar plants crank out refrigerators and televisions, and in some remote towns industrial enterprises operate bus and streetcar lines. Seeing these tasks as a distraction from their main business, established organizations do them with neither enthusiasm nor efficiency, and the ensuing potpourri of programs is weakly coordinated and the first to be harmed when something goes awry.

Production of consumer goods for private purchase, a sore point made more tender in the late Brezhnev years, is the best illustration. Soviet light industry plants, which manufacture mostly for the mass market, still find themselves at the end of the supply queue. The resultant slack in production is taken up by heavy industry (including the defense production ministries), which makes half of all non-food goods, among them all vehicles sold to the consumer and most home appliances. Years of exhortation have not annulled among the captains of heavy industry "the attitude that the production of articles for the consumer is something of secondary importance."[59] Subjected to little direction from above, they produce a jumble of models that are designed within individual plants, mutually incompatible, and frequently out of touch with consumer needs and tastes. They thus inflict upon the Soviet household no fewer than 130 refrigerator models (most of them outdated), 70 kinds of vacuum cleaners, 56 different television sets, 50 table radios, 40 sewing machines, and 34 electric razors. Economies of scale are rarely achieved because of the fragmentation of design and production. The Ministry of Trade, a bureaucratic pygmy compared to the industrial establishment, is notorious for accepting poor products from industry and passing them on to consumers, and only recently has it become more critical of its suppliers. Spare parts and servicing, for which neither the manufacturer nor the retailer accepts much responsibility in the Soviet Union, are left largely to unlicensed private entrepreneurs: "For years the discussion of the shortage of spare parts has gone on, but it is still apparent that they are available only from fast operators and profiteers."[60]

A uniquely perverse outcome has developed in the field of low-priced household goods, known in Soviet parlance as "goods of the simplest selection, not centrally planned." For about 85 percent of these approximately 3,000 items, central control consists solely of national planners in Gosplan assigning global quotas, reckoned in rubles and not in physical units, to the industrial ministries, which are then given carte blanche to decide what to make and distribute. "No one," a trade official grumbled in 1982, "is occupied with coordinating the production of the whole range of the simplest commodities, and in this lies the source of many omissions and failures."[61] Salt has been rubbed in this old wound since the mid-1970s as executives, pressed to meet their basic plans, cut back arbitrarily on the manufacture of household goods. The bottom line being calculated in gross ruble terms, plant managers have often opted for larger, higher-priced items and produced fewer of the cheaper but often more necessary articles. This explains the recent proliferation of shortages of such inexpensive but irreplaceable consumer goods as paper products (of which there is a permanent shortage), tooth brushes, underwear and lingerie, baby blankets and diapers, low-wattage light bulbs, ink, glue, small bottles, aspirin, bandages, light footwear, needles and thread, inexpensive radios, kitchen utensils, ironing boards, axes, spades, garden hoses, wooden stools, key rings, hinges, bolts, shoe polish, electric switches, spark plugs, piston rings, typewriter ribbons, bath soap, and washing machine detergent. It is an object lesson, once again, in Soviet regression even as overall economic and social capacity continues to expand.

Minimal reforms with this result may be worse than no change at all. An individual might, after all, be philosophical about not owning a washing machine; when the machine he does own cannot be repaired or stands idle for lack of detergent, he is apt to be less forgiving. Such experiences fuel popular disillusionment, the underground economy, and demands for more responsive policies and structures.

The Danger of Crisis

What can be concluded about the seriousness and dynamics of Soviet miseries? One answer, offered by a fair number of observers in the West as the Brezhnev regime drew to an end, is that the USSR today is a society in crisis, that it has come to a turning point in which the very continuance of the Soviet order is at stake. This thesis, in my view, is invalid. It understates the rulers' resources and overstates their problems.

In cataloguing the leadership's worries, one must never lose sight of its strengths and assets. The Soviet system of government is closing out the seventh decade of its existence, making it one of the longest-lived and most firmly established of the world's political regimes. It has weathered more than its fair share of trials and shocks: civil war, forced-draft industrialization and the violent transformation of the countryside through collectivization, the great purges, invasion and occupation by Germany in a war with 20 million Soviet casualties, de-Stalinization, the overthrow of Khrushchev, the petrifaction of the late Brezhnev period. The resilience of Soviet power can hardly be doubted. It is based in large part on sturdy instruments of control—rule by a single party with a monopoly over personnel decisions, formal and informal censorship, a nationalized economy, political police and armed forces that possess nearly all weapons in the society, denial of free assembly, comprehensive political education, and the like—none of which shows signs of cracking. The telltale mark of a political system in mortal danger is violence, and political violence has been kept to a singularly low level in the Soviet Union. There have been impromptu strikes, the occasional street demonstration, a few aircraft hijackings, and scattered acts of terrorism. But little blood has been spilled, and the authorities have not had to strain to limit the fallout from such incidents. Among the forces aligned against the regime, there is barely a soul who either advocates its forcible overthrow or sees any realistic chance of this happening.[62]

The regime's solidity rests also on a record of positive achievement. Whatever its defects, it has made the country a world military power, safe for the first time from foreign invasion, the proprietor of an empire in Eastern Europe and the patron of far-off dependencies. It has thus been bound up in the public mind with Russian nationalism, an emotion which, as the case of Stalin proves, can also exert a hold on members of the society not of Russian ethnic origin. The regime has maintained order and facilitated the normal workings of a complex society over an immense and diverse territory. Its economic and scientific programs, at great sacrifice, have ferried peasant Russia into the space age. Industrialization and free public schooling have drawn millions of Soviets from humble backgrounds into rewarding professional and administrative careers. Cradle-to-grave social services and safeguards, expanded under

Brezhnev for rural dwellers, give Soviet citizens a security few would happily surrender. All told, the Communist Party's accomplishments represent a cache of political capital on which it can draw for some time.

Granted that it has been jarred by recent events, basic support for Soviet institutions has thus far not really been softened. As one thoughtful observer puts it, "there is no evidence that [the] perceived legitimacy of the system has lessened . . . among any but the relatively small contingent of dissidents and critically minded intellectuals." Much as there has been a welling up of pessimism, especially in the middle class, there is still a residue of optimism about the future, "a feeling that in the very long run things will turn out all right."[63] Preliminary results of the Soviet Interview Project, a massive survey of recent emigrants from the USSR to the United States, show a considerable degree of satisfaction with important regime norms even among individuals who voluntarily left the country. Fifty-two percent of the expatriates questioned, for example, strongly favored a system of state medicine such as exists in the Soviet Union, and 13 percent favored it somewhat; 38 percent fully endorsed public ownership of heavy industry, with 11 percent showing some approval; a good deal of support was also voiced for Soviet-type education, and a surprisingly large minority sympathized with the Soviet approach to criminal justice. Interestingly, the Soviet Interview Project is turning up many findings reminiscent of those of the Harvard Project, which polled several thousand refugees from Stalin's Soviet Union in the early 1950s.[64]

To help keep the recent failures of the Soviet regime in perspective, it must be remembered that many of them have been failures at the margin. Economic growth has been slowed, but the economy has not ceased to grow, let alone given indications of breaking down. There is a shortage of steak but not of bread, of stylish clothing but not of plain suits and work boots, of living space but not of basic shelter. Some Soviet problems would not have happened at all but for previous successes. The Stalinist economic model, for instance, would not be under scrutiny today had it not succeeded in promoting economic development to the point where the model is diminishing in effectiveness. There would be no ecological controversy in the Soviet Union if breakneck industrialization had not occurred, no mass striving for better careers and consumer goods if state education and steady economic progress had not stoked popular expectations, and fewer infant deaths if Soviet doctors had not cut down on stillbirths.

Although the regime's difficulties are more plentiful and imposing than ten or twenty years ago, some problems are offsetting rather than mutually reinforcing. Think of the growing second economy. It is a source of corruption and in many ways a rival to the state economy for the loyalty and energies of Soviet citizens. It is also, however, a safety valve for the disaffected and a provider of goods and services not supplied by the state. In certain parts of the country, it may alleviate ethnic tensions as well. A new study of Uzbekistan, the most populous of the Moslem republics, concludes that the indigenous population draws major material benefit from its concentration in agriculture, services, and the light and food industries. Whereas Russians and other Europeans in Uzbekistan fill the leading positions in heavy industry and many of the professions, the Uzbeks themselves prefer to work in sectors well situated for crossover into individual enterprise, much of it illegal. Employment in the agricultural and services branches furnishes direct access to materials and products in short supply, which can then be traded in the underground economy, and in many cases allows earnings higher than those of the Russians. Extensive Uzbek participation in the second economy also "works to stifle the articulation of dissatisfaction in a direct political sense," in that those involved frequently circumvent or violate Soviet laws and can ill-afford to draw attention to themselves by making political demands.[65]

It is also instructive, before being carried away with the trouble the Soviets are in, to weigh their difficulties against those of other countries. The Soviet Union is far from alone in suffering from higher adult mortality rates and a widening gap between male and female life expectancy. It displays in an exaggerated form demographic symptoms found in a number of other developed societies.[66] On economic matters, it may be overdoing it to say, as does one American commentator, that talk of declining growth and structural problems in the USSR "could describe any country in the world."[67] Still, it is all too tempting in reciting the litany of Soviet woes to forget that the capitalist economies suffered from stagflation in the 1970s and deep recession in the early 1980s, that cash wages in the United States (adjusted for inflation) are barely what they were ten years ago, and that there are more than 25 million men and women out of work in Western Europe and North America.

Making due allowance for its deficiencies, the USSR still possesses the second largest economy in the world (third by some measures, behind Japan as well as the United States). It leads all other countries in the production of steel, cement, and many types of chemicals and machinery. With giant reserves of natural gas, oil, coal, and hydropower, it has the most favorable long-term energy balance of any industrial power. The Politburo's headaches do not include, as those of the cabinets of the liberal democracies have lately, sky-high budget deficits, key industries ravaged by foreign competition, a wobbly international banking system, race riots, or separatist movements. The Soviet Union is not a society polarized along ethnic or socioeconomic fault lines, nor is the corruption and ineptitude of its political class at all comparable to that of a Ferdinand Marcos or a Jean-Claude Duvalier.

None of this is to make light of Soviet problems. They are legion, they are real, many of them are worsening, and they are having a cumulative effect. While the Soviet system has not arrived at the point of crisis, it clearly is headed in the wrong direction, raising the specter of grave trouble down the road. Some Soviet leaders guardedly conceded as much in the early 1980s. Writing in the party's theoretical journal in 1981, Konstantin Chernenko, then Brezhnev's closest confederate in the leadership, enjoined the party to recognize anew the importance of serving the "proper interests" of all segments of society. With Poland obviously in mind, he warned that otherwise, "our policy risks losing its firm social base, its support on the part of the masses." Poor analysis of social problems and disregard of the interests of particular classes and groups are, he said, "fraught with *the danger of social tension, of political and socioeconomic crisis.*"[68] Andropov several times struck a similar chord during his brief leadership. "It is necessary to pay dearly for one's mistakes in politics," he told the Central Committee in June 1983. "If the party's bond with the people is lost, into the resultant vacuum come self-styled pretenders to the role of spokesman for the interests of the working people"—an unmistakable allusion to Lech Wałęsa and the Solidarity union.[69]

Which problems are most capable of shearing "the party's bond with the people"? Which will command priority attention because they have the potential of realizing the admitted danger of a general crisis of the Soviet system? For a problem to be critical in this sense, it must satisfy two criteria. First, it must be severe enough to affect the essential well-being of society and the cooperative relations among its members. Second, it must be urgent, calling for prompt action, as distinct from a condition that is stable or worsens only slowly.

Some of the problems on the Soviet agenda, while much more than trivial, fail to qualify as critical by the touchstone of severity. Genetic engineering, water and air pollution, traffic tie-ups, and city planning will agitate many officials and citizens in the years to come and be the subject of letters to the editor and learned conferences. They may act as well as a drain on resources needed to resolve more basic problems, as, say, concern over pollution does in relation to some kinds of industrial growth. But they are not so threatening as to force their way onto the leadership's core agenda. The problems of health care, bad as they may be, are also non-critical from a political perspective. The rise in mortality rates after the mid-1960s provoked little reaction at the time outside a restricted circle of administrators and experts. Equally important, the Soviets managed in the middle and late 1970s to stabilize the increase in death rates for one of the worst affected groups, infants, and to reverse the trend decisively in the Moslem republics and more moderately in the Baltic and Slavic areas.[70] Infant mortality was lessened by upgrading hospital maternity wards and clinics, enlarging the supply of qualified obstetricians and pediatricians, organizing more child care classes, improving the distribution of infant formula, and so forth. There can be little question that Soviet health standards in general can resume their historic upward movement. For this to happen, funds will have to be allocated to treatment, research, and prophylaxis, and this will require that health's share of the state budget, which gradually fell after 1965, rise once again. But we are speaking here of a straightforward matter of resources, not of system capacity.

Still other Soviet problems do not meet the test of urgency. This surely is true of most demographic issues. The regime will continue to grope for an "effective demographic policy," but no Soviet leader in the 1980s is likely to give top priority to influencing through means of dubious reliability family-planning decisions that will not be reflected in manpower levels until after the turn of the century, long after he is out of power. The same holds for the reduction in opportunities for Soviet youth to enter desirable professional careers. Once any society has passed through the early stages of industrialization and the most prized occupational slots have been filled (and the children of the winners given a head start in competing for plum positions in the next generation), it is difficult if not impossible to retain the high rates of upward mobility realized at the outset. For the individuals involved, the problem may be severe; for the government, it cannot be urgent, for there is no tangible remedy short of upending other policies (such as career security for qualified incumbents). The 1984 amendments to Soviet elementary and secondary education seem to recognize the intractibility of the problem, which they deal with mostly by changes in the relative size of curriculum streams (in favor of vocational training at the expense of generalist education) seemingly aimed at reconciling youths from the lower classes to not entering university.

The Soviet Union's nationality problem is not so easily dismissed, yet here again it is important to keep the issue in perspective. Soviet ethnic relations are too often discussed by foreign observers in apocalyptic language, sometimes as if the Soviet multinational state were on the verge of collapsing like a house of cards. Careful reflection suggests this, too, is not a critically urgent problem. The Soviet regime has in the past been extraordinarily adept at using sticks and carrots to keep the non-Russian minorities pacified. Two or three generations into the future, population dynamics alone may make fundamental change inescapable. Over the next ten years or so, however, and even several decades beyond, the situation seems entirely manageable.

Russian hegemony in its present form is in no immediate peril for several reasons. The most important is that ethnic conflict will continue to be moderated by the same set of systemic constraints and buffers that help make the Soviet regime as a whole so stable—checks on communication, administrative and political controls, and the like.

In addition, crucial realities of the nationality issue itself will keep it well below the boiling point. First, demographic trends, distressing though they may be to the Russians, will leave them and their Slavic cousins numerically ascendant long into the twenty-first century. Russians, Ukrainians, and Belorussians will comprise about 65 percent of the USSR's population in 2000, three times the Moslem proportion.

Second, political leverage will not automatically spring from demographic growth. Political power is an independent Russian resource. Control over the Soviet state and Communist Party will be used to ensure that as much power as possible is passed on to future Russians.

Third, the dominant Russians will go on enjoying the advantage of territorial and political coherence and centrality. The ethnic minorities will remain on the periphery, penetrated by large Russian settler communities (24 million Russians lived outside the RSFSR in 1979, making up almost a fifth of the population there), relatively remote from one another (and in some instances hostile to one another), and able in most cases to communicate with one another only in Russian.

Fourth, there is reason to believe that the region that poses the greatest demographic challenge—Central Asia—will long remain receptive to Soviet rule. This is primarily because of government policies, among them modernization of the economy and of social services (especially successful when compared to neighboring Asian countries), Soviet tolerance of native traditions (including Islam), and leniency toward the indigenous second economy. The vast majority of Soviet Central Asians seem content with the regime and would find the arguments of an Ayatollah Khomeini, which have wreaked such havoc across the Iranian border, "very difficult . . . to understand, let alone endorse."[71]

Fifth, Moscow will have the opportunity of carrying forward the one great success of nationality policy under Brezhnev: Russian-language training. Between 1970 and 1979, the proportion of non-Russians knowing Russian as a first or second language rose from 49 to 62 percent; the ratio is much higher among urban residents and younger people and in republics, such as Uzbekistan, where it was given a high priority by the local leadership. Bilingualism, in which members of other ethnic groups are able to function in Russian for economic and other state purposes, without relinquishing their particular identity, may very well be the cornerstone of the Soviet nationality policy of the future, and it will be building on solid past successes. The intensified teaching program unveiled in the late 1970s and affirmed in 1983 should keep the trend in train.

There is an item on the Soviet agenda that is sufficiently severe and urgent to be truly critical, one that could lead to a general crisis of the regime. That is the problem to which this chapter has repeatedly turned for examples—the problem of the economy. For the Soviet Union, the central question of the 1980s and 1990s is that of its sputtering economic engine and of the social ramifications of economic stagnation.

Economic difficulties are the most common precipitant of trauma and change in politics. In well-nigh all industrial societies today, economic and socioeconomic issues dominate political discourse. The Soviet Union is no different: elite and mass opinion alike take it as a given that economic and related problems are and will remain of overriding importance. The regime's rhetoric, action program, and deepest anxieties all revolve around the economy. The population, for its part, sizes up the state today more than ever by how it delivers material goods and services. And no section of the establishment, no matter how coddled, has been insulated from economic stringency. Even Soviet military officers, traditionally a privileged group, were reported in the late Brezhnev period to be "forced to become nervous and to waste valuable time waiting in queues" for food. According to another report in the military press, underinvestment and poor personnel practices in the army's retailing network had bred bad services, spoiled goods, and "interruptions in supply," with hoarding and black markets as a consequence. All these "call forth justified indignation on the part of the residents of the garrisons."[72]

Furthermore, the health of the economy has a direct bearing on many of the non-economic issues facing the Soviet system. Prized foreign policy goals are implicated, as has been more emphasized in recent Soviet discussions, since military competitiveness and the international prestige of Soviet-style socialism are harder to sustain with a sluggish economy. The weapons systems of the armed forces, the principal vehicle for projecting Soviet power abroad, depend increasingly on technologies coming out of civilian science and industry and not just out of the nine defense production ministries: new materials and alloys, hardware and software for communications and data processing, manufacturing and miniaturizing techniques, directed energy, and the like.

At home, almost all major interests would be poorly served by continuing economic malaise. Soviet communists have been no less inclined than American liberals to see economic growth as a surrogate for painful, redistributive choice among competing priorities. The worse the economy does, the more those conflicts—guns versus butter, schools versus hospitals, the holders of jobs versus the aspirants to jobs—have to be sorted out and defused. The more also ethnic harmony will be injured, for retarded growth in an unreformed Soviet economy would aggravate both the rivalry for jobs between natives and Russians in the non-Russian republics and the competition for investment funds that pits region against region. Unless economic productivity and growth prospects are improved in the built-up Slavic and Baltic republics, the manpower shortage will present the regime with two options either of which is likely to inflame ethnic relations: involuntary importation of millions of Central Asian workers into the European USSR and Siberia, which could both anger the Central Asians and create ethnic ghettos in Slavic cities; or, equally unpalatable, redirection of new investment and maybe even existing industrial plant into the Moslem regions.

It is on economic and socioeconomic issues that the gap between regime performance and popular expectations has grown most dangerously in recent years. There are no grounds whatever for the Kremlin hoping that the present economic crunch will prove to be transitory and that developments a few years hence will ring in new and easy prosperity. Arable land, capital, raw materials, energy, labor—all the abundant and cheap grist that once fed the mill of extensive economic growth has become scarce and expensive, and will only become more so as the 1980s give way to the 1990s.

To make matters worse, the Soviets by the early 1980s were the victims in economic policy of several vicious circles, that is to say, of negative trends that feed on themselves. Three stand out. One is the contribution of inadequate incentives to poor work motivation and, therefore, to low productivity, which in turn reduces the total available for rewards. A second vicious circle is built around the substitution of private for public responses to economic needs. This spins off worlds of activity not under the regime's direct control and at variance with its values. A third stems from the investment crunch beginning in the late 1970s. A capital goods glutton for half a century, the Soviet economy was put on a diet because the economic growth that sustained new investment was wavering and the Brezhnev Politburo was unwilling to rank investment ahead of maintenance of levels of mass consumption and military spending. With the emergency need for investment in oil and natural gas development further tightening the bind, the Soviet leaders were, in the opinion of many analysts, heavily mortaging future economic growth.[73]

To sum up: the agenda of Soviet politics is indeed a cluttered and a disquieting one. The combination of the resurgent problems of neglect and the novel problems of success, dwindling payoffs to old solutions, the accentuation of ethnic tensions, the inability of the regime to meet rising expectations, social atomization in such forms as corruption and the second economy, the failures of faint-hearted reforms—all are of concern, and all are harbingers of more trouble ahead. The Soviet system is not yet in crisis, but unless its new leaders can brake downward trends, especially in the economy, the day cannot be put off indefinitely when it will be.

3
Succession and the Changing Soviet Elite

The succession to Leonid Brezhnev was keenly anticipated by Sovietologists in part because it would make for good political theater. At a deeper level, they knew how much rides in a single-party dictatorship on who the leaders are and how they behave. The impending change would terminate almost two decades of continuity in the Kremlin, and it would do so against a backdrop of economic and social mismanagement. The transfer of power, it was also understood, would affect not just the General Secretary but the entire Soviet hierarchy. Officials recruited into leading positions under Joseph Stalin would finally exit en masse, their places to be taken by a younger generation.

These things being agreed, wildly differing predictions were offered of what exactly would result from Brezhnev's departure and the attendant displacement of generations. Three main points of view were propounded in the West. The first brought out the succession's potential for inducing conflict and instability. Its authors emphasized the severity of Soviet problems and the regime's lack of constitutional procedures for choosing a top leader, something that had been done only three times before in its history. These, it was speculated, might fracture the leadership and open the door to an insurgent faction from within the party or perhaps from the military or KGB. A second set of analysts submitted that the succession would confirm the status quo. Postulating that shared values outweigh differences within the Soviet elite, they foresaw that party unity would hold and that new bosses, after a period of adjustment, would end up acting much like the old. The third hypothesis was that the succession would open up avenues for reform in the Soviet Union. From this perspective, the competition for top office had often in the past been a catalyst of change, and a parallel of sorts could be drawn between the imminent Brezhnev succession and the reforms touched off by the death of Stalin in the 1950s.

While the early evidence does not jibe perfectly with any of these theories, it fits best with a modified version of the third. Not only did Brezhnev's death not precipitate a political cataclysm or usurpation of party authority, but equilibrium was preserved through the death and replacement of two short-lived successors, Yuri Andropov and Konstantin Chernenko. The transition has not ground out a replica of the Brezhnev regime, either. Brezhnev's style and important parts of his program have been disowned by new leaders, starting with Andropov and then, after a lull under Chernenko, more forcefully by Mikhail Gorbachev. All things considered, events to date are most supportive of the reform prognosis, although with the caveat that actual reforms have fallen short of rhetoric and have been gradual in pace, limited in scope, and counterbalanced by controls. Andropov, the victor in the first heat of the succession, was not in power long enough to make much more than promises, and Gorbachev, though a far more robust leader, has focused in the early going on leadership style, personnel, and public policy rather the essentials of the Soviet system. The shift toward moderate reform, tentative though its results have been, would not have been possible at all without changes in the Soviet elite. At the top, Gorbachev has labored, with no small success, to build a change-minded coalition. Intermediate and lower levels of officialdom have been rocked by forced retirements, new staffing procedures, and the long-delayed influx into influential positions of a generation that reached maturity after Stalin. The future of innovation in Soviet politics hinges on further developments within the elite.

The Andropov-Chernenko Interregnum

The turning points of the struggle to succeed Brezhnev, including all changes in the Politburo and Secretariat of the Communist Party since 1976, may be tracked in the Appendix, *A Soviet Leadership Chronology*. The jockeying for position began during the dénouement of Brezhnev's reign and culminated in the seizure of control by a new leadership group centered on Mikhail Gorbachev. Throughout this time the Politburo, the party's nerve center, continued to make the crucial decisions about leadership, but it did not do so in a vacuum. Prudence dictated that the contenders and their supporters keep one ear cocked to opinions in the party and beyond. Under party statutes, the larger Central Committee could overturn a Politburo decision on the choice of leader, as it had done on one prior occasion (in June 1957, when Nikita Khrushchev successfully appealed to it). Accordingly, along with backstage plotting and alliance-building, the rivals in the several phases of the Brezhnev succession played a crude kind of image politics, each seeking to signal to wider audiences how he would treat elite and mass interests.

The fray was joined in earnest during the final year of Brezhnev's life. A stabilizing force within the oligarchy was eliminated by the death in January 1982 of Mikhail Suslov, the seventy-nine-year-old overlord of propaganda and foreign relations, legendary for his ascetic devotion to party doctrine and his lack of ambition for the General Secretaryship. Suslov's death made leadership politics more fluid and was a stroke of luck for Andropov, the head of the KGB since 1967, for an unwritten premise of succession politics since Stalin had been that a new General Secretary was to be chosen from among the tiny number of politicians sitting on both the Politburo (which averaged twelve members during this period) and the Secretariat (usually about ten men strong), the collective overseer of the party bureaucracy. The barrage of rumors and information leaks about disarray in the Kremlin and corruption in Brezhnev's entourage seems to have helped create the presumption that the country's top policeman was the natural person to occupy the empty seat in the Secretariat. In late May 1982 a plenum of the Central Committee awarded Andropov the deceased Suslov's position as chief party ideologist. From that moment forward, portraying himself as a principled realist who could deal firmly with official misconduct and underlying economic problems, Andropov was a leading candidate to succeed Brezhnev.

His chief rival was Chernenko, now the senior secretary responsible for cadres selection. For many years previously Brezhnev's alter ego in party administration. Chernenko was undoubtedly the favored candidate of Brezhnev, who was reported by the fall of 1982 to be considering resigning one or more of his posts in his friend's favor. This forced everyone to take Chernenko seriously, yet it also underscored how closely he was tied to the political apronstrings of his patron. Besides Andropov and Chernenko, only two other men doubled as Politburo and Secretariat members in 1982, and both were badly handicapped. Gorbachev, the newest and youngest face in the Politburo and its specialist on agriculture and consumer affairs, was hobbled by his relative youth and inexperience. Andrei Kirilenko, an old associate of Brezhnev's who had nonetheless retained some autonomy, had during the 1970s been considered heir-apparent but was by now in such bad political odor that he was mysteriously scratched from the unofficial Politburo lineup five weeks before Brezhnev's death.

In choosing Yuri Vladimirovich Andropov on November 12, 1982, two days after Brezhnev's heart gave out, the oligarchy handed the torch to a tough and resourceful politician with lengthy and varied service to the party cause. Born in a Russian railway clerk's family in 1914, Andropov did odd jobs before enrolling in a vocational institute for water transport personnel, from which he graduated in 1936. By the time he joined the party in 1939, he was well launched on a career as a Komsomol (Young Communist League) and party administrator in Yaroslavl' *oblast'* (region) and the Karelian area on the Finnish border. Narrowly escaping a postwar purge in Karelia, he was transferred to the Central Committee's party cadres department in 1951. In 1953 he was reassigned to foreign policy, first as counsellor in the Soviet embassy in Hungary and then as ambassador. Andropov returned to Moscow in 1957, working briefly in party personnel management and then assuming responsibility as department head in the Secretariat for liaison with other ruling communist parties. He was made a full secretary in 1962. In May 1967 he was appointed chief of the KGB, in which capacity he was co-opted to candidate (non-voting) Politburo membership in June 1967 and to voting membership in April 1973. It was from here that he took over Suslov's portfolio in 1982.

Andropov's background in some senses differed from his predecessors'. His fifteen years in the KGB, the longest term as chief in its history, made him the first Soviet leader to have had prior custody of the secret police. His having acquitted himself there, in Brezhnev's estimation, in a "clean and irreproachable" way, showed he could be trusted with still more power.[1] Altogether, Andropov had amassed twenty-seven years in national administration, whereas Brezhnev and Khrushchev had but a dozen years between them and were fundamentally products of the provincial party machine. Not having worked at the local level since leaving Karelia in 1951, Andropov saw the world primarily through the prism of the central Soviet bureaucracy. His KGB experience, in particular, seemed to impress on him that Moscow's directives were often sabotaged by venal or inept subordinates—as good an explanation as any of his penchant for "discipline" after November 1982. His many years in the capital also ingrained in Andropov respect for the research institutes that flourished there in the 1960s and 1970s, and he had been one of the first party officials to involve academics as policy consultants. Among the policy-oriented intellectuals who enjoyed his early patronage were Fedor Burlatskii, Georgi Arbatov, and Aleksandr Bovin.[2] Andropov also was unusual for his exposure, via the foreign service, Central Committee apparatus, and KGB, to foreign affairs and the international environment.

In choosing Andropov, the Politburo could not possibly have intended a radical break with the status quo. His age (sixty-eight at appointment) and his physical frailty, which must have been well known to his confrères, made it most unlikely that he would have the stamina to change a great deal, even if he wanted to. However accurate the early reports of Andropov as bon vivant and fan of Western jazz, he was a stickler for ideological propriety and on most essential points a defender of the mainstream political culture of the Soviet Union. In his meager formal training and long career in party administration, he resembled closely the typical official of his generation. That he did not demur at running the KGB—or, as Soviet leader, at callously defending the September 1983 downing of an unarmed Korean airliner by Soviet interceptors, with the loss of 269 lives—was a reminder that he put the interests of the regime above all others. His surface charm cloaked a hardness beneath, summed up by an aide's comparison of his character to "a fine feather bed you jump into only to find that the mattress is filled with bricks."[3] The fact remains, though, that Andropov had also been known as a politician of urbanity, honesty, and a modicum of compassion, "the most educated and progressive party figure" in the opinion of some intellectuals.[4] He spoke favorably of economic reforms in Eastern Europe, Soviet relations with which he supervised from 1957 to 1967. His approval extended to the economic liberalization instituted in Hungary by János Kadár, whom he had helped make Hungarian party leader when still Soviet envoy to Budapest. While Andropov manifestly had no intention in 1982 of carbon-copying the Hungarian reform, his actions were to demonstrate a conviction that Soviet problems had accumulated to the point where something had to be done.

Andropov's starting point in November 1982 was to see to his own power position. One way he did this was by using his office as a pulpit, communicating with an air of authority and often addressing himself to the population as well as to officialdom. An ostensibly unrehearsed appearance at a Moscow machine tool plant in January 1983, followed by a solo article in the party's theoretical journal, *Kommunist,* bespoke a desire to use mildly unorthodox channels to get his message across. By June 1983 Andropov had appropriated both of Brezhnev's non-party offices, those of Chairman of the Defense Council and Chairman of the Presidium of the Supreme Soviet. Of greater political moment was his aggressive use of prerogatives in the area of personnel. Where Brezhnev for years had let most incumbents age gracefully in office, Andropov took a different tack, starting with the tongue-lashing in his inaugural speech of officials who "simply do not know how to work."[5] The sacking of senior officials, at a clip not seen since 1964, began within days. Transport Minister Ivan Pavlovskii was the first prominent government functionary to go, on grounds of incompetence, and he was soon joined by Interior Minister Nikolai Shchelokov, against whom the accusation was corruption. The Andropov broom was slower to reach into the party organs, but by late March 1983 the first major regional boss, Nikolai Bannikov of Irkutsk, had been retired, and many more firings were to ensue.

Andropov's personnel strategy was executed by allies who assumed great importance in the politics of the succession. On the party side, the details of placement were handled by an ex-regional first secretary, Yegor Ligachev, plucked in April 1983 from the obscurity of Tomsk oblast in Siberia and made head of the Central Committee Secretariat's section for assigning party officials (the "organizational-party work department"). At about this time Mikhail Gorbachev was given supervisory responsibility for party staffing, and he retained this when Ligachev was made a full member of the Secretariat in December 1983. Within the state bureaucracy, Andropov found a willing helper in Geidar Aliyev, the new First Deputy Chairman of the Council of Ministers. Aliyev, originally a KGB officer, had since 1969 been party first secretary in the southern republic of Azerbaidzhan, where much was made of his stern measures against corrupted and inept bureaucrats.

Aided by Gorbachev, Ligachev, Aliyev, and others, Andropov started to winnow out old-time Brezhnev clients and more generally to bring fresh blood into the Soviet elite.[6] In his truncated reign, he engineered the replacement of one-third of the heads of Central Committee departments, almost one-quarter of the regional first secretaries of the party, and one-fifth of all the ministers in the Soviet government. Andropov's threat in June 1983 to have administrative staffs reduced across the board might have been the pretext for further changes, but it was not implemented.[7] At the peak of the political pyramid, in the party Politburo and Secretariat, the Andropov changes were slower but not inconsequential. One Politburo member (Grigori Romanov of Leningrad) was brought into the Secretariat and thus into the innermost group, one outsider (Vitali Vorotnikov, the new premier of the RSFSR) was added to the Politburo, two Politburo candidate members (Aliyev and Mikhail Solomentsev) were co-opted to full membership, and there was one new Politburo candidate (Viktor Chebrikov, the KGB chief) and two new secretaries without Politburo rank (Nikolai Ryzhkov and Ligachev). Only one Politburo member was retired, Kirilenko in November 1982, although one member and a candidate member died in 1983.

What did Andropov accomplish with his power, which waxed even as his physical strength waned? Certainly, hopes about early political and ideological liberalization were dashed. Andropov called in nebulous terms for "further democratization" of the political process, but practical results were few. Some unclogging of information channels can be detected in the introduction of press communiqués on the weekly meetings of the Politburo (hitherto shrouded in secrecy), the printing in *Izvestiya* of biographic cameos of all new members of the Council of Ministers, and Andropov's several denunciations of stage-managed public meetings. Policy debates by specialists were somewhat enlivened, especially over economic issues, while newspapers carried more critical letters from their readers. In June 1983 legislation was passed providing for some worker participation in industrial management.

On balance, however, the leadership under Andropov tightened up rather than slackened state controls over the individual. From Soviet citizens, it demanded above all, as innumerable editorials and posters proclaimed, "discipline and order" (*distsiplina i poryadok*), qualities that seemed to matter more to the leadership the greater the flux in its own ranks. One unappealing manifestation was a further tightening of the political screws on the arts and stepped-up harassment of dissidents. In the economy, penalties were stiffened for underfulfillment of production quotas, violation of "planning discipline" through renegotiation of targets, and slothful behavior on the job. These, combined with more favorable weather, helped push production statistics slightly up in 1983.

But Yuri Andropov did considerably more in office than crack the disciplinarian's whip. He also took the first halting steps toward reconsidering policies and structures allowed to ossify under Brezhnev. Admittedly, concrete changes (to be discussed in Chapter 4) were slow and deliberate, a pace seemingly dictated by Andropov's reading of the political barometer as much as by his health. Andropov took pains to reassure conservative elements that no snap decisions would be taken or the contribution of loyal communists slighted, telling party veterans that "not a single valuable grain" of their experience would be forgotten. Still, there is no mistaking that Andropov varied markedly from the 1964–82 baseline in terms of style and definition of the condition of the Soviet system. Without faulting Brezhnev personally, Andropov put the regime's backlog of problems squarely at the head of the Soviet political agenda. He urged the party "to see the facts as they are" and "not to embellish anything," the unspoken message being that the truth previously had been embellished. The Soviet Union needed, he declared, a period of self-analysis and therapy in which past oversights and errors were made up for and the way prepared for future advances: "We must soberly realize where we find ourselves. To jump forward would mean to take on unrealistic objectives; to dwell on our accomplishments would mean not to take advantage of all that we possess. What is demanded of us today is to see our society in its real dynamics, with all of its possibilities and needs."[8]

Andropov's voice was often that of the moralist, warning society against spiritual decay and especially aggrieved by the mismatch between words and actions. He flayed corruption among officials, shirkers in the work force, hypocritical and ritualized propaganda campaigns, and the unfulfillable promises of the long-ignored 1961 Communist Party Program. Other times, Andropov struck a more cooly analytic note, lauding rational inquiry and science as a guide to action: "To be frank about it, we to this time have not studied to a sufficient extent the society in which we live and work and have not completely uncovered the laws peculiar to it, especially the economic ones. Therefore, we are often forced to act . . . by way of the extremely irrational method of trial and error." He spoke grandly of the need for "an integrated strategy of social development," and advocated, more than any earlier head of the party, learning from the successes and failures of other communist lands. For all his distaste for trial and error, however, it was only by this route that Andropov seemed prepared to proceed. He stated unapologetically in an early speech that he himself had "no ready-made recipes" for resolving Soviet difficulties. He may have had reformist instincts, but he had nothing approaching a clear reform plan or strategy.[9]

Andropov's comments on issues ranged far and wide, but his predominant concern was with the Soviet Union's stalled economy. Less notable than his observations about specific problems, considerably more trenchant than Brezhnev's, was his attribution of the overall malaise of the economy to poor leadership and incentives and not just the peccadilloes of individual bureaucrats and workers. The country now needed to devise, by his reckoning, "measures capable of giving greater scope of action to the colossal creative forces walled up in our economy." One possible inference from such a statement was that there had to be an economic restructuring to free up the initiative of producers, and it was on this possibility that Andropov had put his finger briefly in an address in November 1982: "Recently not a little has been said about the need to expand the independence of [industrial] associations and enterprises, collective and state farms. I think the time has come to get down to a practical decision on this question."[10]

Andropov was adamant that economic innovations be "carefully prepared and realistic" and not negate the central precepts of socialism. But he made it equally plain that, as he put it in his last public speech, he wanted major decisions (*krupnye resheniya*) on the economy, not another bout of the minimal reforms that typified the Brezhnev period: "We cannot be satisfied with our pace in shifting the economy onto the rails of intensive development. . . . It is obvious that in looking for ways to resolve new tasks we were not energetic enough, that not infrequently we resorted to half-measures and could not overcome the accumulated inertia quickly enough. Now we must make up for our neglect." This would require, he said, "changes in planning, management, and the economic mechanism" by the start of the next five-year plan in January 1986. As of his final message on domestic policy, read to the Central Committee on his behalf in December 1983, Andropov was sticking to this schedule, saying that the small steps taken and the slight improvement in the economy in 1983 were "only a beginning."[11]

A beginning was all Yuri Andropov would be given to make. He was much the oldest person ever to be made General Secretary, exceeding Brezhnev's age at accession by ten years and Khrushchev's by nine, and his chronic health problems soon became acute. Only three months after he succeeded Brezhnev, Andropov's kidneys failed and dialysis treatment was begun. There was no official admission of his condition, but enough was said by his frequent absences from important functions and, when he did show up, by his emaciated features and shaking hands. Though he was stated in the posthumous medical bulletin to have tended to party business until January 1984, he was last seen in public August 18, 1983. Andropov died February 9, 1984, and was buried beside Brezhnev in Red Square.

The selection of Konstantin Ustinovich Chernenko to succeed Andropov as General Secretary was not easily made, for it took four days to announce, twice as long as for Andropov. It in no way settled the longer-term leadership issue. Chernenko, six months shy of his seventy-third birthday (four years older than Andropov in 1982), was so weakened by emphysema that he could barely make it through a ten-minute speech at Andropov's funeral. His medical condition alone, to say nothing of his other qualities, branded him an interim leader from his first day in office. Creakily going through the motions for thirteen months, he turned out to be the most ineffectual and transient General Secretary ever.

Born of peasant parents in the Krasnoyarsk *krai* (territory) of central Siberia in 1911, and a party member since 1931, Chernenko had remarkably skimpy credentials for holding so exalted a post. His formal education was limited to two years in a school for party organizers and a correspondence degree from a teacher's college, earned when he was forty-two. He began his career in low-level Komsomol work in 1929, spent three years in the border guards in the early 1930s, then held a string of positions in the party's ideological apparatus in Krasnoyarsk, Penza oblast, and the Moldavian republic. Two years after becoming head of the propaganda department of the Moldavian central committee, chance brought him into the political orbit of Leonid Brezhnev, when the latter was named Moldavian first secretary in 1950. Moving to Moscow when Brezhnev became a Central Committee secretary in 1956, Chernenko from 1960 on worked as one of Brezhnev's personal aides, first in the Presidium of the Supreme Soviet (which Brezhnev chaired from 1960 to 1964) and then in the Central Committee Secretariat. It was a sign more of Brezhnev's growing authority than of his own that he was appointed head of the Secretariat's general department, which handles internal party communications, in 1965. Made a national party secretary in 1976 and a member of the Politburo two years later, Chernenko grew in influence as Brezhnev's health worsened and was rarely far from the ailing leader's side. Brezhnev's trust enabled him to nose out other confidants such as Andrei Kirilenko, from whom Chernenko took over responsibility for supervision of party personnel.

Chernenko had little to recommend him except his association with Brezhnev. According to one insider's account, some of the older members of the Politburo, particularly Aleksei Kosygin and Suslov, considered him a parvenu, "lacking the qualifications for becoming their colleague, much less those fitting him to become their leader."[12] He was a dull and mumbling speaker in public, humorless and given to monologues and interruptions in private. Americans who saw him at the 1979 Vienna summit with President Jimmy Carter thought he behaved more like Brezhnev's valet than a policy-maker. Incredibly, Chernenko had never run a major Soviet organization on his own before February 1984. Presenting Chernenko with a seventieth birthday award in September 1981, Brezhnev's main salutation was that he could not "remember an instance when you forgot something, even if the thing was at first glance insignificant." Chernenko's reply was pure sycophancy: "Our years of joint work I consider to be the happiest, brightest, and most productive of my life. Work together with you is a great school of life, a school of wisdom and party-spiritedness in the highest sense of these words."[13]

None of this is to say that Chernenko's mind was shut to all innovation. There are inklings that he was trying by the late 1970s to distance himself from some of Brezhnev's policies. One survey of Chernenko's writings and speeches before Brezhnev's death found that he had "sought the support of progressive, reform-minded elements within the party" and appeared determined to prove that he was not a Brezhnev clone.[14] Although his economic ideas were hazy, Chernenko seems to have favored some reduction of overcentralization. Despite his extended service in central administration—a year longer than Andropov's—he evinced an unusual interest in political participation, being the most prominent advocate within the Soviet hierarchy of closer contact with the population. As Central Committee secretary, he sponsored the establishment of party bureaus for polling public opinion and greater responsiveness to citizens' letters and complaints. In 1980–81 he warned more strenuously than any other member of the Politburo that a Solidarity-type crisis could engulf the Soviet system if the populace were sufficiently alienated by economic and social failures.

After being bested by Andropov in November 1982, Chernenko seemed politically orphaned and slated for retirement. He had taken over the senior Secretariat position in the ideological realm held by Suslov and Andropov before him, but he was far removed from the economic decisions that most interested Andropov. Denuded of his pre-1982 patronage powers, he was hard pressed even to protect close clients.[15] His major acts were to nominate Andropov for his big appointments and to deliver a depressing paean to ideological and cultural orthodoxy in June 1983. When Andropov's early enfeeblement and death unexpectedly handed Chernenko a second shot at the leadership, he did not waste it. His chief assets in February 1984 were undoubtedly his familiarity and the certainty that his rule would be brief. Elevating him to General Secretary extended the careers of aging members of the leadership and put off a little longer the choice of a member of the younger political generation. That Chernenko won without the assistance of Brezhnev testified to inner reserves and suggested that there was a kernel of truth to Brezhnev's comment in his memoirs that Chernenko was a "convinced fighter" for his beliefs with "an ability to win people over."[16]

Chernenko made a credible beginning as General Secretary, receiving foreign statesmen and expounding his views in speeches. In April 1984 he was elected ceremonial head of state, raising his hands in jubilation in the Supreme Soviet chamber. Chernenko's references to Andropov were uniformly laudatory, declaring that the best memorial to his predecessor would be "to continue and through collective efforts to move forward the work begun under Yuri Vladimirovich." He stressed his intention to persevere with Andropov's crackdown on bribery and embezzlement, and the stripping away in November 1984 of the military rank of the disgraced ex-Interior Minister, Shchelokov (once Chernenko's colleague in Moldavia), backed up his words. Chernenko echoed Andropov on the need for "a serious restructuring of our economy's management system, of our entire economic mechanism." He specifically endorsed Andropov's notion about increasing material rewards for productivity as well as the major experiments in industrial management and planning begun in 1984. He had harsh words for "any kind of conservatism and stagnation" and reprimanded unnamed skeptics "who do not at all wish to reckon with changed conditions."[17]

What with his long and intimate connection with Brezhnev, it came as no shock that Chernenko was not prepared to ascribe economic and other failings to the late General Secretary directly. His rallying cry in office was "continuity in policy" (*preyemstvennost' v politike*), and in this Chernenko tried to have things both ways, that is, to proclaim equal fidelity to Andropov's legacy and to

Brezhnev's. The party, he said, had to "rely on everything that has earlier been accomplished," this "without belittling" anything.[18] On many practical questions, Chernenko's approach owed more to Brezhnev than to Andropov. When it came to cadres, he sharply braked the trend begun under Andropov toward pensioning off older officials. The only personnel decision carried out with any sense of urgency was the demotion in September 1984 of Marshal Nikolai Ogarkov, the Chief of General Staff of the armed forces, which bore the marks of a civilian leader seeking to rid himself of an excessively zealous military subordinate. Chernenko made some moves to build a personal office loyal to him, but staffing changes in the Central Committee apparatus, in the Council of Ministers, and among the regional party secretaries once again occurred at the leisurely tempo typical of the Brezhnev years. At the summit of the system, Chernenko was the only General Secretary in the party's history not to push through a single change in the ranks of the Politburo or Secretariat. Save for Defense Minister Dmitri Ustinov, dead of cancer in December 1984, the collective leadership that buried Chernenko in March 1985 was the same that had elected him thirteen months earlier.

Chernenko as General Secretary neither made nor, it would seem, contemplated major decisions on the burning issues of the day. He chaired a party committee on revising the old party program of 1961, but its work was not concluded. The Central Committee met only twice with Chernenko at the helm. The first time, in April 1984, it endorsed changes in the elementary schools that increased their orientation toward vocational training, as well as a slight widening of the powers of the local soviets, as Soviet municipalities are called. In early October Chernenko revealed formation of a "commission of the Politburo on the improvement of management and the heightening of the effectiveness of the economy." When the Central Committee convened later that month, however, it was to vote through a costly irrigation and river diversion plan for Soviet agriculture that smacked of the extensive economic approach of the Brezhnev years.

Speculation about Chernenko's own approach was rendered academic by the worsening of his emphysema and other afflictions, which brought his administration to an early and rather pitiful end. For the third time in as many years, the Soviet media in the winter of 1984–85 waged a moronic campaign to pretend that a mortally ill leader had nothing worse than the sniffles. On March 1, 1985, *Pravda* carried a photograph, evidently posed in Chernenko's hospital suite, purporting to show him receiving congratulations on his recent election to the RSFSR Supreme Soviet. Eleven days later it announced, on page 2, that Chernenko had died of lung and heart failure. Page 1 was reserved for the appointment of Mikhail Sergeyevich Gorbachev as General Secretary.

Gorbachev's Running Start

Gorbachev, a dark horse in the early heats of the leadership race, was by the time of Chernenko's death patently the front-runner. The stretch drive might actually have been the easiest part of the contest for him. According to then Foreign Minister Andrei Gromyko, who nominated Gorbachev as General Secretary at the Central Committee session of March 11, 1985, Gorbachev had for an unspecified time been unofficial stand-in for Chernenko. "He led the Secretariat, as is well known. He also chaired sessions of the Politburo, in the absence of Konstantin Ustinovich Chernenko. He performed brilliantly, without exaggeration."[19] Equally strong clues that Gorbachev's victory was rigged well in advance were provided by the announcement of his appointment only five hours after the death notice and by the top billing then given in the press to Gorbachev rather than to the customary eulogies of the fallen leader. It is entirely possible that a deal was struck at the time of Andropov's death, providing for Chernenko to be interim General Secretary but for Gorbachev to be his right-hand man and automatically to succeed him. This would help explain the absence of changes in the Politburo and Secretariat after February 1984: newcomers might have jeopardized the deal.

Whenever exactly the bargain was sealed, there were palatable and, as best we can fathom, more conservative alternatives to Gorbachev. Grigori Romanov, born in 1923 and about halfway in age between Chernenko and Gorbachev, was the most obvious. Romanov's career had been made in his native Leningrad, where, after discharge from the army on account of war wounds, he received an engineering education at night school, worked in the shipbuilding industry, and rose within the local party machine, becoming oblast first secretary in 1970. A strong Russian nationalist, a hard-liner on culture and dissent, and said to be domineering in personal relations, Romanov won Brezhnev's attention by his efforts to raise industrial productivity and improve city and regional planning in Leningrad. His reward was a candidate's seat on the Politburo in 1973 and full membership in 1976.[20] Andropov brought him to Moscow in June 1983 as Central Committee secretary for military, defense-production, and police affairs, which made him the only person besides Gorbachev to have joint Politburo-Secretariat membership upon Chernenko's death. Although Romanov did not receive especially prominent press play after relocating in Moscow, he did have some success in promoting former Leningrad colleagues.

Had the Politburo been willing to vary precedent and consider a candidate not on the Secretariat, one possibility in earlier rounds would have been Defense Minister Ustinov (born 1908), who prior to 1976 had been a Central Committee secretary. That option, however, was removed by Ustinov's death in December 1984. A more plausible contender, if only because he was healthier and younger (born 1914), was Viktor Grishin, the durable Moscow party boss. Grishin, like Andropov and Chernenko, did not have a proper higher education. He was known within the establishment for his slyness, lack of imagination, and currying of favor with successive party leaders. As second secretary (to Nikita Khrushchev) in the Moscow oblast party committee in 1952, he had been important enough to win election to Stalin's last Central Committee. Grishin took over the national trade union federation in 1956 (earning Politburo candidate membership in 1961), and was made party first secretary in the city of Moscow in June 1967 and a full member of the Politburo in 1971. His close watch over the strategically placed Moscow organization and assiduous tending to the material wants of high bureaucrats were much appreciated by Brezhnev and, it seems, by Chernenko. Although the capital city organization was not as important as it once was in the party, it gave Grishin superb contacts in the central administration. Among those with whom he had worked in the past was Ivan Kapitonov, a Central Committee secretary and for the eighteen years before Ligachev's arrival from Tomsk the head of the organizational-party work department.[21]

Mikhail Gorbachev was a great deal younger than any of these men, having been born in a peasant family in March of 1931, the same year that Brezhnev and Chernenko joined the party as adults.[22] He hailed from Stavropol' krai, a sunny, grain-growing region in the south of European Russia, on the northern approaches to the Caucasus mountains. Gorbachev's law degree, received in 1955 from the country's leading university, Moscow State University, made him markedly superior in education to his rivals (and to all his predecessors as General Secretary), and this had been supplemented by an agronomist's diploma later in the 1950s. He had been active in the Komsomol at law school and evidently decided at this time to pursue a political career. He went straight into salaried work in the Komsomol apparatus in Stavropol' and stepped up to party administration in 1962, with a special but not exclusive focus on agriculture, the predominant economic activity in the area. Only eight years later Gorbachev was named first secretary of the Stavropol' krai committee. In this capacity, he was appointed a full member of the Central Committee in 1971—the same year as Chernenko, who was twenty years his senior.

In November 1978 Gorbachev was suddenly transferred to Moscow to become Central Committee secretary for agriculture, substituting for a former Stavropol' first secretary, Fedor Kulakov, who had died in office (a rumored suicide) several months earlier. He became a candidate member of the Politburo one year later and a voting member in October 1980, the last to be co-opted before Brezhnev's death. Gorbachev's star shone still brighter after November 1982, when Andropov picked him to supervise party organization and economic decision-making at the highest level. Under Chernenko, his domain was expanded to take in party ideology and foreign policy, putting him in the same position of presumptive heir as Chernenko and Andropov previously. A headline-winning trip to Britain in December 1984 underlined Gorbachev's standing as number two man in the regime.

Gorbachev's meteoric rise can be attributed to several factors. Brainpower and a good formal education were certainly among them. The first person with legal training to make it into the Politburo since Lenin's day, he has impressed foreigners who have met him with his quick grasp of facts and analytical ability. This does not make Gorbachev an intellectual, for he betrays none of the patience with abstractions that demarcates the man of ideas. Politics, not philosophy, is Gorbachev's forte, and here he moves like someone born to the art—self-assured, at home in a crowd, comfortable with the use of power. A human touch and sense of humor are balanced by the combativeness that has flared in his travels abroad. Gromyko made reference to Gorbachev's pugnacity in his nomination speech, reporting that Gorbachev "expresses his position directly, whether this is to the liking of his conversation partner or not completely to his liking." Events since March 1985 have borne Gromyko out.

In contradistinction to both Andropov and Chernenko, Gorbachev entered top office directly from work in the provinces, and he logged less than six-and-a-half years in central administration before becoming General Secretary. This created a natural constituency for him among regional politicians, a group whose status had declined since the early Brezhnev era but who still constituted nearly 40 percent of the voting members of the Central Committee elected in 1981. At the same time, Gorbachev had been assiduous at forging ties to powerful Moscow-based officials. He surely enjoyed Brezhnev's confidence when he broke through into the leadership in 1978, at the peak of Brezhnev's power, and, equally important, he kept it despite the General Secretary's tendency to tire of younger politicians.[23] Gorbachev gave signs of having a rapport of sorts with Mikhail Suslov, aided perhaps by the fact that Suslov many years earlier had been Stavropol' first secretary. And he evidently got along especially well with Yuri Andropov, who, coincidentally or not, was also a native of Stavropol' krai and took his annual vacations at its famous hot springs. Had Andropov lived a little longer, one guesses that he would have been able to ditch Chernenko and have the succession pass directly to Gorbachev.

As the oligarchy agonized over the selection of a long-term successor to Brezhnev, three things appear finally to have tipped the scales toward Gorbachev. One was his relative youth and physical vigor, the attractiveness of which must have grown after the experience of watching three aging party chiefs in a row die a slow death in office. While some in the Politburo might have preferred to anoint yet another septuagenarian, thereby saving their own positions and giving them another chance to debate the leadership question in the near future, it is not inconceivable that the Central Committee would have mutinied at such an attempt. A second advantage was Gorbachev's expressed support for an admixture of discipline and policy innovation similar to that which Andropov tried to put into effect. Of all the contenders, Gorbachev was the one who spoke most animatedly of the need for economic modernization and for whatever institutional changes were needed to effect it, insisting all the while on firm control over political side-effects. The third factor was his tactical agility and apparent ability to blur and reconcile, at least temporarily, differences within the party. "It often happens," Gromyko said in laying Gorbachev's nomination before the Central Committee, "that problems, both domestic and foreign, are very difficult to make out if you follow the law of 'black and white.' There can be intermediate colors, intermediate links, and intermediate decisions. And Mikhail Sergeyevich always knows how to find such decisions." Indeed, some members of the Politburo may have mistaken Gorbachev for another consensus leader in the Brezhnev mold, finding out too late that he was prepared to inject a greater dose of conflict into elite politics than had been seen since Khrushchev.

The change of style in March 1985 from Chernenko to Gorbachev, at fifty-four the youngest incoming General Secretary since Stalin in the 1920s, could hardly have been more dramatic. Here was a party leader who could climb stairs on his own, put in a normal day at the office, commit himself to meetings with foreigners at prearranged times, deliver a speech audibly and if need be without note cards, and pose for pictures in a well-tailored suit and with an attractive wife, Raisa, at his elbow.

In April 1985, at the first regular plenum of the Central Committee after Chernenko, Gorbachev unveiled his chosen slogan—"acceleration (*uskoreniye*) of the socioeconomic development of our society"—one seemingly calculated to telegraph the difference between the new era and what was now disparaged as the "quiet life," a code phrase for the laconic approach of Chernenko and Brezhnev. The key ingredient of acceleration would be what he called, borrowing a phrase from Andropov, "the restructuring (*perestroika*) of the economic mechanism." Economic reform of some kind, in other words, was high on Gorbachev's agenda from the start.[24]

To augment the impression of vigor and purposiveness, Gorbachev in the spring and summer of 1985 ventured forth from the Kremlin on excursions reminiscent of Khrushchev's populism but done with a sharper eye to television coverage. Foraying through

Moscow, Leningrad, and provincial centers, he dropped in on factories, building sites, stores, hospitals, housing estates, and military bases, glad-handing with onlookers and firing off comments and questions on what he was seeing. His speeches were short on specifics, long on bombast that the country under his leadership was on the march again. "The question might arise," he declared to metal workers in Dnepropetrovsk, "of whether we are not making too sharp a turn." Not so, he said. "The other approach would be more peaceful, but it does not suit us. The times dictate that we act exactly this way."[25] On July 2, 1985, as a further token that he meant to be an activist leader, Gorbachev excused himself from the prestigious but largely ritualistic position of head of state. Nominating Andrei Gromyko for the honor, he stated that the General Secretary should "concentrate as much as possible on organizing the work of the central organs of the party."[26]

Style apart, the abruptest turn effected by Gorbachev in his early period in office was in the realm of machine politics, where Andropov's staffing changes had been slowed to a crawl by Chernenko. Gorbachev clearly wanted them resumed and accelerated. At the April 1985 plenum, he drew a direct link between personnel policy and regime performance. "Certain leaders," he observed, "occupying one and the same post for a long time, stop looking for the new and habituate themselves to shortcomings." The antidote was "more active movement of our leading personnel." In case anyone had missed the message, Gorbachev reiterated it in a table-thumping speech in Leningrad the next month: "Of course, all our cadres should be given the chance to understand the demands of the moment and reform themselves. But those who are not inclined to reorient themselves or, worse, who impede the resolution of new tasks, should simply get out of the way and not interfere. We cannot put the interests of one person above the interests of our whole society." It was the death knell of the Brezhnev formulas of respect and trust in personnel, which implicitly granted indefinite tenure to officials. Yegor Ligachev formalized the indictment at the Twenty-seventh Party Congress in February 1986: "It is well known that the necessary trust in personnel was often replaced [under Brezhnev] by a careless credulity and, in essence, an absence of checking. Proper words about a careful attitude toward cadres sometimes covered up an indifference and all-forgivingness. The line about stability of personnel was often perverted to mean its complete immobility."[27]

At the apex of the Soviet hierarchy, where this immobility was most pronounced, Gorbachev struck with a vengeance. Andropov and Chernenko had discarded only one Politburo member and secretary between them (Kirilenko, who in fact was earmarked for retirement before Brezhnev's death), and neither had as General Secretary settled scores with his erstwhile chief rival (Chernenko and Gorbachev respectively). Yet, Gorbachev on July 1, 1985, less than four months into his administration, had Grigori Romanov ejected from the Politburo and Secretariat into early retirement, ostensibly for health reasons but without a word of thanks. Premier Nikolai Tikhonov, an eighty-year-old mainstay of Brezhnev's Dnepropetrovsk clique, was divested of his government office on September 27 and dropped from the Politburo the following month. His replacement was Nikolai Ryzhkov, the fifty-six-year-old party secretary for economic coordination appointed in Andropov's first month. On December 24 Viktor Grishin lost his Moscow position, followed shortly by his second secretary, the mayor of Moscow, and his other close associates. His expulsion from the Politburo occurred February 18, 1986. Grishin fared worse than Romanov and Tikhonov in that he was raked over the coals for arrogance and conservatism by his replacement, Boris Yel'tsin.

Also ousted in Gorbachev's first year were two octagenarian candidate members of the Politburo (Vasili Kuznetsov, the first deputy head of state, and Boris Ponomarev, a Central Committee secretary) and two of Ponomarev's fellow secretaries (Ivan Kapitonov and Konstantin Rusakov).[28] A useful bonus from Gromyko's appointment as head of state in July 1985 was that, while staying on the Politburo, he relinquished operational control of foreign policy to Gorbachev's new Foreign Minister, Eduard Shevardnadze. Yet another Politburo veteran, Dinmukhammed Kunayev, the party first secretary in Kazakhstan and a close friend of Brezhnev, was directly attacked in the central press in early 1986, and his prospects for retaining his post seem dim.

Into the inner sanctum of Politburo members, candidate members, and Central Committee secretaries (numbering twenty-six individuals as of mid-1986), Gorbachev was able in one year to pull in no fewer than twelve newcomers—the same number as in the last ten years of Brezhnev's reign. Four others had their status elevated within the ruling group. Seven of the sixteen persons thus advanced were provincial party secretaries, or had been in their previous position. The backgrounds of the others were eclectic. Five of today's twelve Politburo members have gained their seats under Gorbachev: Ryzhkov, Shevardnadze, the KGB's Viktor Chebrikov, and Central Committee secretaries Ligachev (the de facto second secretary, overseeing ideology and organization) and Lev Zaikov (Romanov's successor in the military sector and responsible also for economic coordination). Add to their votes those of Gorbachev himself and of the three members promoted under Andropov, and Gorbachev on routine issues ought to have a solid Politburo majority. Besides Gorbachev, only three other Politburo members—Gromyko, Kunayev, and the Ukrainian party leader, Vladimir Shcherbitskii—are carryovers from the Brezhnev Politburo. Of the seven Politburo candidates, five earned this position under Gorbachev, as did seven of the ten Central Committee secretaries apart from the General Secretary (to whom may be added Ligachev, an Andropov appointee). Five of the new secretaries made their debut in a single batch in March 1986, one of them Aleksandra Biryukova, the first woman in the leadership in twenty-five years.

At middle layers of the establishment, functionaries have lost their positions in droves. Surviving cronies of Brezhnev have been but one subgroup hit by personnel changes that, measured by the number of offices changing hands, are the most sweeping of the entire post-Stalin period.[29] *Pravda* went so far before the Twenty-seventh Congress as to print several letters calling for an across-the-board party purge (*chistka*). Gorbachev disclaimed this suggestion in his congress report, but stated that the party was carrying out a non-violent and more selective "cleansing" (*ochishcheniye*). In the sprawling government service, ministers, including economic ministers singled out by Gorbachev for criticism, were being retired from the outset. The pace was picked up after Ryzhkov supplanted Tikhonov as Chairman of the Council of Ministers in September 1985. Ryzhkov paid special attention to his deputy chairmen, who together with him make up the Council's Presidium and coordinate whole policy sectors. Five of eleven deputy premiers were retired and six new ones appointed in Ryzhkov's first three months, and another demotion, coupled with two new appointments, occurred in June 1986. The most important addition has been Nikolai Talyzin, now a first deputy to Ryzhkov and the chairman of Gosplan; Talyzin was made a candidate member of the party Politburo shortly after his promotion.

Within the party apparatus as such, Yegor Ligachev still bears overarching responsibility for personnel, but the staffing changes have been directly orchestrated since June 1985 by the new head of the organizational-party work department, Georgi Razumovskii. Razumovskii's mettle was tested in Krasnodar krai, where local corruption was egregious enough to have received Kremlin attention before Brezhnev's death and where, under first secretaries Vitali Vorotnikov in 1982–83 (until his recruitment for higher duties by Andropov) and Razumovskii in 1983–85, the local leadership was, in Razumovskii's proud description, "almost completely renewed."[30] Sixteen years younger than Ligachev and more indebted to Gorbachev, Razumovskii was made a Central Committee secretary in March 1986 (remaining as department head) and may be destined for greater things in future.

Table 1 summarizes the effect of personnel changes on specific segments of the Soviet elite as of mid-1986 and gives an idea of how Gorbachev compares as a machine politician with the three other General Secretaries of the 1980s. The contrast between Gorbachev and Andropov, on the one hand, and Brezhnev and Chernenko, on the other, could hardly be starker. Moreover, of the two, Gorbachev's rates of turnover were appreciably higher than Andropov's, more than double in some categories. In the bulk of the cases under both Gorbachev and Andropov, those weeded out by the minipurge have been retired honorably. Yet, again, there is a difference of emphasis between the two, in that Gorbachev has mostly discontinued the Andropov practice of publicly thanking high-ranking retirees (Tikhonov is one of the few exceptions) and has provided fewer of them with sinecures.[31] Open disgrace has also become more common under Gorbachev, especially if corruption is alleged. Cases in point would be Politburo member Grishin and the powerful regional politicians Mukhamednadzar Gapurov and Turdakun Usubaliyev, first secretaries in the Central Asian republics of Turkmenistan and Kirgiziya, both of whom were fired in late 1985.

TABLE 1
Turnover of Top Soviet Officials, 1981–86

	Percent Turnover (With Percent Due to Death in Office in Brackets)				
	General Secretary				
	Brezhnev (III/3/81 to XI/10/82)	Andropov (XI/12/82 to II/9/84)	Chernenko (II/13/84 to III/10/85)	Gorbachev (III/11/85 to VII/1/86)	Percent of 1986 Officials Not in Office in 1981
Politburo members and candidate members[a]	9 (9)	19 (14)	10 (10)	28 (0)	53
Central Committee secretaries and department heads	4 (4)	34 (0)	4 (0)	68 (0)	86
Council of Ministers Presidium (chairman and deputies)	0 (0)	20 (0)	7 (7)	60 (0)	79
Other members[b]	5 (2)	20 (0)	12 (1)	41 (1)	67
Regional first secretaries of party[c]	9 (1)	23 (1)	11 (1)	33 (1)	66
Top officials of union republics[d]	14 (7)	26 (5)	12 (0)	35 (0)	72

[a]For this category only, officials were considered as a group and turnover includes only removal from group as a whole. For other categories, turnover also includes change of position within group.
[b]Excludes heads of union republic governments, who nominally are members of USSR Council of Ministers.
[c]Regional party committees in five largest republics only (RSFSR, Ukraine, Belorussia, Uzbekistan, Kazakhstan). Moscow city counted as an RSFSR region.
[d]Includes party first secretary, second secretary, and head of government for all republics except RSFSR, for which there is head of government only.

The cumulative effect of staffing decisions taken since 1981, mostly in the spurts under Gorbachev and Andropov, is registered in the last column of Table 1. Renewal has been slower among the Politburo barons than lower in the system, as could have been predicted, but even here more than half of today's members and candidate members were not in their positions at the conclusion of

Brezhnev's final party congress in 1981. Newly promoted since 1981 are roughly nine in ten national party secretaries and department heads, four in five members of the Presidium of the Council of Ministers, two in three of the other government ministers, and better than two in three republic and regional party bosses.

The exodus of the old guard has been slower from the Central Committee, the broadly based collection of party notables that normally convokes twice a year to ratify Politburo decisions but could have a significant impact during a crisis. Fifty-nine percent of the members of the 1981 Central Committee still alive were re-elected in 1986, markedly less than the 89 percent of the surviving 1976 members returned in 1981 but, in all likelihood, more than Gorbachev would have preferred. The 1981 members re-elected in 1986, plus ten 1981 candidate members elevated to full voting status between congresses, come to more than half (59 percent) of the 1986 Central Committee. Their proportion is higher than it would otherwise be because, unaccountably, the Central Committee was trimmed in size (by twelve members) from 1981, contrary to the post-Stalin practice of inflating successive committees so as to make it easier to bring in adherents of the leader. The 41 percent new members must be assumed to be the core of Gorbachev's following in the 1986 Central Committee, though the holdovers from 1981 should also contain a large contingent of strong Gorbachev supporters.

With the new leadership team rapidly taking shape, what line will they pursue? What, aside from getting rid of tired and corrupt bureaucrats and constructing his own machine, is the Gorbachev program? Policy particulars will be set aside until Chapter 4. The main thing to convey here is that, building on the comparatively gentle criticisms put forward by Andropov, Gorbachev has in words if not yet much in deeds repudiated Brezhnevism. In this he is like the major Soviet leaders of the past, all of whom defined their programs in large part in reaction to the actions of their predecessors (and Leonid Brezhnev can be considered Gorbachev's real predecessor, if Andropov and Chernenko are counted as transitional figures). After months of oblique criticism, Gorbachev delivered the heaviest anti-Brezhnev broadside yet at the Twenty-seventh Congress in February 1986:

> Giving what was achieved [during the Brezhnev years] its due, the leadership of the CPSU [Communist Party of the Soviet Union] considers it its duty to speak honorably and directly to the party and people about omissions in our political and practical activity, about unfavorable tendencies in the economy and the social and cultural sphere, and about the causes of these phenomena. During the course of a number of years, and not only because of objective factors but due above all to reasons of a subjective nature, the practical actions of the organs of the party and state lagged behind the demands of the time, behind life itself. Problems in the development of our country accumulated more quickly than they were resolved. Inertia, a freezing of administrative forms and methods, a lessening of dynamism in our work, the growth of bureaucratism—all this wrought no small harm on our cause. Stagnation began to manifest itself in the life of our society.
>
> The situation demanded changes, but in our central organs and at the local level, too, a peculiar psychology began to prevail: that of trying to improve matters without changing anything. But this does not happen, comrades. As they say, if you stop for a moment you have stopped for a mile. We cannot avoid the resolution of pressing problems. Such a position costs the country, the state, and the party too dearly. So let us speak about this out loud![32]

One of Gorbachev's persistent themes has been precisely the need to air problems "out loud." Bidding for public support, as well as for better input and feedback on policy questions, the leadership under Gorbachev has peeled back the limits of permissible discourse in many if not all areas. It has nurtured the beginnings of a thaw in Soviet culture. The principle of publicity (*glasnost'*) has been urged on the state media, and a number of executives have been replaced by officials more sympathetic to the new line. The two most important changes occurred in February 1986. Mikhail Nenashev, the editor of the RSFSR daily *Sovetskaya Rossiya*, one of the newspapers most critical of officialdom, displaced the Andropov appointee Boris Pastukhov as head of the publishing industry. And Richard Kosolapov, the conservative editor of *Kommunist*, the party's theoretical tribune, was removed in favor of the much less orthodox Ivan Frolov. A professional philosopher who made a name for himself by attacking Trofim Lysenko and championing freedom of expression for scientists, Frolov had in 1977 been fired as editor of *Voprosy filosofii*, the main philosophical journal.[33]

This having been said, Gorbachev's priority in office to date has been economic and socioeconomic reform, not political reform. Like Andropov, he has had something to say about almost every issue under the sun and has spoken expansively of "imparting dynamism to our society . . . in all spheres." But his chief interest from the outset has been in the economy. "The development of Soviet society," he said at the April 1985 plenum, "will be defined in decisive measure by qualitative shifts in our economy, by the transfer of it onto the rails of intensive growth." The USSR's economic woes he dated from the early 1970s, when the ambiguous Kosygin reform of 1965 was scrapped at Brezhnev's behest. Decelerating growth since then, he argued, has subjected the regime to worsening pressures from every angle, which could not be alleviated by shuffling resources around. "We cannot take the path of dismantling our social programs," Gorbachev said of consumer demands. But simultaneously, in the face of the external challenge from the United States, "We cannot allow anyone to achieve military superiority over us." Portraying economic modernization and renewal as the way out of the bind, Gorbachev sold his message with appeals to a mix of motifs: responsiveness to the average citizen, the power of modern science and technology, traditional Russian nationalism, and Marxism-Leninism.[34]

Gorbachev's early utterances on the economy, though categorical on the need for bold decisions to bring about improvement, were as evasive as Andropov's had been on just how this could be achieved. Like Andropov, a number of his initial decisions were essentially disciplinarian, the firing of tired administrators and the campaign against alcoholism being the prime examples. But in addition, and without providing specifics, he issued a cannonade of statements about "basic restructuring" of the economy, "perfection of the economic mechanism" (a phrase employed by Chernenko as well as Andropov), and "activation of the human factor." In one speech, Gorbachev remarked cryptically that economic restructuring could begin without any overall design: "It would be intolerable to go slowly in the expectation of some kind of new instruction or orders from above." In a talk in Minsk in July 1985, he seemed to be saying that many of the needed changes could be in place by the end of 1985—the same unrealistic deadline put forward by Andropov two years earlier.[35] No further reference was made to this as the year drew to an end.

The published debate, merely the tip of the iceberg, made it as obvious as ever that there were deep differences within the leadership and the wider elite as to how the economy could best be modernized, with sharp disagreements on questions of principle such as whether market mechanisms could be employed. Gorbachev's attention, meanwhile, seemed in the second half of 1985 to gravitate to shorter-term tasks, above all the drafting of the 1986–90 five-year plan. The draft plan ratified by the Twenty-seventh Congress and given final approval in June 1986 jacked up targeted rates of GNP growth to roughly 3.5 percent in 1986–90 (versus the 2.2 percent achieved in 1981–85) and to about 5 percent in 1991–2000, which would be a return to the pace of the late 1960s.

Gorbachev's address to the party congress in February 1986 signified an escalation of his verbal commitment to far-reaching institutional changes in the economy. For the first time, he used the loaded word "reform" (*reforma*) to sum them up—indeed, at two points he brandished the phrase "radical reform" (*radikal'naya reforma*). "It is obvious," he said in the more direct of them, "that economic management is constantly in need of perfecting. But our situation now is such that we cannot limit ourselves to partial improvements—a radical reform is necessary." Retreating from his previous optimism, he conceded that such a reform would be a long time in the making, would have to be closely studied and debated, and would be introduced in stages. Ticking off recent initiatives (see Chapter 4), Gorbachev said that these were only the beginning of the road. "For the restructuring of the management mechanism in our country, with its enormous and complex economy, are needed time and energetic efforts." There could be difficulties and errors along the way, but the main thing would be "to move step by step in the chosen direction, rounding out and perfecting the economic mechanism on the basis of the acquired experience, getting rid of everything that is obsolete or has not proved itself."

Gorbachev's new gradualism seems to spring from his own more sober thinking but also, without doubt, from awareness of the reluctance of colleagues and underlings to move more quickly. Several times in his congress speech, Gorbachev alluded to political obstacles to economic change. He complained of Soviet functionaries who, like the hero in a nineteenth-century Russian novel, draw up fancy schemes but do nothing about them. "It is impossible to accept the position of officials like this. We simply cannot go along with them. Even less can we go along with those who hope that things will blow up and we will return to the same old rut." He exuded particular frustration at opposition on ideological grounds, which he described as widespread. "Unfortunately, the position has gained wide currency that any change in the economic mechanism is to be seen as almost a retreat from the principles of socialism. In this connection let me emphasize the following: the highest criterion in improving management, as in the entire system of socialist productive relations, must be socioeconomic acceleration, the consolidation of socialism in reality."[36] The statement sounded a lot like the famous saying of Deng Xiaoping in China about it not mattering whether the cat is black or white, so long as it catches mice.

A glaring gap thus far in Gorbachev's vision of the Soviet future is his inability or unwillingness to connect it to the past. He has failed to place his program in historical context. He has condemned Brezhnevism without censuring Brezhnev by name. He has not rehabilitated Nikita Khrushchev, even though he was recruited into politics under Khrushchev, attended his first party congress in 1961 (when Khrushchev had Stalin's body removed from Lenin's tomb), and seems more akin to him in spirit than to the leaders who followed. Nor, for that matter, has he had anything directly to say about Yuri Andropov, who put him on the doorstep of power and first raised questions about Brezhnev's policies.

Soviet history does not supply an attractive and noncontentious model of moderate reform that Gorbachev could easily embrace as his own. Wholesale identification with Khrushchev is dangerous because of memories of his "harebrained schemes" and, of course, the fact that Khrushchev was in the end a political loser. Nonetheless, certain Kremlinological signs during Gorbachev's first year (one of them the appearance of an article praising Gorbachev's policies by Khrushchev's son-in-law, Aleksei Adzhubei) perhaps point to an intent to place the Khrushchev period in a more flattering light.[37] As will be discussed in Chapter 4, some of the stirrings in the arts now harken back consciously to the post-Stalin thaw.

The campaign in the spring of 1986 to commemorate the twenty-fifth anniversary of Yuri Gagarin's pioneering space flight, which took place at the height of Khrushchev's power, continues the pattern, and may represent a first effort to find a historical prop for regime legitimacy other than World War II, the obsession of the Brezhnev years.

Another, though imperfect, forerunner may be found in the so-called New Economic Policy (known to most Soviets as NEP), introduced by Vladimir Lenin, the founder of the Soviet system, at the end of the Russian Civil War in 1921, and abrogated by Joseph Stalin at the end of the decade.[38] NEP gave Russia a mixed economy and the Bolsheviks an economic and political rapprochement with the peasant majority of the population, albeit as a temporary expedient. Perhaps as a trial balloon, Gorbachev, in announcing changes in Soviet agriculture at the Twenty-seventh Congress, invoked the NEP precedent and Lenin's policy of *prodnalog*, the "tax in kind" levied on the peasants which left them free to sell surplus produce on the open market. The new measures, Gorbachev maintained, were "a creative utilization of Lenin's idea of the tax in kind applied to contemporary circumstances." A bit later in his report, Gorbachev excerpted a Lenin speech from about the same time on Soviet financial policy, which under NEP gave leeway to private traders and small firms.[39] It will be fascinating to see if he returns to this analogy or articulates another one.

The Dynamics of Succession and Elite Conflict

Enough is now known about the Soviet succession of the 1980s to hazard some generalizations and some implications for larger questions. One easy conclusion to draw is that dire predictions about political chaos as an outgrowth of the succession have not been realized. Three leaders have died and been replaced in rapid sequence, as many as in the entire preceding history of the Soviet state. The process has been orderly and peaceful. The rules of the succession game, though still not set down in a binding, written constitution, have been abided by and, in the process, strengthened. The fact that the party's senior ideological secretary in each instance became the new General Secretary suggests the inclusion of a new and stabilizing clause in the tacit understanding about succession politics. If such a line of succession has become the accepted one, it limits the potential for disruption by designating a successor everyone can live with before the incumbent has died.

Events also refute the claims heard in the West in the early 1980s that the Communist Party was ceding important ground to the military establishment and the KGB. If anything, the Brezhnev succession has reinforced the dominance of the party apparatchiks and especially those, like Gorbachev, with a background in provincial administration. There is not a whit of evidence that warring groups within the party courted the military or the police, as happened in China in the 1960s and, in a more limited way, in the Soviet Union after Stalin's death. Nor is there anything to suggest that either the army or the KGB played kingmaker to the benefit of Andropov or anyone else. Too much was made at the time of Andropov's KGB experience and of Defense Minister Ustinov's apparent support of him in November 1982. Andropov, however many years he served as the Politburo's man in the KGB, was in the final analysis a party politician who would have been a leadership also-ran without strong support in the party apparatus. Marshal Ustinov, likewise, had been a civilian administrator for all of his career prior to becoming Defense Minister, working for decades in the defense industry and serving in the Central Committee Secretariat from 1965 to 1976. There seems to have been no love lost between Ustinov and some of his deputies from the career military, notably Chief of Staff Ogarkov, who regularly criticized the same military-industrial complex that Ustinov spent most of his life building. Nor can we assume military-KGB accord on all issues. Aside from areas of agreement, there are also innate tensions between the two organizations, fed by officers' memories of Stalin's police-administered purges and by their awareness that the KGB's "military counterintelligence" branch is one of the major watchdogs over them.[40]

It is absurd to think that after Andropov a selection procedure heavily influenced by the army or the KGB would have resulted in the appointment of Chernenko. Lacking direct connections with either organization, Chernenko was the first Soviet leader since Stalin not to have seen active duty in World War II. One of his few decisive personnel changes was to demote Marshal Ogarkov and substitute the less truculent Sergei Akhromeyev as Chief of General Staff. When Ustinov died three months later, the new Defense

Minister was the seventy-three-year-old Sergei Sokolov, a staid military bureaucrat with none of Ogarkov's drive and fire. In 1985, one would have thought that the military and KGB would have lined up behind Grigori Romanov, a war veteran, an arch-conservative on culture, a former engineer in a defense plant, and the Central Committee secretary supervising army and police affairs. But the winner, of course, was Gorbachev, who had no military or KGB ties that we have heard of and who conspicuously excluded the military high command from the reviewing stand at Chernenko's funeral. Under Gorbachev, Marshal Sokolov has been consigned to candidate status in the Politburo, the first time the Minister of Defense has not had a regular Politburo seat since 1973. He is thus outranked by KGB chief Chebrikov, Foreign Minister Shevardnadze, and the national party secretary for military affairs, Zaikov.

It may be that Western observers were misled by the militarization of U.S.-Soviet relations after 1980 into thinking that Soviet domestic politics, too, was being militarized. Uniformed officers, and Marshal Ogarkov in particular, gained new visibility as defenders of regime decisions on matters such as arms control and the Korean Air Lines fiasco. This, however, hardly proves that the military or the secret police have been running the entire Soviet Union. There has been since Stalin's death a deep-seated consensus within the civilian party organs against any pronounced upgrading of KGB or military power, and nothing has happened to crack that consensus.

Were the power of the army or KGB to be much greater today than under Brezhnev, we would expect them to be receiving payoffs in terms of appointments. The two organizations, in other words, would be exporting personnel into the civilian ministries, Central Committee apparatus, local party organs, and so forth. With the military, this is simply not happening. Its own hierarchy is being renewed, though with no evident sense of urgency.[41] It is not reaching out into other organizations.

The KGB's reach has been longer, but not much, considering that Andropov headed that organization for fifteen years. While Geidar Aliyev's KGB experience (all acquired before 1969) may have helped him into Andropov's Politburo, his career has since stalled and he was passed over for Chairman of the Council of Ministers in favor of Ryzhkov. The one new regional leader of the party to come out of the KGB is Boris Pugo, the Latvian first secretary appointed under Chernenko, and even Pugo served twice as long in the Komsomol as in the KGB. Only the Ministry of the Interior, the civilian police force under fire for corruption, was penetrated by KGB cadres to any significant extent after Brezhnev—Vitali Fedorchuk, Andropov's immediate successor as KGB chief, was made head of the ministry in December 1982—and the KGB here had to share prominence with new party organs in the ministry supervised by local party committees and headed by an official, Viktor Gladyshev, recruited directly from the Central Committee apparatus. Fedorchuk, moreover, was in January 1986 replaced as Interior Minister by Aleksandr Vlasov, a local party secretary evidently on close terms with Gorbachev.[42]

It is easier to trace the limits of military and KGB influence during the succession period than to say with confidence how power and authority relations have evolved within the central agencies of the party and state. The position of the new General Secretary is of primary interest. It has been suggested that a "law of diminishing secretaries" makes each Soviet leader less powerful than his predecessor, while only within his period of office has his power vis-à-vis his colleagues increased.[43] The second generalization seems applicable to the Gorbachev era, but the first need not be. Gorbachev's bulldozing style, exerted on an aging leadership full of members ripe for retirement, has allowed him to make rapid progress in consolidating his power. If he develops a consistent and activist program and continues to display the political aplomb of his first year in office, he may turn out to exercise considerably greater influence over policy than Brezhnev before him. He is already in a far stronger position than either Andropov or Chernenko, both of whom inherited a Politburo and Secretariat that they did little or nothing to change.

Nonetheless, Gorbachev can by no stretch of the imagination rule by fiat. As it has been in the past, so it is today that the new party leader must struggle to build and exercise authority after obtaining the peak post.[44] Many of the colleagues with whom any General Secretary begins his term are not particularly beholden to him, and he presides over an unwieldy administrative machine that responds slowly to even the sternest directives. Some of the tools used to buttress the party chief's position in the past are no longer available. Political terror and violence are not, without re-Stalinization of Soviet politics, and leadership cults are both harder to mount (it took Brezhnev a decade to get his under way) and less credible than in years gone by.

Machine politics has been a crucial instrument in the hands of previous party bosses. It has worked, as in the United States, primarily through the manipulation of appointments. After Stalin made these a prerogative of the General Secretary in the 1920s, successive heads of the party have settled long-time cronies and associates in sensitive posts. Their substantial ability to rig intraparty elections has been turned to recruiting new supporters and packing decision-making bodies with them, up to and including the Central Committee and Politburo. Brezhnev, in addition to selectively hiring and firing, was able to win a further measure of support among the broad office-holding class merely by granting to most of them security of tenure.

In the 1980s, use of these customary techniques has become more problematic than before. The last was a one-time-only device: once stable tenure had come to be accepted as the norm by many officials, no new leader could reap political benefit merely by affirming it. As for favoritism toward old and new acolytes, this is now made more awkward by collective decision-making at the top. Oligarchy can be subverted, but only gradually, for the General Secretary must take care not to raise the hackles of his peers.

The pattern of political and administrative careers colors the use of the patronage weapon still further. Particularly under Brezhnev's tutelage, the mobile party generalist, easily reprogrammed, gave way to a much more professional and specialized type of official, who was expected to be technically competent and steeped in the particular agency or locality in which he worked. Promotion from within poses a serious obstacle to the Kremlin patron, be it the General Secretary or someone else, who seeks to colonize outlying parts of the bureaucracy by carrying out periodic shakeups and sending in his loyalists.[45] It means also that high-ranking politicians, having advanced along more structured career paths, have acquired smaller and less diverse "tails" of clients, as the Soviets say, than was true previously. Andropov and Chernenko, from the older generation, were forerunners of this trend, but Gorbachev and his rival Romanov exemplify it perfectly. Gorbachev spent his entire administrative career up to 1978 in Stavropol' krai, and his duties in Moscow until after Brezhnev's death centered on the same policy area, agriculture, that had preoccupied him in Stavropol'. Romanov had never worked outside of Leningrad before 1983, and when he came to Moscow it was mostly to supervise an economic sector (defense industry) that is of great importance in his home city.

Gorbachev surely will do the best he can to land former Stavropol' associates in positions of influence. Of his several successes to date, the main one has been the November 1985 placement of Vsevolod Murakhovskii as First Deputy Chairman of the Council of Ministers and chief of the new super-ministry for agriculture. Murakhovskii was head of the Stavropol' city Komsomol committee when Gorbachev was hired there in 1955 and the two men worked at close quarters until 1978, when Murakhovskii succeeded Gorbachev as party first secretary of the krai.[46] Gorbachev may enjoy a special kinship with officials from other southern territories near Stavropol'—Interior Minister Vlasov (who was party first secretary in two neighboring regions, most recently Rostov oblast), party cadres chief Razumovskii (from Krasnodar), and Foreign Minister Shevardnadze (from Georgia) being good examples. And Gorbachev may also have forged a bond of trust with a few individuals who worked in central agricultural administration under his supervision after 1978—several functionaries from the older generation, for instance, or, among the high fliers, Nikolai Kruchina, the former first deputy head of the Central Committee's agriculture department, who was named head of the party chancellery in 1983.[47]

Compare Gorbachev's patronage base to Brezhnev's—fattened by his work in widely dispersed parts of the country—and you see the extent of his problem. Bear in mind also that Gorbachev is the first General Secretary since 1953 (leaving Andropov and Chernenko aside) to have done all his provincial work in the Russian Republic, the only one of the fifteen union republics not to have its own republic-wide party organization. Nikita Khrushchev had a large and potent Ukrainian machine, which Brezhnev in a way inherited in 1964, but Gorbachev had no RSFSR party machine to get his hands on before or after March 1985. In short, Gorbachev has had no choice but to rely heavily on organizational tactics other than old-style patronage to increase his power. Two of these have stood out.[48]

First, Gorbachev has formed coalitions with politicians previously independent of him and possessing their own sources of support, by and large in one or another of the provincial party organizations. All General Secretaries have done this, but Gorbachev has done it more than others and will have to persevere with it longer into his term. One such alliance has been struck with administrators from the Urals and western Siberia, adjoining areas rich in heavy industry and defense plants and far enough from Moscow for their officials to share a certain frontier esprit de corps. The beneficiaries include Yegor Ligachev (from Tomsk and Novosibirsk), Nikolai Ryzhkov and Boris Yel'tsin (from Sverdlovsk), and a number of lesser lights, some of whom may feel more of an affinity for their regional comrades than for Gorbachev.[49] An entente of a different kind has been established with the Leningrad organization, the second most important local unit of the party after Moscow. Here Gorbachev in effect decapitated the organization by dethroning Romanov, the former Leningrad boss. Only after this did he offer major promotional opportunities to one-time Romanov subordinates such as Lev Zaikov, Yuri Solov'ev (the current Leningrad first secretary, now a candidate member of the Politburo), Boris Aristov (the new Minister of Foreign Trade), and Anatoli Dumachev (put in charge of Soviet vocational education).[50] In Uzbekistan, a purge of protégés of the late first secretary, Sharaf Rashidov (who died in October 1983), has been accompanied by disclosures of a Rashidov "personality cult" and of Rashidov's "belittling of the role of the elective members of the party organs."[51] In this way, Gorbachev and the new first secretary, Inamzhon Usmankhodzhayev, have tried to rally support among local officials previously overshadowed by Rashidov.

Gorbachev's second organizational tactic is potentially of far-reaching importance. Especially in the party apparatus, he has launched a frontal assault on the Brezhnev policy of promotion from within and has used a more interventionist personnel policy to offset organizational biases, fight corruption, and fashion a bureaucratic coalition sympathetic to him and his program. Technical competence is still a prerequisite for appointment, but a premium is now being placed on general political orientation and on administrative experience outside the given organization. As officials are bounced from niche to niche, Gorbachev's intent seems to be to create a more mobile and a more insecure national elite, less balkanized and more responsive to his will. The movement directly into major government ministries by provincial party secretaries like Murakhovskii (State Agro-Industrial Committee), Shevardnadze (Foreign Affairs), Vlasov (Interior), and Vladimir Klyuyev (Light Industry) seems to reflect this integrating spirit.[52] The five national party secretaries appointed after the Twenty-seventh Congress include two persons without previous experience in party administration (Biryukova, from the trade unions, and Anatoli Dobrynin, the long-time Soviet ambassador to Washington), and another (Aleksandr Yakovlev) who until July 1985 was director of a research institute and was ambassador to Canada for ten years before that.

At the regional level, where control of the party machine must be maintained and party policies directly touch the population, the Brezhnev policy is now said (in Ligachev's words) to have "led in a number of cases to self-isolation, stagnation in work, and other negative phenomena," including ethnic tension. Now to be fostered is "the exchange of experienced officials," that is, their rotation between center and periphery and from one city or region to another.[53] The new policy, which may have been in the works under Andropov but did not come to fruition until Gorbachev's accession, has had a prompt impact. Whereas most regional first secretaries under Brezhnev (and Andropov) were local officials elevated within the same region, 78 percent of the RSFSR first secretaries appointed under Gorbachev have had as their most recent assignment work in a central agency. Most often this has been as one of the "inspectors of the Central Committee," working out of the organizational-party work department, whose staff seems to have expanded quickly under Ligachev and Razumovskii. Fifty-six percent of the new regional bosses are known to have had some prior experience in the region of appointment, but only 15 percent came directly from such a position. The commonest pattern has been for local politicians to be recruited from their home regions, seasoned in Moscow, and then returned to take charge of their area of origin.[54]

Gorbachev's twin efforts to construct alliances with semi-independent politicians and stimulate inter-regional and inter-agency mobility should influence elite politics in interesting ways. We have already seen the level of discord go up within the establishment, as Brezhnev's consensual and meticulously balanced policies are modified and leaders inimical to the new ways are shown the door. And yet, despite Gorbachev's signal success so early in his term at eliminating adversaries, pruning out dead wood, and bringing new recruits into the party leadership, his own coalition bands together individuals from quite disparate backgrounds and very likely with differing approaches to policy. They will have a natural interest in preserving collective decision-making, and that is exactly what some of them have been saying. It is not so surprising that it was Yegor Ligachev, who today exercises wide powers but never worked in proximity to Gorbachev before 1983, who made the point most firmly at the Twenty-seventh Congress: "It is important to underline that in all cases, whether it concerns domestic or foreign policy, pressing problems or strategic questions, the Politburo and Secretariat act collegially, under conditions of high exactingness and open exchange of views."[55]

Of the newcomers to the leadership, very few have any prior career association with Gorbachev. They thus will tend to form with him only the weakest of patronage bonds, that based merely on recent appointment.[56] Their cooperation will be assured on issues of ordinary scope and significance, but they will not necessarily be as faithful in times of adversity as Chernenko and Tikhonov were to Brezhnev, or as willing to follow the leader down new paths as Gorbachev may want. A Ligachev or a Ryzhkov will have to be persuaded, not commanded, to go along. Promotion of functional rivals may help keep independent members of the Politburo in check—a game Gorbachev is probably playing with Ligachev, for example, by promoting Aleksandr Yakovlev as a counterbalance in the ideological and propaganda area. But it will be some time before younger officials, dependent on Gorbachev from an earlier point in their careers, arrive in the leadership, and even they are apt to have multiple loyalties.

If transfers and crossovers grow more common within the bureaucracy, coalitions will become more complex and quite likely more fleeting. Rising politicians can also be expected to have followings bigger and more varied than is the rule today. Patronage politics may thus regain some of its lost importance. It will largely be up to Gorbachev to define whether the politics of patronage assumes the traditional form of dividing up spoils or is adjunct to the politics of policy. It was the latter politics that brought him to power, and it will retain its primacy if he is serious about pursuing economic reform.

Generational Change and the Itch for Improvement

Behind the jousting for high office, another great change has been occurring, this in the Soviet elite as a whole. Whereas the post-Khrushchev succession of the 1960s had little effect on the age structure of the elite, a massive shift of generations is now in train and will continue for the rest of the 1980s, perhaps longer. It is lifting into power individuals with substantially different life experiences, more critical of Soviet failings than their predecessors, and with more of the itch for improvement so readily apparent in Gorbachev.

Generational change was staved off for as long as humanly possible by those who would suffer from it, old men born soon after the turn of the twentieth century. Call them the Brezhnev generation, after the future General Secretary (born in 1906), who, like thousands of others, was a beneficiary of Stalin's savage prewar purges of the Old Bolsheviks. Catapulted into positions of great responsibility in their thirties or younger, the Brezhnev generation maintained a near-stranglehold on top office for decades and only began to let go in the 1970s. Its members used their long years in power to justify staying there, and their role at climactic points in Soviet history like the industrialization drive and World War II as a source of moral authority. Sixty is the legal retirement age for Soviet men, but this is normally waived for individuals in management positions. Political figures are more reluctant to bow out than most, probably because in a society dominated by politics their drop in status and privilege is unusually steep. For members of Brezhnev's age cohort, the determination to hold on was fortified by an exaggerated sense of their own indispensability. It has been obligatory, as one party spokesman explained in the late 1960s, "to display the maximum of sensitivity" in broaching the pensioning-off of even ill-qualified members of the old guard. "Often it is difficult to blame such a person for lagging behind, for not studying. [He points to] his difficult youth, the war, his important assignments, [how] he himself barely noticed how his life flew by as he worried about things necessary to the party and state."[57]

The handing over of power has been further obstructed by the lingering effects of World War II. Soviets born approximately between the 1917 Russian Revolution and the mid-1920s bore the brunt of the slaughter at the front, and those who survived were often cheated of the advanced technical training needed for the best political and managerial posts. This wartime generation has served as a poor bridge between men in the age bracket of Brezhnev, Chernenko, and Andropov and those born in the second half of the 1920s or the 1930s and reared under greatly different conditions. For simplicity's sake, I will call the latter group the Gorbachev generation and take a year of birth of 1926 as a cut-off point. In their forties and fifties, they were making inroads in the late Brezhnev period, but they were still a minority in the most senior positions.[58] Only 27 percent of the members of the 1981 Central Committee, Brezhnev's last, had a date of birth after 1925. Mikhail Gorbachev was the only member of the Politburo or Secretariat to fall into this category.

Brezhnev's death removed the biggest roadblock to the succession of generations. First Andropov and now Gorbachev have moved members of the Gorbachev generation into prime positions. Four of the twelve members of the Politburo are now individuals born in 1926 or later—Gorbachev (born in 1931), Ryzhkov (1929), Shevardnadze (1928), and Vorotnikov (1926). So are three of the seven candidate members of the Politburo—Nikolai Slyun'kov and Talyzin (both born in 1929) and Yel'tsin (1931)—and four of the seven secretaries without Politburo rank—Biryukova, Vadim Medvedev, and Viktor Nikonov (all born in 1929) and Razumovskii (1936). Years of birth can be dug up for 273 of the 307 voting members of the new Central Committee elected in 1986, and 150 of these, or 49 percent of the total, belonged by my definition to the Gorbachev generation. Fifty-six of 68 new members for whom a birth date is known were born after 1925, and, assuming a similar distribution of ages among the unknown members, some 58 percent of the entire Central Committee membership would now consist of members of the Gorbachev generation. This is well over double their proportion of the 1981 Central Committee.

What is the significance of the turnover of generations? Will the Soviet Union be governed any differently as a result? One commonsense finding of studies of political personnel in other countries is that ambition and vigor in office are inversely related to age.[59] In today's Soviet Union, having seen the difference between Chernenko and Gorbachev, with twenty years between them, few will dispute that the new Gorbachev-appointed Chairman of the Council of Ministers (twenty-four years younger than his predecessor), the new deputy premier for defense matters (twenty-one years younger), or the new mayor of Moscow (twenty-nine years younger) will bring greater vitality to their offices.[60] Soviet social scientists provide some more systematic data to back up this conclusion. One survey of factory directors in Sverdlovsk oblast in the early 1980s discovered that managers older than sixty, regardless of their "great experience and enormous knowledge," find it "more and more difficult with the passage of the years to lead production collectives." The article, which conjured up so well problems at the highest levels of the Soviet system, recommended that the title of honorary director be conferred on reluctant retirees, with a stipend attached, and that they be replaced by younger, more aggressive persons.[61]

The impatience and therefore, perhaps, the effect of a new generation are apt to be all the greater when they have waited a long time for the opportunity. In the Soviet case, however, there is an odd wrinkle. When it looked at the deputies of the plant directors, the Sverdlovsk survey reported the "not quite normal phenomenon" of understudies who are only a few years younger than their superiors and are their natural successors but have been kept in the wings for so long that they have lost their élan. "As a result, the directors are left without bold deputies, deputies with initiative. . . . This increases the load on the people at the top, who are already at the 'heart attack level' of leadership." Some directors had only themselves to thank because, "fearing competition from able assistants, they themselves choose passive ones." If new managers were to be dynamic, the study concluded, recruiters would have to skip over the weary and demoralized second tier and go straight to the younger, better educated, and more enterprising chief engineers of the factories.[62] As many Soviet readers would have gathered, this portrait of industry was a fetching microcosm of the Soviet regime of the late Brezhnev period in its entirety: aging bosses convinced of their irreplaceability, unchallenged by lackluster lieutenants, but afraid to gamble on the youth and talent a grade or two below. If the analogy holds true, it would make especially good sense to anticipate a reinvigoration of Soviet institutions as the equivalents of the Sverdlovsk chief engineers finally claim their patrimony.

Harder to judge is the likely effect of generational change on the direction of Soviet policy, as opposed to the energy with which policy is executed. Will the new rulers have beliefs or priorities any different from the old? Comparative studies find differences across political generations of several kinds: life-cycle differences that diminish as members of the successor generation mature; differences stemming from conscious rejection of the values of the established generation; and more measured differences that reflect the evolutionary change of attitudes over the life experience of the younger generation.[63] Life-cycle differences are not likely to be pronounced in the Soviet elite, for the simple reason that, barring a drastic change of policy, most new appointees to senior positions will be of late middle age, well past the point where the idealism and inquisitiveness normally associated with youth will have rubbed off. Delayed promotion, coming after self-selection into a political career and years of socialization, militates also against the second pattern, that of overt rebellion against the elders.

But more subtle differences, reflecting a formative experience dissimilar in certain ways to that of the Brezhnev generation, are another matter. Such differences are to be anticipated in the mentality and behavior of the Gorbachev generation now coming into its own in Soviet politics. It has lived through dissimilar times from its forebears. For one thing, officials in Gorbachev's age group had no hand in founding the Soviet system's basic political and economic institutions. Brezhnev participated in the bloody collectivization of agriculture at the end of the 1920s, as apparently did Chernenko. And Brezhnev, Chernenko, Andropov, and Suslov all helped bring under Soviet control non-Russian territories (Moldavia, Karelia, and Lithuania) annexed by Stalin during the war, a process accompanied by mass deportations and police terror. The coming generation had no part in these events. It is too young to have been implicated in Stalin's witch hunts and killings, having entered political life in most cases after his death. Unthreatened by de-Stalinization, it had less reason than older colleagues to be traumatized by Khrushchev's boisterous reforms. Conversely, it had less cause to identify with the lead-footed conservatism of the Brezhnev years. The setbacks of the 1970s, coming at the prime of these men's careers, seem to have had a more wrenching impact on them. Unlike their elders, they know the consequences of present failures will be in their laps. Many surely were thinking privately under Brezhnev what a journalist was able to say publicly only in 1986—that too many senior officials had "the habit of putting off the resolution of pressing problems . . . until the time when it will be possible to go on pension and pass the problems on to other people."[64]

Members of the maturing Gorbachev generation are also quite different in their material expectations. Since the Soviet standard of living has steadily risen for all or most of their lives, they have come to take for granted what their parents saw as frills and to aspire to more. Whereas for the senior generation, "all this was a novelty—refrigerators, vacuum cleaners, separate apartments, hot water," for them, especially those born after the mid-1930s, the features of a modern consumer society "are all natural, all a norm of life."[65] This greater exactingness has been generated not only by past economic growth, but by formal education, acquired by members of the emerging generation without interruption by war or work and without discrimination on the basis of class origin. By and large, they are both technically and in a general cultural sense considerably more sophisticated than their predecessors. More of them are from urban rather than peasant backgrounds. They have come of age in the least repressive intellectual climate in Soviet history and have had the greatest exposure to the outside world.

It would be fallacious to expect the Gorbachev generation to turn the Soviet Union upside down. It shares with the veterans of earlier marches fundamental values—faith in one-party rule and the state-owned economy, a fear that relaxation of political controls may produce anarchy, identification with Soviet achievements—and a general assumption that its best interests lie with the Soviet system roughly as they know it. Many of its members, particularly among the economic managers, seem persuaded that there is a technical solution to every social and economic problem, something that will not change until still younger administrators, born after the war and given some training in the social sciences, take command in the 1990s.[66] Prepared to draw on foreign knowledge and practice, most of them do not go on to accept Western ideas holus-bolus. "I would have to say," Gorbachev said to French journalists inquiring about his generation's world-view in September 1985, "that we do not look on socialism as some kind of consumerist society, that we will not adopt here the standards of the Western way of life. But that which is useful we will use."[67]

The Gorbachev generation in the Soviet elite could not be called "liberal" in the conventional Western meaning of the word, for it places collective and state rights before those of the individual. Nor is it internally homogeneous. There are significant divisions within it along ideological, programmatic, bureaucratic, territorial, ethnic, and other lines. That Gorbachev has quarreled with a number of his age peers underlines the point.[68] Indeed, as could be expected from the less conformist environment within which they grew up, there appears to be considerably more diversity within his generation than in preceding ones.[69] Its being in power will neither obviate these tensions nor reverse basic beliefs and operating assumptions. What we are likely to see, rather than destabilization or black-to-white transformation, is a reshading of the greys.

For all that divides them, what many members of the Gorbachev generation share is a desire to make the existing Soviet order work better, without necessarily transforming it. They subscribe to no single plan or strategy, and may eventually fall out over the particulars of one, but they do exhibit a common mood, an itch for improvement. This much was clear by the late Brezhnev period. It could be detected in public policy debates and, to the limited extent that foreigners have access, in private discussions as well. If one looks, as an indicator, at speeches delivered at the 1981 party congress by the provincial party leaders (the largest set of speakers), generational differences are discernible. Party first secretaries born in 1926 or later paid much less attention to ideological questions than the older secretaries. They were considerably less likely to urge old-fashioned extensive development of either agriculture (usually entailing big outlays for irrigation) or industry (building new factories) or to expatiate on the need for better central management of the economy. They were more interested in pushing innovative, intensive solutions to economic problems (involving research and development, retooling, updating of infrastructure, better work incentives, and the like). Party secretaries from the Gorbachev generation were almost twice as likely as older ones at the conclave to bring up the need for enhancing consumer welfare via housing construction, better personal services and environmental protection, and production of more household goods and food. When they mentioned consumer satisfaction, it was often in the context of boosting worker motivation and productivity. The younger men also devoted twice as much attention to one specific strategy for decentralization of decision-making, namely, the beefing-up of local coordination of economic and social development at the expense of the Moscow planners and ministerial head offices.[70]

The desire for improvement is etched as sharply in the broad discussions of social and economic problems found in the Soviet media of the late Brezhnev years. Younger officials and scholars, though not free to deride the accomplishments of the older generation, often spoke in a self-conscious way about generational blockage. They wrote of how the system of economic management developed in the 1930s "has sunk deep roots . . . into the imagination of the administrative apparatus, many of whose officials consider it the sole possible one," and of how the resulting myopia had kept many older officials from facing the system's shortcomings. They took issue with "attempts to work in the old ways under new conditions and setting store exclusively by the experience of the past." They argued the need to punch through the rind of custom and routine, especially in the economy: "Improvement of economic planning and management . . . demands a creative approach, a certain boldness, and experimentation. Otherwise, we cannot overcome inertness and stagnation in economic work, we cannot get away from traditions and habits that have had their day." They heaped scorn on the hoary theory that problems like alcoholism, corruption, ethnic conflict, and the housing shortage are "survivals of the past," with no basis in modern Soviet society. "When we speak of 'survivals,' " one critic said a few months before Brezhnev's death, "the impression is created that these phenomena are residual and insignificant," whereas in truth certain of the country's problems were not only persevering but were noticeably worsening. Repetition of the old alibis, she continued, "oversimplifies the situation, unjustifiably idealizes real life, prevents us from seeing the full outlines and extent" of the problems.[71]

Mikhail Gorbachev, the first member of his generation to sit in the Politburo, has tapped sentiments like these in his surge to power and his opening policy moves. As he plans for the long haul, he would be foolish not to keep on doing so. Members of his own age cohort, or at least the more restless among them, would be the natural base to turn to for support, recruits for important offices, and ideas for moderate economic and social change. They represent the most obvious political force available for mobilization behind whichever strategy for innovation and modernization Gorbachev settles on. Their ambitions frustrated by the Brezhnev gerontocracy and their material and other aspirations unmet by the current performance of the Soviet system, they are his to woo and win.

The problem with Gorbachev so far is that he may be moving too slowly to take best advantage of the generational factor. This statement does not contradict the evidence presented above about the high rate of replacement of officials since March 1985. Officeholders are indeed being retired in record numbers, but, as the statistics on the 1986 Central Committee confirm, many members of the Brezhnev old guard remain for now in their positions. More important, Gorbachev has shown a willingness to cooperate with politicians from the wartime and Brezhnev generations, in addition to his own, and he has made virtually no moves to promote Young Turks substantially younger than himself. In a little noticed passage in his May 1985 Leningrad speech, Gorbachev voiced reservations about proceeding too quickly with rejuvenation of the elite: "It is sometimes said that there are not enough young people [in leading positions], that we need to open the way for youth. This is true, . . . but the main thing is that it is necessary to intelligently combine . . . experienced and young cadres. This is the most reliable guarantee against inertness and stagnation, and also against adventurism and voluntarism."[72] Others, by contrast, have called openly for rapider promotion of younger officials and for changes to the party rules limiting the time senior politicians can serve in office.[73]

There is no way of divining whether Gorbachev's approach stems from genuine conviction or from tactical considerations. On the latter point, he may wish not to affront older colleagues, not to be upstaged himself by more vigorous persons, or not to be saddled early in his administration with associates young enough to have decades to go until retirement. Whatever the motivation, a fair number of Gorbachev's major allies have been individuals anywhere from one or two to fifteen years older than himself.

For example, three of the five new members of his Politburo, two of the five new candidate members, and three of the seven new Central Committee secretaries were born before 1926. Yegor Ligachev and Lev Zaikov, the only two politicians besides Gorbachev to hold dual Politburo-Secretariat positions, were born in 1920 and 1923 respectively, and Aleksandr Yakovlev, the coming power in the ideological realm, was born in 1923. When members of the Gorbachev generation have been promoted, it usually has been persons at the older fringe of the group. In 1986, eight years after coming to Moscow, Gorbachev remains the youngest member of the Politburo (Yel'tsin, a candidate member, is only several months older), and there is but one secretary (Razumovskii, born in 1936) younger than he. At middle levels of the elite, Gorbachev's appointments have on average been little if any younger at the date of promotion than officials promoted by other General Secretaries in this decade. In the Council of Ministers, for instance, new Gorbachev ministers have averaged fifty-six years of age, one year younger than Andropov's appointees (and five years younger than Chernenko's) but one year older than Brezhnev's in 1981–82 and a year older than ministers named by Brezhnev in the decade 1966–75.[74] Among the regional party leaders, those promoted under Gorbachev have been fifty-four years old on average, which is one year younger than the Chernenko appointees but three years older than Andropov's and a year older than even Brezhnev's.

Table 2 presents the outcome of what might be termed a high rate of renewal but a low rate of rejuvenation of the Soviet establishment. It has been no mean achievement to lower the average age of Politburo members and candidates by six years in 1985–86, or to produce the sharp drops in age recorded in the party Secretariat and the Presidium of the Council of Ministers. Average dates of birth are advancing in all segments of the elite. But the youth trend has not occurred in all positions—among regional and union republic officials average age is almost identical to what it was in 1981—and, even where it has occurred, the result is precarious. The aver-

TABLE 2
Changing Age Profile of Top Soviet Officials, 1981–86

	Average Age (With Average Year of Birth in Brackets)				
	End of 26th Congress (III/3/81)	After Death of Brezhnev (XI/10/82)	After Death of Andropov (II/9/84)	After Death of Chernenko (III/10/85)	Gorbachev in Power (VII/1/86)
Politburo members and candidate members	68 (1913)	68 (1914)	68 (1916)	69 (1916)	63 (1923)
Central Committee secretaries and department heads	67 (1914)	67 (1915)	67 (1917)	68 (1917)	61 (1925)[a]
Council of Ministers Presidium (chairman and deputies)	65 (1916)	67 (1915)	69 (1915)	69 (1916)	60 (1926)
Other ministers[b]	64 (1917)	65 (1917)	63 (1921)	64 (1921)	60 (1926)
Regional first secretaries of party[c]	57 (1924)	57 (1925)[d]	57 (1927)[e]	57 (1928)[f]	57 (1929)[g]
Top officials of union republics[h]	57 (1924)	57 (1925)	57 (1927)	57 (1928)[i]	58 (1928)[j]

[a]No information on 9 of 28 secretaries and department heads.
[b]Excludes heads of union republic governments, who nominally are members of USSR Council of Ministers.
[c]Regional party committees in five largest republics only (RSFSR, Ukraine, Belorussia, Uzbekistan, Kazakhstan). Moscow city counted as an RSFSR region.
[d]No information on 10 of 140 secretaries.
[e]No information on 10 of 141 secretaries.
[f]No information on 8 of 141 secretaries.
[g]No information on 36 of 141 secretaries.
[h]Includes party first secretary, second secretary, and head of government for all republics except RSFSR, for which there is head of government only.
[i]No information on 3 of 43 officials.
[j]No information on 10 of 43 officials.

age age of the 1986 Central Committee is sixty, which is a slight two years younger than the 1981 Central Committee (even if the average date of birth is seven years later, 1926 as compared to 1919).[75] The Politburo is now the same age as it was in the mid-1970s. If further changes were not made, it would be the same age in 1991 as it was in

1981, in the moribund late Brezhnev period. In all categories, despite the brisk turnover of individual officials, average ages hover around sixty—the threshhold beyond which the Sverdlovsk study concluded executives find it physically difficult to carry out their duties.

The danger thus is that the Gorbachev generation may get a firm grip on the gears of power only to find it has become too old to do much with them. Top Soviet officials today are certainly considerably younger than they would be if Brezhnev's immobilism had been continued. But they are still primarily men who in most industrial societies would be on the verge of retirement. Gorbachev thus will have an important choice to make by the end of the 1980s. One option, which conceivably he has been planning all along, will be to sever all ties with the old guard, replace many of the older individuals appointed under his aegis at the beginning of his term, and make room at the very top for younger supporters like Yel'tsin and Razumovskii. It would not be too early then to start bringing a post-Gorbachev generation into leading roles. If it is Gorbachev's intention to carry out such a shakeup, the age of a Ligachev or Zaikov will be a convenient excuse for his removal. The alternative for Gorbachev is to stay with those who threw in their lot with him during the succession struggle and to allow the Soviet elite once again to age with its leader. The ineluctable effect of this strategy would be for his regime's decision capacity and spark to dwindle the same way Brezhnev's did, and with many of the same consequences.

4
Reform and the Soviet Future

The picture of the pilgrim at the crossroads has been used in countless cartoons to depict the plight of the government forced to select between diverging strategies. For the present-day Soviet Union, the comparison would be truer if the traveller were imagined coming to the end of a well-demarcated highway and peering ahead at territory that is uncharted. The road trod since the mid-1960s having petered out during the Brezhnev succession, a choice must be made, but without signposts and without assurances that the path taken will not intersect with others.

Only now, as new leaders take charge and commitments begin to be made, can we start to say with any confidence which trajectory is most likely to be followed. Oversimplifying for analytical purposes, the main alternatives as to the near future of the Soviet system can be distilled to several: the far-fetched possibility of revolution; the several species of reform (radical, moderate, and minimal); conservative prolongation of the status quo; and reaction.[1] What would each of these strategic options entail? And what can be said in sum, building on what we know about trends in Soviet society and in the Soviet elite, about the odds of adoption?

The Unlikelihood of Fundamental Change

The most drastic alterations of the status quo are also the least likely to be in the cards. The Soviet system is well imbued with checks and stabilizers that guard against them. Revolution would entail the total and violent annihilation of the Soviet order as we now know it. Radical reform would bring basic change, but by evolutionary and peaceful means. And the reactionary or neo-Stalinist solution would wrench the USSR forward into the past, back to a more repressive and closed society.

Revolution: The collapse of the system. A Soviet dissident, the late Andrei Amalrik, once inquired whether the regime would survive until 1984.[2] As that Orwellian year recedes into memory, with no apocalypse and no rumblings of one, revolutionary collapse seems prohibitively unlikely. The reason is that the prerequisite of such an upheaval—a global, acute crisis of the Soviet political and social system—does not exist at this time. As we argued in Chapter 2, mass and elite discontent is still directed in the main at the performance of the Soviet system and not at its existence. Plentiful though the regime's worries are, they are not so awful that it will soon buckle beneath them. The usual portents of collapse, in particular widespread disorder and violence, cannot be found in the Soviet Union today.

To be sure, the leaders have recently spoken uneasily about the potential for political crisis. At the Twenty-seventh Party Congress, Boris Yel'tsin, the new head of the Moscow party organization, used prophetic language to impress this upon the delegates: "We must not be mesmerized by our country's relative political stability. How many times can we commit the very same mistakes, ignoring the lessons of history?" Yel'tsin did not answer his own question, but left the impression that there would not be too many more times. In his generally less alarmist speech, Yegor Ligachev, the second-ranking of the national party secretaries, allowed that "the political stability of Soviet society . . . is to a large degree determined by the party's correct social policy."[3] By extension, incorrect policy could trigger political instability.

Such an outcome, however, does not yet loom on the horizon. The Soviet system's legitimacy, moored in familiarity, past successes, and Russian nationalism, is too great. For, say, the next decade, there is little likelihood that this legitimacy will crumble. If economic and other troubles snowball, the possibility cannot be excluded that the regime's position will become precarious, though this assumes the problems at their severest and leadership wit and competence at their feeblest. Even were the regime's base to be sapped to this degree, the sinews of control are so pervasive and durable that it could persist for some time on their strength alone.

There are only two plausible ways by which the party's grip on the population might soon be shattered. One is through defeat in a major war, of the magnitude that dealt a mortal blow to Russia's tsarist regime in World War I. Lost wars erode social solidarity, offend nationalist feelings, and often pull disaffected military officers and their troops into the main political arena. Barring the mutual suicide of nuclear war with the United States, this is a contingency against which the Soviet Union's awesome military power is an adequate shield. The other script for disaster would involve detonation of massive ethnic conflict. This may possibly await the Soviet Union at some future time, all the more so if there is any truth to long-term population projections now being done in the West (and not accepted by all scholars) which foresee that Russians in the year 2080 will make up only 27 percent of the Soviet population, all Slavs 41 percent, and the main Moslem groups 42 percent.[4] But the nationality problem, while serious and perhaps fatal in the long run, ought to be containable well into the twenty-first century, when the consequences of the demographic surge of the Moslems will make themselves felt. Whither it will carry the Soviet system is for politicians several generations from now to anguish over.

Radical reform: Transformation from within. Next to revolution, radical reform of the Soviet system by pacific and more gradual means would be the most audacious course. Reshaping the system in its totality, radical reform would be distinguished from the less sweeping varieties of reform by its concentration on the fundamentals of institutions and ideology. In politics, it could be expected to bring liberalization and a quotient of democratization. Without necessarily replicating a Western constitutional democracy, it would extend citizens' liberties, multiply their opportunities for political participation, and make the state more directly responsible to them through electoral and other mechanisms. Radical reform would also have important economic consequences, probably involving some considerable displacement of state planning by the market.

A peaceful transfiguration of the one-party Soviet dictatorship could come about in either of two main ways: from above, at the behest of the regime; or from below, forced by society. The prototype of radical reform from above in a Soviet-type society is Czechoslovakia's "Prague Spring" of 1968. Although the officials and intellectuals who initiated it and rallied public support for it wanted to cure a miscellany of economic and other ills, their imaginations were kindled primarily by an ethical and political vision.[5] "Socialism with a human face"—with a competitive political process, an end to censorship, and greater civil rights—was inspired by the country's democratic and constitutional heritage, embodied in the interwar Czechoslovak republic, and by humanist ideals carried over from the party's days in opposition, which ended only in 1948. The dream died tragically in the occupation of Czechoslovakia by Warsaw Pact armies, directed by Soviet generals, in August 1968.

Radical, politics-centered reform has been promoted by several major factions among the Soviet dissidents. The "party democrats" of the 1960s, epitomized by the historian Roy Medvedev, wanted changes not dissimilar to those tried by Dubček. Andrei Sakharov, the physicist and Nobel Peace Prize laureate, has spoken for a rather different tendency, more Western-oriented and less socialist in its economics. The new manifesto prepared by a previously unknown group calling itself the Movement for Socialist Renewal, leaked to Western journalists in the summer of 1986 and propounding freedom of speech, legalized opposition, and a swing toward private enterprise, exceeds both Medvedev and Sakharov in its enthusiasm for radical reforms from above. In no case do these views find enough resonance in influential circles to get them a serious hearing. One perceptive observer reports that Medvedev's party democrats "are at present almost completely unrepresented in the highest reaches of the party," and the same could surely be said of Sakharov and the Movement for Socialist Renewal.[6]

There has been a discernible opening up of the Soviet political process under Mikhail Gorbachev, as will be discussed below. But the chance of a "Moscow Spring" breaking out any time soon, of a sudden efflorescence of personal rights aimed at the authoritarian heart of the system, is remote. Russia's democratic tradition remains too weak, and the effervescent politics of its Revolution is now too distant to have much effect. The regime's mistrust of the population and dedication to maintaining its vanguard role, by force if necessary, are far greater than was the case in Czechoslovakia.

Disincentive is added by the danger of destabilization due to the USSR's internal ethnic diversity and external ties. Within the Soviet Union, new political freedoms would in all probability be used to agitate for home rule and even secession by the Ukrainians, Baltic peoples, some of the Soviet Moslems, and many of the other non-Russians. If it allowed political parties to form and compete without restriction, full-blooded democratization might lead to the breakup of the multinational Soviet state. The same goes for the Soviet bloc in Eastern Europe. Aspirations for radical reforms would soar there the moment they had taken hold in the Soviet Union, and in most parts of the region would spur efforts to win greater autonomy from Moscow. Radical reform will thus be opposed by many Russians who might otherwise welcome it but will not run the risk of losing their empire.

If would-be Alexander Dubčeks lurk in the upper or middle echelons of the Soviet Communist Party, they are doing a superlative job of keeping their convictions to themselves. Soviet theorists stoutly reject any diminution of either the "leading role of the party" (the party's control over politics) or "democratic centralism" (the leadership's control over the party). Do-gooders in Eastern Europe or the non-ruling parties may espouse institutionalized "pluralism" or some other brand of "bourgeois democracy" in society and the party, the Soviets say, but "practice shows that where 'pluralism' flourishes it leads only to the loss of the party's fighting efficiency, to the erosion of its ideological foundations and class boundaries, in a word to the conversion of the party into some kind of motley conglomeration of ideologically disconnected groups and groupings."[7] Although the words are Chernenko's, from 1982, there is no evidence as of yet that Gorbachev and his peers will wander much from them.

Granting that Gorbachev wants the Soviet dictatorship to become more benevolent and open-minded, he intends it to remain a dictatorship nonetheless. His report to the Twenty-seventh Congress endorsed extension of "socialist self-government" (*sotsialisticheskoye samoupravleniye*), but this kind of phrase has been abused by so many Soviet ideologists in the past that there is no telling whether he intends to breathe meaning into it. Elsewhere in the report, Gorbachev paraded many of the stock Soviet terms about political structures and even saluted the KGB and its "struggle with all kinds of encroachments on our state and social system."[8] Some political controls may be modified, yet it is to be doubted that any present or prospective Soviet leader will tear up the basic authoritarian credo of Leninism.

The second brand of radical reform, from the grass roots up, was to be found in communist Poland in 1980–81. Here an independent trade union movement sprang into being and, in league with other social forces, unseated party leaders Edward Gierek and Stanislaw Kania, pried astonishing concessions from the regime, and eventually prompted Wojciech Jaruzelski's rearguard coup of December 1981. Solidarity's 10 million members took in one-third of the membership of the Polish Workers' Party. Could such a thing happen in the Soviet Union?

Insofar as the Polish uprising was "a classic case of protest produced by disappointed rising expectations," there is a temptation to see some parallel.[9] Regime performance has also been slipping behind public expectations in the USSR. The rash of spontaneous work stoppages in the late 1970s and early 1980s (the 1980 walkouts at the Togliatti and Gorky automotive plants, set off by local food shortages, being the biggest ones) evoke thoughts of Poland. There was even a gallant attempt in 1977–78, led by an embittered ex-foreman from the Donbass coal region, Vladimir Klebanov, to found what he called the Free Labor Union for the Defense of Workers. A more ephemeral Free Interprofessional Association of Workers (SMOT, in the Russian acronym), organized around self-help "cooperatives," was also started up in 1978. Scattered words of support of Solidarity appeared in Soviet samizdat publications during and after the Polish crisis. The very virulence with which Moscow execrated Solidarity, and the attention paid it in domestic propaganda and intra-party debates over the meaning of "contradictions" in communist societies, bespeak real apprehension.

With this the resemblance between the two countries ends. Solidarity's genesis at the Gdansk shipyards occurred during the fourth spasm of mass blue-collar protest in Poland in twenty-five years, going back to the Poznan demonstrations of 1956. It came on the heels of a decade of egregious mishandling of the economy that stoked mass aspirations without delivering the promised rise in living standards. Its victim was a regime, installed by Red Army bayonets after 1945, that had at no time earned more than the barest legitimacy. Equally to the point, the communist revolution in Poland, having sunk only shallow roots, left important areas outside state and party domination, among them the Roman Catholic church, a free-thinking and Westernized intelligentsia, and a large private sector in agriculture. Each of these contributed generously to Solidarity's sixteen months of glory.

The Soviet system, by way of contrast, is twice as old and far more fully consolidated than its Polish counterpart. It was forged in a much more thoroughgoing and bloodier revolution, and the ensuing Stalin terror obliterated all overt resistance and left few pockets of autonomy. Home-grown and never the puppet of a foreign power, the regime is able to mine national pride, especially among Russians, in the country's economic advance and rise to superpower rank. It was, indeed, anti-Polish nationalism as much as anything that was used to sour Soviet workers on Solidarity in 1980–81.[10] The Soviet government's repressive machinery dwarfs that of any of its counterparts in Eastern Europe—the mind boggles at the thought of the Kremlin letting a Lech Wałęsa become a media personality or tolerating "flying universities," underground printing presses, or the other channels through which Polish dissent built up a head of steam.

It should come as no surprise that the Soviet wildcat strikes of the late 1970s and early 1980s were easily crushed, like all those before them, and that the fledgling free trade unions, with never more than several hundred active supporters, were swiftly strangled by the KGB. Faithful to Russian tradition stretching back before 1917, and in contrast to Poland, relations between worker activists and nonconformist intellectuals in the Soviet Union have been hobbled by differences in self-image and an absence of mutual trust. Klebanov, the would-be union organizer, was rebuffed by prominent middle-class dissidents from whom he sought assistance, including Andrei Sakharov. A foreign journalist who questioned Sakharov about the affair discovered that he "displayed a patronizing prejudice against the people in the group, asserting that such simple workers as those Klebanov had signed up could not possibly have any idea what risk they were taking by trying to organize."[11]

Gorbachev has paid Solidarity the compliment of saying that it was not a "workers' protest against socialism" so much as "a difference of opinion with distortions of socialism in practice that pained the working class."[12] In the USSR, he did not have to add, the party will fight any attempt to decide in the streets or in independent union halls what is a distortion and what is not. The stumbling blocks to effective demands for radical reform being made from below are very high. The Soviet Union has not yet faced even dress rehearsals comparable to the Polish riots of 1956, 1970, and 1976. Soviet citizens, far from taking to the barricades, have in recent years withdrawn into private pursuits and apathy. Industrial workers remain the group that will draw the most nervous glances from the regime, but they lack the opportunity, heritage, intense grievances, and allies to mount a serious challenge at this time. The official trade unions remain meek executors of orders, with the union chief installed in 1982 during the wave of post-Solidarity concern, Stepan Shalayev, still being treated as a functionary of secondary importance. No other social group seems destined to raise the banner of democratizing reform any time soon, and no broad coalition is in the making. Poles are said to have a tradition of believing in miracles; Russians do not.

Reaction: Back to Stalinism. Some observers—including a fair number of emigrés from the USSR—have forecast radical movement in the reverse direction. They have in mind a restoration of many of the features associated with the acme of Joseph Stalin's rule: leader worship; rampant insecurity for office-holders; hypercentralized, secretive, and doctrinaire decision-making; strict abridgment of the population's freedoms, including its present right to select employment voluntarily; mass terror by police thugs and periodic purges of real or fancied "enemies of the people"; priority in the economy for investment, heavy industry, and armaments over consumers; and Russocentric xenophobia toward foreigners and countries outside the Soviet camp.

Neo-Stalinist trends undoubtedly were in play, along with others, in Brezhnev's Soviet Union. Some Soviets evinced a misplaced nostalgia for Stalin, the "strong boss" (*krepkii khozyain*) of an earlier and ostensibly simpler age, and some a thumbing of their noses at the establishment by gestures such as the hanging of a Stalin portrait. A smaller number, officials and ordinary citizens, consciously favored a thoroughgoing re-Stalinization of Soviet life. They blended at the edges into what Alexander Yanov calls the "Russian New Right," a disparate grouping of extreme Russian nationalists, religious fundamentalists, and, in the atypical case, racists and anti-Semites.[13] At the fringe of the fringe are the self-described Soviet fascists, who made an appearance in some cities starting about 1980. These were mostly bands of working-class toughs given to short haircuts, racial hatred, and fistfights.[14]

In the 1980s and 1990s, even an avowedly reformist regime will make selective use of repressive methods and of bits and pieces of the Stalinist legacy. Gorbachev has done this, presiding in his first half-year in office over ornate celebrations of the fortieth jubilee of victory in World War II and the fiftieth anniversary of the "Stakhanovite" movement, named after the Donbass miner whose feats in shoveling coal were used by Stalin's regime to lash fellow workers on to greater effort. Wholesale re-Stalinization, however, is something else again. The odds are stacked tall against it.

The Stalinization of the Soviet Union, beginning a decade after the Russian Revolution, was not a bolt from the blue. As historians have established, the country lay prone to the fate that befell it. Mass illiteracy and semi-literacy, millions of people set adrift by revolution and civil war, profound economic dislocation, a relative isolation from the world at large, a small and unrepresentative ruling party only recently escaped from conspiratorial politics and infatuated with an untried ideology with a strong messianic streak, a prevalent identification of the state with the Russian nation—all left Soviet Russia vulnerable to Stalin's assault. Stalinism both completed the severing of the old social bonds and cemented new ties between individual subjects and an overweening central authority.[15] Now, a half-century later (and three decades after de-Stalinization), the Soviet Union is a very different place. It has near-universal literacy, is reasonably settled in its ways and mores, and is far less divorced from world developments and opinion. With its larger and more assertive non-Russian communities, it would be much more resistant today to the shrill Russian nationalism embraced by Stalin.

The Soviet Communist Party, too, is a different organism. Ten times larger than in 1930, its ethos is blandly managerial and it is all but devoid of ideological fervor. It has recanted Stalin's murderous thesis about the "intensification of the class struggle," said to accompany the building of socialism and to justify the annihilation of all opposition. It accepts, as Yuri Andropov said in a reiteration of the post-Stalin position shortly before becoming General Secretary, "the existence of diverse, non-identical points of view and interests," and deems that "the failure of the interests of various social groups to coincide does not end in antagonism."[16]

Mikhail Gorbachev gave the fullest statement about Stalinism of any Soviet leader since Khrushchev in a February 1986 interview with the French Communist Party's newspaper, *Humanité,* which was reprinted in the Soviet press:

> Thirty years have now passed since at the Twentieth Party Congress the question of overcoming Stalin's personality cult was raised [in Nikita Khrushchev's Secret Speech] and the Central Committee's resolution on this question was adopted. We must say frankly that these were not easy decisions for our party to take. It was a kind of test in party principles and devotion to Leninism.
>
> In my view, we passed it with merit and have drawn the proper conclusions from the past. These relate to the life of the party itself and of Soviet society as a whole. We see as a crucial task the further development of intra-party democracy and of socialist democracy more generally, the strengthening of the principles of collegiality in our work, and the widening of publicity (*glasnost'*). The party and its Central Committee demand modesty of people elected to leading posts and instill in communists impatience toward flattery and toadyism. We acknowledge and will continue to acknowledge the enormous significance of the preservation and solidifying of socialist legality, and we will constantly keep our law-enforcement agencies under strict control.[17]

Gorbachev, though as nationalistic as most Russians, seems ill-disposed to the nativism and chauvinism common to both the New Right of the Brezhnev period and to Stalin's regime. One of the major personnel changes of his first year in office was to make Aleksandr Yakovlev, a declared foe of Russian ultra-nationalism, the head of the Central Committee's propaganda department and, in March 1986, the Central Committee secretary supervising party communications and cultural policy. Yakovlev had in 1973 been demoted from his position as acting head of the propaganda department to ambassador to Canada after penning an attack on Russophiles who "attempt to bring back the past."[18] At the same time as Yakovlev was elevated to the Secretariat, Vasili Shauro, the head of the Central Committee's culture department since 1965 and always considered more receptive to the New Right, was retired. His replacement, Yuri Voronov, is, by Soviet standards, liberal in orientation, and held a high media position (editor of *Komsomol'skaya pravda*, the youth newspaper) under Khrushchev.

Could the unique social and cultural chemistry that made Stalinism possible be recreated from above? Could a zealous and flint-hearted strongman retrace Stalin's steps despite differing conditions? This cannot be absolutely ruled out, because there are no ironclad constitutional and political safeguards against it in the Soviet Union. And yet, this possibility is one of the more unlikely. The hurdles to be cleared today are much higher than the first time around. Thanks to Stalin, Soviet politicians now comprehend what full-blown Stalinism is like. When the leaders claim tersely to have extracted the "proper conclusions" from the Stalin experience, as Gorbachev did in his *Humanité* interview, they are speaking volumes. Some, perhaps many, in the political class may long for a strong father figure in the Kremlin and even for certain of Stalin's long-abandoned policies. But collectively they have no interest in restoring the Kafkaesque atmosphere, groveling before the tyrant, and dread of extinction so much their lot in the high Stalin era. Nikita Khrushchev was thrown out for threatening the elite's preserve far less.

The economic and social content of the primal Stalinist model also loads the dice against re-Stalinization. Its genius was an unstinting use of state power to develop a primitive industrial economy. Its waste of economic inputs, serflike work force, and low rates of technological innovation would run against the grain of the complex and demanding Soviet society of today. It is precisely the clinging to some of the more outworn of the socioeconomic institutions developed in the 1920s and 1930s that lies behind many of the

Soviet Union's current difficulties. To resuscitate flagrantly coercive methods might shake free some economic reserves and yield one-time gains in productivity, but this would not be an easily sustainable strategy.[19]

It has sometimes been thought in the West that the secret police and/or the military could be the architects of a new Soviet totalitarianism. This was not how Stalinism arrived in its first incarnation, for that was very much the work of the Communist Party and its leader, whose police and army generals were agents but not equal partners. The KGB, elements of which might well object to reformist changes of any kind and aspire to re-Stalinization, has historically not exercised much independent influence over grand decisions. At Stalin's death in 1953, the police ran a vast internal empire, had millions of citizens in labor camps, and could make the most senior politician's knees tremble. All of this power, far surpassing that of the KGB today, could not prevent either de-Stalinization or the undoing of their own autonomy.

The army figured prominently in the recent re-establishment of harsh political controls in Poland. The Polish military did not so much push its way into politics as get pulled in by a regime that, mired in political and economic crisis, needed its aid to restore order and rebuild party authority. The imposition of martial law and the installation of General Jaruzelski as head of the party represented a partial abdication of the discredited civilian party to the armed forces. Even if the Jaruzelski regime (which aspires to economic reform as it struggles to reassert political control) can be considered neo-Stalinist, there seems little prospect of events soon taking a similar turn in Moscow. The Soviet party's authority would first have to implode as thoroughly as the Polish party's did, and this cannot be shown to be happening. Furthermore, it is probably not a coincidence that reminders of the preeminence of the civilian apparatus of the party have been more frequent and more barbed since martial law was declared in Warsaw—a tocsin intended, one guesses, for any general who begins to fantasize about becoming the Soviet Jaruzelski. Party spokesmen have belittled the idea "that any army, including a socialist army, is somehow a force that is 'above [social] classes,' an instrument for regulating the political relations of the entire nation." In a proper communist system, such a task is reserved to the party alone.[20]

The Realistic Alternatives

Conservatism and minimal reform. If there is to be no swerve toward revolution, radical democratization, or re-Stalinization, the choices for the Soviet Union's near future can be narrowed down to several. One option, widely predicted in the West, would be for the regime to muddle through on essentially the post-1964 Brezhnev course. Preservation of existing institutions, values, and policies would remain its arch objective. In addition, intelligent conservatives today, as Brezhnev and his colleagues did in their early years in power, could and probably would make small, consensually based adjustments to policy and technique. The aim would be to relieve some of the worst symptoms of underlying problems while causing a minimum of discord and inconvenience for vested interests. In the economy, this would mean continuing to walk what has been called the treadmill of the minor administrative reforms of the 1970s, palliatives and localized experiments requiring later adjustment in a never-ending series of tinkering changes.[21]

We can be sure that Mikhail Gorbachev and whoever sits around the Politburo table with him in the 1980s and 1990s will want to perpetuate the essence of the Soviet order—its Leninist ideology, single-party system, and state-owned economy. All well-anchored political systems, East and West, rely on leaders and elites who remain committed to certain of the system's central and irreducible features. But the Brezhnev leadership, especially as its vigor was drained in the 1970s, far outdid this normal conservatism. Its excessive concern with stability gave rise to petrifaction, distortion of priorities, and a failure to follow through on even minimal reforms.

As has been discussed in this essay, the exaggerated conservatism of the Brezhnev leadership grew first and foremost out of the specific historical circumstances that polarized the Soviet elite in the 1960s and caused Nikita Khrushchev's overthrow. They took office united by a resolve to govern in an orderly manner and to halt the reformist excesses of the Khrushchev years, particularly the assaults on the corporate interests of different parts of the establishment and the perceived derogation of Soviet traditions wrought by the de-Stalinization campaign. Brezhnev's agenda was largely set, therefore, by the aspirations and failures of his predecessor.

Counter-reformism was strongly reinforced by factors of personality and elite composition. Leonid Brezhnev was an ideological conservative who was essentially content with Soviet reality and conceived of himself as a kind of chairman of the board, not a policy entrepreneur. Nonincremental innovation, whether originating in the General Secretary's office or somewhere else, was further retarded by the proliferation of political veto points. The "charter of oligarchy" at the summit of the system, "respect for cadres" below, recruitment and promotion of officials along structured lines within agencies and territories, "scientific" decision-making premised on deference to experts and operating agencies—all increased the amount of political work needed to change policy. And this was when the aging of the Soviet elite was depriving it of the inflow of energy and ideas that accompany normal turnover. As one post-Brezhnev critic saw it, "the extremely long stays of leading party cadres in the very same posts . . . [led] to the formation of the habit of resolving questions in the very same ways, without taking notice of the changes in the situation."[22]

Brezhnevism both fed on important Soviet opinions and, as the regnant philosophy, generated powerful props of its own. It congrued with a conservatism within the elite and the population at large that, as Stephen Cohen phrases it, "is at once prideful and fearful and thus doubly powerful."[23] The pride was in the country's achievements, the fear that significant change would turn into a disaster, as many would say it has at earlier watersheds in Soviet history. These attitudes did not evaporate in November 1982, as the selection of Konstantin Chernenko even as lame-duck leader demonstrated. At present, Brezhnevism without Brezhnev would surely be favored by many of those who lived with it and benefited from it. The repeated references by Gorbachev to the need for "psychological reorientation" testify to the huge advantage that the Brezhnev approach derives from inertia and precedent.

Academician Tat'yana Zaslavskaya, the Novosibirsk-based scholar who is one of the most vocal partisans of economic reform, recently gave as a concrete illustration the attitudes of plant-level management toward greater enterprise autonomy from central planners. Factory directors who tried under Brezhnev to expand their decision rights were punished for their pains, and others learned from their failure. "That is why at the head of enterprises you now sometimes find people who are capable only of carrying out directives from above . . . people who are opposed to everything that contradicts either their narrow understanding of the public interest or their group interest."[24] In this and other realms, moreover, the policies and institutions that Brezhnev embalmed were by and large inherited from the Stalin era—meaning that now most of them are more than half a century old. Other communist countries in which deep economic and other reforms have been launched have typically spent twenty or twenty-five years under the unreformed system—Hungary in the 1960s, for example, or China in the late 1970s. Soviet conservatives defend practices that have had twice as long or more to entrench themselves.

Moderate reform. Although the forces conducive to a neo-Brezhnevite mix of conservatism and minimal reform should be recognized, they should not be overemphasized. In the final accounting, they will probably carry less weight than those supportive of a program of moderate reform. Moderate reform refers to a strategy of controlled change somewhere between radical and minimal reform. Since its focus would be on public policy and the machinery needed to fulfill change, and not on the most basic institutions and beliefs, it would fall well short of radical reform. It would be, to put it another way, significant reform *within* the Soviet system but not a fundamental reform *of* it. Unlike minimal reform, however, the change involved would be enough to disrupt some important procedures, challenge old habits, and precipitate controversy and conflict.

The political conditions of the Brezhnev succession are the most important variable impelling the leadership toward moderate reform. Stalin's rule ended in demented preparations for a final purge, and Khrushchev's in frantic redrawing of the organization chart. Brezhnev's end point was political stagnation, all the more alarming to some because it coincided with incontrovertible evidence of economic and social decay. Just as Khrushchev strove for de-Stalinization and Brezhnev for de-Khrushchevization, the new leaders seem bent on de-Brezhnevization. The shakiness of the first steps taken by Andropov, and the equivocation under Chernenko, probably increased the interest in some quarters in an emphatic change. Many of the more restive members of the elite must have been thinking like the regional first secretary (Yuri Petrov of Sverdlovsk oblast) who explained to the Twenty-seventh Congress that he was tired of waiting for action on the economy: "How long are we just going to talk, write, and argue about this? . . . It is impossible, comrades, for us to remain in suspension for decades."[25]

Gorbachev's speech to the congress, with its assault on inertia, self-flattery, and the illusion that the party could "improve matters without changing anything," now stands as the regime's definitive position on Brezhnevism. His Kennedyesque call for accelerated economic and social development, more an encapsulation of mood than of a precise program, is the best indication of the path he intends to mark out. The attempt to get the country moving again connotes a change in speed more than of direction or final goal. It is a summons to moderate reform, by my definition, but not, as best we can tell from the details furnished so far, to radical reform. Gorbachev has used the phrase "radical reform," but loosely and in reference to economic changes only. Some changes in political process are proposed by the Gorbachev coalition, but these will be within a framework of continued authoritarianism.

As with the Brezhnev Politburo, the quirks of character and small-group relations, as well as the consequences of larger-scale trends within the elite, are shaping regime strategy. One may quibble about how to categorize Andropov, and about whether to take note of Chernenko at all, but there can be little doubt that Gorbachev envisages himself as a tough-minded reformer out to realign the Soviet elite and to save the Soviet system by modernizing it. By temperament he is as different from Brezhnev as Brezhnev was from Khrushchev. Indeed, while on points such as formal education and career progression Gorbachev is exemplary of his generation of Soviet officials, in certain other ways—the delight in long speeches and harangues, the tendency toward self-dramatization, the populist or pseudopopulist hankering to deal directly with the people and thereby to threaten noncooperative members of the establishment—he resembles nothing so much as an updated and well-groomed version of Nikita Khrushchev. This shone through in the shirt-sleeve tours taken in his early months in office and in the new round of field visits and Kremlin audiences begun after the Twenty-seventh Congress. Like Khrushchev, too, Gorbachev accepts conflict, open and clandestine, as an inevitable concomitant of his policies.[26]

Kremlin decision-making remains oligarchic, but Gorbachev, taking astute advantage of tactical opportunities, is already emerging as an assertive General Secretary. Still obligated to get the collective's approval for changes of policy, he is more of an activist than Brezhnev ever was in influencing the terms of private and public debate. He and his allies have speedily made major changes in personnel and, maybe of greater importance, in personnel policy. Following on Andropov's early lead, he has revoked Brezhnev's implicit contract about security of office and has set the Soviet elite in political and physical motion. Although many of Gorbachev's closest collaborators are older than he, officials from his generation, more fretful about Soviet failures and more ready to try judicious innovations, are streaming into positions long closed to them. The politics of elite patronage and placement in the years ahead promises to be more volatile and, if Gorbachev's first year in office is any indication, more closely tied into policy debates.

Behind these political maneuvers and countermaneuvers is a tally of economic and social difficulties that, as is ever more openly recognized in the Soviet Union, has lengthened steadily in recent years. The proliferation of problems has made the elite and the population more receptive to reformist leadership. It also carries the danger of exhausting these same leaders in the fighting of political brushfires. A litmus test for Gorbachev and his supporters will be whether they can step back from micro-problems long enough to look at macro-problems in a systematic way. In an economic and political system in which deadlines and quotas must be met come what may, it will be tempting to imitate Brezhnev in dealing with emergencies one by one—the shortfall in oil production one day, the congestion of the railroads another day, the Chernobyl' reactor fire the next. It is easy to see how the often-noted resistance to innovation within the Soviet firm could be reproduced at the level of the system as a whole, as surely happened under Brezhnev.

Supposing that Gorbachev is able to rise above micro-problems, and to achieve with the passage of time a clearer action plan than he has hitherto done, one thing augurs reasonably well for moderate reform. That is the degree of the Soviet Union's present problems—serious enough to demand changes, as Gorbachev said at the congress, but not yet so lethal as to call the regime's survivability into question. "Perhaps the hardest lesson to learn for governments sensitive to the needs of reform," one scholar cogently writes of reform in general, "is the importance of introducing reforms from a position of strength. Reforms which appear to be granted under pressure from events and the demands of more radical groups can only further weaken the regime, strengthen the radicals, lead to more extreme demands from more groups, and provoke a counterrevolutionary backlash."[27] A Soviet leadership as self-contented as Brezhnev's Politburo of the 1970s would see no particular need for big innovations in policy. A leadership as beleaguered as the Shah of Iran in the late 1970s or the Polish government in the early 1980s might be readier to try temperate reform, but with less prospect of success than Gorbachev and his confederates have today. The longer the regime procrastinates, the more it fritters away the advantage of strength. A unique window of opportunity exists today for moderate reform. A decade ago, that aperture was not yet open because the problems of the Soviet system were not sufficiently grave; a decade hence, it may be slammed shut by problems that have become too much so.

Six Points of Moderate Reform

A rough sketch of the likely and possible features of moderate reform can be inferred from the debates conducted and the actions taken since the death of Brezhnev, and especially since the accession of Gorbachev. Gorbachev on some points is essentially expanding on initiatives taken by Andropov; on others, he has been more his own man. Since words have not always been backed up by action, we are forced in certain areas to speculate as judiciously as can be done.

The new leaders have prescribed changes in many areas of Soviet life. As revealed to date, however, the agenda for moderate internal reform encompasses predominantly economic and socioeconomic issues. Most are related one way or another to the ambition to increase growth rates, though in each case considerations of political power and authority also figure. The main exception is the opening up of the media and the arts, which is a political reform pure and simple. This I will deal with last, as its ultimate significance is very much a riddle. Of the primarily economic and socioeconomic issues, five stand out. Inculcation of discipline and order, the least venturesome measure, has been pushed the furthest. The manipulation of resources to achieve economic and social ends has thus far been inconclusive, and it may well be that Gorbachev has more modest or more muddled objectives here than have been ascribed to him. Encouragement of private economic initiative is still mostly at the talking stage, but prospects have brightened for a shift in policy in agriculture and maybe in other areas. New incentives to mobilize the "human factor" in the labor force have been agreed upon in principle, with some avenues of implementation more likely than others. Last and most nettlesome is the possibility of overhaul of the whole system of planning and management, where even under the best of circumstances debate, preparatory work, and indecision probably will continue for some time.

Discipline and order. One of Yuri Andropov's earliest decisions as leader was to issue a clarion call for "discipline and order." Though overdue, it did not come as an abrupt break, and it had the added virtue of furnishing, at low cost, prompt if limited gains. "Putting things in order," he remarked in early 1983, "really does not demand any capital investments at all, yet it has an enormous effect."[28]

The Andropov law-and-order offensive at first directed its fire broadly. It flung at both rulers and ruled a volley of rhetoric that some have likened to the orders of a drill-sergeant, others to a neo-Calvinist injunction to gain secular salvation through hard work.[29] Andropov sent a shock wave through the elite by firing some senior officials, dressing down others, and stressing, as he said in several speeches, that discipline was for everyone "from worker to minister." Rank-and-file citizens were subjected to "Operation Trawl," which authorized police sweeps through stores, theaters, and public baths in search of workers absent from the job and unleashed the police and volunteer street patrols on loiterers, alcoholics, wife-beaters, ticketless streetcar riders, and urban dwellers without residence permits. Operation Trawl wound down in the late spring of 1983, after which more concerted efforts were brought to bear in two main areas.

The first was the workplace, where laggards, drunkards, and truants were implored and bullied to shape up. August 1983 amendments to the labor code put teeth into the campaign by more precisely defining shirking (more than three hours of unjustified absence from the job) and increasing workers' financial liability for damage caused. For those missing shifts or punching in intoxicated, it also authorized managers to reduce their vacations, dock their pay, and even lay them off without first clearing it with the factory trade union committee. These and like measures are stated to have cut working time lost to absenteeism and tardiness by 15 to 25 percent in various parts of the country.[30] Soviet managers themselves were hit by heavier penalties, up to and including dismissal and public humiliation, for failing to meet planned targets or attempting to renegotiate them. The railway bureaucracy, which under a new Transport Minister, Nikolai Konarev, made some headway against congestion, was held up as an early paradigm of effective discipline.[31]

The second prong of Andropov's offensive jabbed at corruption, a blight that spread in the 1960s and 1970s and, as other societies have learned, would sooner or later have devastating effects on the system as a whole if unchecked. Andropov's Politburo moved quickly to sanction unprecedented press coverage of venality in public office and to make an example of high officials alleged to be deriving illicit benefit from their positions.

The Interior Minister since 1966, Nikolai Shchelokov, was sacked in December 1982; in June 1983 he and another family friend of Brezhnev, Sergei Medunov, the party prefect in Krasnodar krai until July 1982 (when he was removed during the pre-succession skirmishing), were expelled from the Central Committee and the party, the first time this had happened in two decades. Shchelokov's first deputy, Yuri Churbanov—Brezhnev's son-in-law—was rusticated to a provincial post. Rapid promotions were offered to officials known to have exerted themselves against bribe-taking and embezzlement, among them Vitali Vorotnikov, the new premier of the Russian Republic (previously Medunov's replacement in Krasnodar), and Geidar Aliyev of Azerbaidzhan, the new

First Deputy Chairman of the Council of Ministers (who in his home republic in the 1970s forbade senior officials to build dachas or buy personal automobiles). Under Shchelokov's replacement, Vitali Fedorchuk, the barrel-chested enforcer who followed Andropov as KGB chief in May 1982, the ranks of the uniformed police were "purged of unworthy people who are ideologically and morally immature," and new party organs were established in the ministry.[32] Dismissals, disciplinary procedures, and criminal trials were extended to the retailing and service networks, where corruption had mushroomed most rapidly under Brezhnev. In at least three of the most egregious cases, prominent officials were given death sentences. Those caught up in the net must have numbered in the thousands, for accounts of party conferences in early 1984 stated that hundreds of party members and functionaries in individual localities had been ejected from the party for moral transgressions.

Konstantin Chernenko, so intimately associated with the late leader, may well have looked askance at the idea of holding Brezhnev and his coterie personally culpable for the deterioration of official ethics. Chernenko did not, however, stop the broad discipline drive or the specific measures against corruption, and he probably would have taken a big political risk had he tried to do the latter. Uncovering corruption, he said in an early speech, "will be carried out steadily and strictly," with no leniency shown.[33] The campaign, though notched down in shrillness and scope, was continued in the provinces with the major regional purges, supervised by Gorbachev and Ligachev, begun in Uzbekistan and the RSFSR's Rostov oblast in the summer of 1984. Nikolai Shchelokov, who had worked with Chernenko in Moldavia in the 1950s, was deprived of his military rank in November 1984 and died under house arrest the following month.

Mikhail Gorbachev as General Secretary has persevered with the battle against corruption. Demotions and arrests have been reported in a number of central agencies, including those for trade, foreign commerce, civil aviation, and petroleum distribution. One minor member of the Council of Ministers (Talgat Khuramshin, chairman of the State Committee for the Supply of Petroleum Products) was removed for corruption in December 1985 and subsequently expelled from the party. In a symbolic repudiation of nepotism, neither Brezhnev's son-in-law nor his son Yuri was returned to candidate status in the Central Committee in 1986.

The regime has proceeded with cleanups on the local level, overseen since mid-1985 by the veteran of the Krasnodar minipurge, Georgi Razumovskii. These have been especially vigorous in the four Central Asian republics, Kazakhstan, Moscow (since the removal of Viktor Grishin and the city's mayor, Vladimir Promyslov), and several provincial centers in the RSFSR. In Uzbekistan, for instance, "Measures have been taken to cleanse the party, state, and economic organs of persons who had compromised themselves" and criminal charges have been brought against "many former leaders."[34] Reports circulating in Moscow in the summer of 1986 said that 800 trade officials had been arrested in the capital city alone. Officials fearing exposure, or seeking revenge for it, are reported to have fought back in some localities by writing anonymous denunciations of their accusers.[35]

In spite of the resistance, a certain confidence about the outcome can be read into the January 1986 transfer of General Fedorchuk, the career KGB officer, out of the Interior Ministry. His replacement was a party apparatchik, Aleksandr Vlasov, who had been commended for rooting out corruption in his previous position (first secretary in Rostov oblast) but had no prior involvement in secret or regular police work. Gorbachev's keynote address to the Twenty-seventh Congress paid surprisingly scant attention to corruption, implying that he is satisfied that fear of the consequences has at least curbed its growth. New legal instruments for the long-haul struggle were defined by party and government edicts on "unearned income" published May 28, 1986. Penalties for bribe-taking have been differentiated, and all financial transactions of over 5,000 rubles now have to be processed through the State Bank. Citizens making any purchase of more than 10,000 rubles, or building a house worth more than 20,000 rubles, must henceforth make a declaration of the source of the income used, and the Procuracy is empowered to investigate if it perceives an "obvious disproportion" between income and wealth.

In the workplace, Gorbachev has held discipline to be especially vital before technological modernization and organizational changes make the economy more efficient: "During the first stage of the struggle for more rapid development of the economy, we can and must get an essential boost from putting things in order, from raising labor, technological, and state discipline."[36] Brandishing slogans such as "A day's work rather than a day at work!," his didactic approach has been much like Andropov's in 1982–84.

Gorbachev's principal initiative in the realm of law and order has been his declaration of war on alcohol abuse, for the sake of economic efficiency but also of public health and probity. Outright prohibition of alcohol was bruited about under Andropov and Chernenko, but Gorbachev seems to have rejected a dry law as unenforceable. Party and state decrees published May 17, 1985, instituted draconian restrictions on consumption of alcohol. Vodka distilling was ordered reduced by an unspecified amount and production of cheap fruit wines ceased by 1988, outlets were reduced in number by 50 percent and removed from the vicinity of factories, sales were limited from 2 p.m. to 7 p.m., the legal drinking age was raised from eighteen to twenty-one, and the police were given new powers to clamp down on public drunkenness. In some parts of the country, local authorities have levied further restrictions, and militant prohibitionists continue to press for an alcohol ban or, at a minimum, vodka rationing.[37]

The May 1985 decision recognized that a change in popular attitudes toward intoxicants, and not just punitive measures, would be required. It granted a long-expressed wish of pro-temperance forces by sanctioning formation of a mass organization to spread the word about the evils of drink. The founding congress of the All-Union Voluntary Association for the Struggle for Sobriety, whose local branches already had hundreds of thousands of members, was held in Moscow in September 1985. Its first chairman is Academician Yuri Ovchinnikov, a respected biochemist and a vice-president of the Academy of Sciences. The regime has also told Soviet planners to provide additional leisure opportunities by accelerating construction of cinemas, clubs, libraries, and sports facilities. The Soviet media have carried numerous and at times gruesome exposés of alcohol's ill effects and depicted bureaucrats setting a good example by sipping carbonated water and fruit juices at official gatherings. Soviet jokesters have given General Secretary Gorbachev the sobriquet of *Mineral'nyi sekretar'*, or "Mineral Secretary," after the now ubiquitous mineral water.

Lineups of two to three hours to buy alcohol were one immediate result of the limitations. Only time will tell what the lasting effects will be. Gorbachev has proudly reported that alcohol sales for the first half of 1986 were down by 35 percent from 1985, costing the state 5 billion rubles in foregone profits, and Ligachev has asserted that "millions" of Soviets have voluntarily adopted "the sober way of life."[38] But they gave no statistics on distillation of *samogon*, homebrew, which surely will negate some of the drop in state production, or on the compensatory increase in drug abuse that some other sources have mentioned. And no one with any experience of the Soviet Union can believe in miraculous overnight cures for millions of alcoholics. The very enormity of the anti-alcohol crusade makes it clear that the regime knows it has squared off with a resilient opponent.

Resource allocation for growth and consumption. There has been for at least a decade shared uncertainty and deep division within the Soviet elite over how best to marshal resources behind national goals. Boxed into a corner, the Brezhnev leadership in the mid-1970s attempted to elevate immediate consumer and defense needs above economic investment. But the policy was never rigorously adhered to, and actual growth of investment hovered about 1 percent a year above the planned level through the early 1980s.

Although Yuri Andropov seems not to have made up his mind about resource tradeoffs, he mused in public mostly about the plight of the consumer, arguing that the party was obliged "to liquidate completely shortages of goods and services."[39] He advocated investment in world-standard production facilities, yet never indicated that he thought investment's share of national product should vary much. As concerns consumers, a Central Committee resolution in February 1983 promised improvements in the housing situation. Other joint party-government edicts in March and May 1983 provided for the opening of more cleaning and repair shops, more personal services such as hairdressing and film developing, easier rental of consumer durables, more convenient working hours in service establishments, and an immediate "substantial increase" in the output of consumer products, including the small household items and spare parts in such acutely short supply. In late 1983 a special Politburo commission, chaired by Aliyev, began working on a comprehensive program for developing consumer goods production and services.

Chernenko seems to have concurred in these decisions, as none was revoked when he was in power. But Gorbachev's stance on resource allocation has been elusive. It has perhaps been misunderstood in the West, where he has been seen as an all-out industrializer little attuned to the consumer. It certainly is true that Gorbachev from the outset has stipulated that the Soviet Union set higher growth targets and commit the necessary capital to realizing them, especially in high-technology branches. At a June 1985 Kremlin conference, he revealed that the Politburo had rejected Gosplan's draft of the Twelfth Five-Year Plan (for 1986–90) as too unambitious in both growth and investment tempos. It was impossible, he said, "to get by without maneuvering resources and concentrating them in key sectors."[40] Friction over the plan apparently was one factor behind the retirement in October 1985 of the longtime Gosplan chairman, Nikolai Baibakov. Gosplan's new boss, Nikolai Talyzin, outlined draft targets for the Twelfth Plan which were then accepted, with some amendments, at the Twenty-seventh Party Congress and written into law in June 1986.

The 1986–90 plan captures an uneasy compromise on resource allotment. Economic investment will be increased by 23.6 percent, or an average of 4.3 percent a year, which is appreciably more than the 15.4 percent overall increase reported by the Soviets for 1981–85 but not as much as some Politburo pronouncements seemed to herald. Curiously, the investment increase passed on by the congress was 20 percent, while the planned increase for the single year 1986 is almost 8 percent, or nearly double the expected five-year average. The discrepancies not only call into question the internal consistency of the plan but hint at ongoing conflict over the investment share. The biggest shifts are among different categories of investment project. By far the largest chunk of capital, an increment of some 80 percent over five years (and 30 percent in 1986 alone), will go to machine-building, Gorbachev's preferred sector and the one he maintains will lift the economy up by its bootstraps. Special priority will go to facilities producing microprocessors and other microelectronic components, computers and automated systems, precision instrumentation, numbered machine tools, robotics, and machinery for the chemical and oil-refining branches. Also favored will be investment in biotechnology and the development of new materials and manufacturing techniques.[41]

Gorbachev might have wanted to see a steeper growth of investment, but the oscillating figures in the several drafts of the plan indicate that this question is still open. The structure of investment cannot be entirely to his liking, either. Both Andropov and Gorbachev have sought to trim investment in energy, which gobbled up huge amounts after the oil scare of 1977. But the 1984–85 tumble in oil production (which will negatively affect the USSR's foreign trade accounts) apparently pushed the Politburo to expand energy investment by 40 to 45 percent in 1986–90. The cleanup of the April 1986 Chernobyl' accident (the Politburo announcement of July 20, 1986, put the direct costs at 2 billion rubles), plus the as yet unknown costs of designing safer nuclear reactors and retrofitting unsafe ones, may push energy spending up even higher. Gorbachev wants to promote energy conservation, as Andropov tried to do before him, but this will be difficult without changes in management incentives. For agriculture, another profligate spender of the Brezhnev years, the increase in investment has been held at or around the average rate. Congruent with the intensification philosophy, the fastest growth here will be of investment in food and fiber processing and storage (up by 51 percent). On-farm investment, including the irrigation and land reclamation boondoggles that Brezhnev propounded and Chernenko tried to continue in 1984, will be pared.

What, then, happens to the Soviet consumer? Jaded by earlier broken promises, he will be unimpressed by platitudes. It bears emphasis that Gorbachev, for all his passion for higher and redirected investment, has at each turn spoken of the indispensibility of spending on consumer needs and has in fact become more eloquent on this issue as time has passed. In his Twenty-seventh Congress report, after saying that Soviet social programs would be idle wishes without economic acceleration, he assailed "the well-known deviation in the direction of technocratic approaches," to the detriment of "pressing" welfare needs, among planners and economic administrators. Touring the Volga city of Kuibyshev in April 1986, Gorbachev made his most pro-consumer remarks yet:

> I must tell you that there are several problems that we must resolve as a matter of the greatest urgency: housing, food, the quality of goods, . . . city transport, health care. We are speaking here of the need to pull up the whole social sphere, because it has lagged. Look, for example, at how you in Kuibyshev are so enthused about heavy industry, at how we build new capacity, plants, and workshops, but without achieving the desired result. That is because we forget that new plants

> and workshops are a dead thing without a profound concern for people. For the individual to work successfully, he needs a system of services, of daily conveniences, of trade, of health care, he needs good schools and places to relax so he can get his strength up for the new working day. All of this defines people's outlook, their attitude toward work, in a word, the productivity of social labor as a whole. I must say frankly that problems in the social sphere have today become aggravated and have acquired a certain determining character.[42]

Addressing factory workers the next day in Togliatti—the site of a big illegal strike in 1980—Gorbachev asserted that resources had actually been diverted to welfare purposes: "Serious measures have already been undertaken, necessary correctives to planning principles have been made. A reallocation of capital investment into our social program has been carried out." And in June 1986 one substantial reallocation was disclosed, an increase in the target for housing construction for 1986–90 from the 565–570 million square meters endorsed by the party congress in March to 595 million (production was 552 million square meters in 1981–85).[43]

All this prompts the conclusion that Gorbachev all along has had a balanced attitude toward resource allocation. The 1986–90 five-year plan, like Brezhnev's last plan, provides for faster rates of growth of production of so-called Group B industries (light and consumer-oriented industry) than of Group A (heavy industry). As will be discussed in Chapter 5, Gorbachev seems to have preferred the claims of both consumption and investment over those of the military. He is probably less worried about enlarging total investment than about funneling it into priority areas such as computers and sophisticated machinery. And he has an authentic concern with consumer satisfaction, grounded in large part, like Andropov's before him, in the realization that disgruntled consumers make unmotivated workers.

The resource squeeze will still make it difficult to pay out of the central purse for big increases in consumer production and amenities. Hence Gorbachev is moving to accommodate consumer demand in several other ways. The first two will be considered below: encouraging private and cooperative provision of consumer goods and services, and fastening benefits received more tightly to the individual's productivity. Another tactic is to exert greater administrative coordination over consumer-oriented activities which reach beyond light industry and service firms into the heavy and defense industries. Local and regional governments were given new powers here in July 1986, though this has yielded poor results in the past. In Moscow, a member of the Central Committee Secretariat (currently Aleksandra Biryukova) has since December 1983 been assigned full-time to consumer problems.

Party approval was given in October 1985 to the voluminous "Integrated Program for Development of the Production of Consumer Goods and of the Service Sector for the Years 1986–2000" prepared by Aliyev's commission. In hundreds of different categories, from underwear to color television sets to haircuts, it lays down detailed benchmarks for attainment by 1990 and 2000. Although the latter figures are more symbolic than real, the 1990 numbers, especially in the grossly neglected services area (where increases of 30 to 40 percent are pledged), will be harder to ignore than the fuzzier quotas of the past.[44] In a number of areas, the Integrated Program vows accelerated benefits after 1990, and this back-loading can be found in other regime statements as well. The new party program, for example, promises every Soviet family a separate apartment or house by 2000, whereas the 1986–90 plan, even as amended, allows for only an 8 percent increase in state housing construction. Premier Nikolai Ryzhkov stated at the Twenty-seventh Congress that investment's share of Gross National Product might be allowed to fall in the 1990s, to the advantage of consumers—many of whom, admittedly, will be skeptical about this result being achieved.[45]

Two other aspects of the regime's evolving consumer policy should be touched on here. One is the renewed effort to make employers responsible for providing a wider range of amenities to their work force. Suggestions to this effect—covering traditional perquisites such as housing and day care, but also new ones in the area of personal services—can be found in nearly every major recent statement on the economy, including the Gorbachev and Ryzhkov reports to the party congress. Some of these will probably soon be converted into legislation, which will have to provide for greater discretion for the enterprise in the disposition of its resources. This policy, if the past is any guide, will have some beneficial effects but will also breed horrendous problems of coordination.

The second and more innovative lead involves the criteria by which firms manufacturing for consumers are judged. Until now, they have been rewarded for making consumer goods in the aggregate, with little regard for quality. These are transferred to warehouses and stores in the Ministry of Trade, which markets them to consumers. Beginning January 1, 1987, quality control officers employed by a new state inspectorate and not, as now, by the producing ministry will be placed in all factories making consumer goods. Gorbachev has also indicated interest in broadening recent experiments, undertaken in the Baltic republics and the Urals, in vertical integration of manufacturing enterprises with trade outlets. Were this to become the norm, factories would be considered to have fulfilled their assigned plans only when goods had been retailed to consumers, which would make them less able to produce junk with impunity and more concerned with responding to market demand. This scheme, according to published accounts, has been fought tooth and nail by both the industrial ministries and the Ministry of Trade. A small victory is the decision to increase the number of factory-owned stores (*firmennye magaziny*) of the Ministry of Light Industry from the present handful to 200–250 by 1991.[46]

Private, cooperative, and market-oriented enterprise. One of the worst quandaries for the rules-minded regime of Andropov and Gorbachev has been what to do with the small fry in the second economy: the moonlighters, unlicensed fruit and vegetable vendors, itinerant construction workers, sticky-fingered salesclerks and waiters, and so forth. Inhabiting a limbo between legality and illegality, they have increasingly found customers for goods and services that the state cannot or will not supply. Besides posing a law-enforcement problem, their very existence points to an enormous economic reserve which the regime has hitherto bottled up for political and ideological reasons. In this the Soviets have been more rigid than most of their allies in Eastern Europe, including the Hungarians but also the much more orthodox East Germans.

The precedent for private or quasi-private enterprise in the USSR would be the small plots Soviet peasants have been allowed to tend behind their cottages since the 1930s, which occupy about 4 percent of arable land but produce and sell in legal "collective farm markets" 60 percent of the country's potatoes, over 40 percent of its eggs and fruit, and about 30 percent of its meat, milk, and vegetables. Brezhnev, already more permissive than his predecessors, gave further protection to the household plots in 1977 and 1981 legislation. A start was also made on giving city residents patches of land of their own to cultivate, with the crops either being retained for family use or sold.

Whereas Andropov and Chernenko did nothing about private enterprise other than let it be discussed more fully, there are signs that Gorbachev may be moving further. His Politburo in April 1985 ordained expansion of the number of garden plots for urban dwellers by 1 million a year, and Gorbachev strongly defended the move in a speech the following month.[47] A sometimes emotive debate over private entrepreneurship broke out in the Soviet press in the winter of 1985–86. At the Twenty-seventh Congress, Gorbachev argued at the level of theory for a second look at the concept of "socialist property" and for greater acceptance of "the healthy functioning of commodity-monetary relations [a phrase used as a surrogate for market exchange] on a socialist basis."[48]

More concretely, Gorbachev announced a new policy on procurement and distribution of agricultural produce which, though it did not sanctify private property as such, placed greater weight than in the past on self-interest and market-type incentives. Collective and state farms, once they have made their compulsory deliveries to the government, will now be free to dispose of the entire surplus "at their own discretion." Whereas Gorbachev, while citing Lenin's New Economic Policy, did not employ the word "market" (*rynok*) in vindicating his policy, his chief agricultural administrator (and old Stavropol' colleague), Vsevolod Murakhovskii, did. Quite remarkably, Murakhovskii claimed that the approach could be generalized to the entire economy:

> The position put forward in [Gorbachev's] political report on the application under contemporary conditions of Lenin's idea of the tax in kind [the fixed tax on the peasantry that was the cornerstone of NEP] is an example of the creative approach to improving the management mechanism, of more actively utilizing the whole instrument of commodity-monetary relations. [It is impossible to] deny the importance of their active influence on the raising of people's incentives and the efficiency of production. The socialist market (*sotsialisticheskii rynok*)

> must play an important role in increasing the volume and the quality of production. There is nothing to fear in this. The market's limits are defined by the socialist system, by the state's possessing the key positions in production and distribution.
>
> We support this important theoretical position and are persuaded that applying it in the practice of building socialism will exert a positive influence on our whole system of management.[49]

Under the terms of the detailed policy description provided in late March, Soviet farms will be obliged to sell to the state in each year of the 1986–90 plan a prearranged amount of grain and other food products (set in most cases at the average of the 1981–85 sales). Over and above this, the crop can either be conveyed to the government at double the normal price or disposed of through the urban markets, in which prices move freely, or the rural cooperatives, which are to double their sales volume by 1990. For most non-grain products, 30 percent of the state quota can also be met by sales through other channels. Farms will be encouraged to open their own shops in cities in order to market processed foods at prices regulated on the regional level only.[50]

So far as the household plots are concerned, the new agricultural policy marks a step forward inasmuch as it erases for most planning purposes the distinction between food grown on common fields and on the small plots. This will have certain drawbacks for peasants, but these should be more than offset by the new awareness on the part of state administrators that it is in their interest to encourage private production. For the future, additional moral and material assistance will have to be made available to the small producer in order for private production to thrive. The kinds of aid most often mentioned in Soviet publications include: guaranteed access to state feed for household livestock; the extension of credit; the provision of seed, fertilizer, and, most important, small machinery such as works marvels on miniature plots in Japan; help with storage and transport; and, least likely to be granted, enlargement of the maximum plot size from the present 0.5 hectares (about 1.2 acres). Off the farm, the city markets at which the produce is disposed of need physical upgrading, better management, and fewer petty hindrances by local governments and police forces.[51]

The other area in which privatizing changes are possible is that of personal services. If anything, the return in output and goodwill might be greater here than in agriculture. The most prevalent suggestions would allow individuals and small, cooperative firms to build and maintain housing, operate taxicabs and delivery trucks, repair appliances and clothing, provide other household services, and sell prepared foods. Since illegal activity has burgeoned in all these areas, the regime could turn much of this to its ends while reducing the underground economy. Opponents of privatization have argued that it is ideologically suspect, would foster inequality, and would leave citizens vulnerable to "the arbitrariness of market prices."[52] But many others have concluded that private activity is all but impossible to suppress and fulfills a useful function: "There is a demand for private services and there is a corresponding supply. So both sides, you can be sure, will find some way of getting around restrictions."[53] The best response, proponents of change say, is to legalize certain kinds of private activity but subject it to greater regulation and to state taxation.

This is the tack Gorbachev seemed to be taking in his Twenty-seventh Congress speech. He committed the leadership to encouragement of the formation of cooperatives "in production and the reprocessing of production, in the building of housing and gardens, and in the sphere of personal services and trade." He also promised to consider "suggestions for setting in order the labor activity of individuals" in the service sector. This should occur, in keeping with socialist principles, either in a cooperative framework or on the basis of contracts signed with state firms, but one way or another, provision of individual service should be stimulated.[54] The May 1986 measures against "unearned income" will cramp underground entrepreneurs who use state machinery and supplies in their activities, or who illegally act as commercial middlemen. Debate continues unabated, however, on the larger issue of legitimate enterprise by individuals and cooperatives.

New work incentives. All three of the post-Brezhnev heads of the party have recognized the need for new direct incentives to stimulate efficient and high-quality labor. While punishing loafers has been part of their answer, so have several affirmative policies on exploitation of the "human factor" long discussed by Soviet academic specialists.

The most important of these is revamping of the egalitarian earnings structure in effect since the mid-1950s and little modified under Brezhnev. Andropov and Chernenko both endorsed "punishment by the ruble" of inefficient workers. The head of the State Committee on Wages and Social Questions appointed under Andropov, Yuri Batalin, was mandated to slow down rates of general wage increase and to widen pay disparities. But little had been done by the time Gorbachev took office, for the new General Secretary had to call for "the working out of concrete and effective measures" in the area.[55] Gorbachev has now formalized the new outlook into a two-point doctrine of "social justice" (*sotsial'naya spravedlivost'*).

In the first place, Gorbachev and his Politburo want to see earnings differentiated to reflect social value added. He is on record as abhorring *uravnilovka*, or wage-leveling, in forms such as flat pay scales (that in Soviet industry often give assembly line workers as much as engineers), wages based on seniority, and the awarding of undeserved bonuses. Full pay envelopes and end-of-the-year premiums, in Gorbachev's opinion, must go only to the sober and industrious employee, and in general the wage gap between the professional and managerial middle class and manual workers ought to be widened.

The flip side to Gorbachev's "social justice" is a limitation on wealth accumulation and a lessening or, at a minimum, a capping of the privileges accorded members of the political and administrative elite. There is no contradiction here and, indeed, it can be hypothesized that the second tenet is being put forward partly to justify the first—the assumption being that the rank-and-file worker will resist remuneration in proportion to merit and output if the criteria are unclear or are not applied equally to the high official. This issue was held up to surprisingly open public scrutiny immediately before the Twenty-seventh Congress. *Pravda*, in the form of a reprint of a letter to the editor, put the question more provocatively than the censors have allowed it to be put in any official Soviet publication since the 1920s:

> N. Nikolayev of Kazan', a party member since 1940, writes: "In arguing about social justice, we cannot close our eyes to the fact that party, state, trade union, economic, and even Komsomol leaders at times objectively deepen social inequality by taking advantage of every kind of special canteen, special store, special hospital, etc. Yes, we have socialism, and each should receive according to how he works. Let it

> be so, without wage-leveling: the leader will receive higher pay in currency. But in other things there should be no privilege. Let the boss go together with everyone else into an ordinary store and stand with the rest in a lineup—then maybe these irksome lineups would be liquidated sooner. . . ."[56]

The former trade union official who replaced Batalin as head of the wage bureaucracy in January 1986, Ivan Gladkii, has clear marching orders to force a greater spread of earnings in the name of productivity. Technical and administrative problems, bound up with measuring productivity and drawing distinctions at the level of the individual, will make the task difficult and slow, as will the fact that wage stratification for many Soviets "is perceived as almost an infringement on their rights as citizens."[57] Indications are that the regime will proceed largely by loosening central regulation of wages enough to let managers skew rates at the enterprise level.[58]

The second aspect of Gorbachev's "social justice" is potentially incendiary, as reaction to the *Pravda* article demonstrated. Boris Yel'tsin spoke in favor of limiting official privilege at the party congress, but Yegor Ligachev chided *Pravda* for printing the letter and a regional first secretary grumbled about how journalists "who have neither experience nor professional knowledge of party work" cast aspersions on loyal party officials.[59] So far Gorbachev has announced only that a progressive inheritance tax will be imposed on estates. Others have proposed a progressive income tax, a property tax, and payment of rent to the state for land used for gardening or recreation. If Gorbachev wants to cut into closed distribution networks and other forms of administrative privilege, he may have to wait until his political position is more impregnable than it is today. Until then, the leadership will have to live with the not unjustified suspicion among blue-collar workers that they live by different compensation rules from higher-ups.

The regime is showing palpable interest in several other incentive strategies in company with wage stratification. One is to grant the most industrious employees better non-monetary benefits as well as cash. Andropov's August 1983 directive on labor discipline, for example, instructed managers to start giving preference to model workers on waiting lists for flats and vacation passes. A related technique is to augment the availability of large and expensive commodities that only the well-paid, aided perhaps by pooling of resources or extension of credit, can afford. The most thoroughly discussed option here would be to lift restrictions on the building and sale of cooperative housing, which Andropov, Chernenko, and now Gorbachev have all indicated they would like to see expanded from its current 8 percent of total housing construction. One specialist has proposed an immediate tenfold to twentyfold increase in cooperative housing construction, which would make it the dominant mode of providing urban housing in the Soviet Union, and recommends that families able to pay for larger than average apartments be allowed to do so.[60] Gorbachev's congress speech said it was necessary to stimulate cooperative and individual housing construction, and also that the party should investigate the pegging of purchase price and rent to apartment size and quality, which, he implied, should in future be more variegated than at present. All these points were repeated in a Central Committee resolution on housing in April 1986.[61] Preliminary approval has also been given to special housing complexes for young adults, to be financed and partly built by those who will occupy them. The first have been started in Irkutsk, Sverdlovsk, and Moscow.

In addition, the new leaders have shown greater interest in organizational changes in the workplace to induce higher productivity and quality of output. In industry, the preferred form is the work "brigade," which has a long but checkered history in the Soviet Union. The brigade usually consists of several dozen workers who take joint responsibility for producing an end product and in many cases are allowed to elect their own leader. This contrasts to the traditional piece-rate system, which recognizes only specialized and repetitive subtasks and depends entirely on hierarchical control through foremen and managers. December 1983 decrees by the party, government, and trade union federation ordered the overcoming of ministerial resistance to brigade organization and for the first time specified the bonuses to be paid brigade leaders. No deadlines were set and the brigades were to be created "without excessive haste," but implementation has left much to be desired. Industrial ministries have been accused of "percentomania" (about two-thirds of all workers are now formally enrolled in brigades, many of which exist only on paper) and of "attempts to 'insert' the brigades into the present . . . system of planning and management" rather than to improve the system.[62]

Gorbachev has been less interested in the brigades in industry than in experimenting with new modes of work organization in agriculture. In a major speech in March 1983, when Andropov was still alive, Gorbachev praised a mechanism dubbed "collective contracting" (*kollektivnyi podryad*), a rural counterpart to the industrial brigade. Under this arrangement, a brigade or a smaller "link" (*zveno*), the second comprising perhaps a dozen peasants, contracts with a collective or state farm to perform a task and is paid for contract compliance. The brigade or link theoretically is free to shop around for the best contract. The number of farmhands covered by such agreements is supposed to have risen by about 50 percent in 1983, to nearly 500,000; more recent statistics are not available.[63]

A variant entitled "family contracting" (*semeinyi podryad*), in which the contracting party is a nuclear or extended family, has lately drawn extended comment in the press. The family, which may agree to feed publicly owned livestock, raise labor-intensive crops, or repair farm machinery, can be leased land and equipment. It cannot hire labor, which is furnished by the family members themselves. Gorbachev referred favorably, though briefly, to the family contract system at the Twenty-seventh Congress. There is great antagonism to the idea among ideological purists, who rightly see it as quasi-privatizing, and agricultural bureaucrats. The method, a recent survey reports, "encounters not simply inattention or underestimation . . . but a sharply negative attitude."[64] Advocates of the family system have their work cut out for them.

A final policy choice bearing on work incentives has to do with the pricing of consumer goods and services. Like most of the millions of prices in the Soviet economy, those in the consumer sector (with the major exception of food sold in the collective farm markets) are fixed by a government agency, the State Committee on Prices. For most vital commodities, they have been stable for decades—state meat prices, for example, remain at their 1962 levels. Given the magnitude of repressed demand, stored in the mountains of savings built up in the 1960s and 1970s, any freeing up of consumer prices would be sure to lead to their general inflation and to the restoration of equilibrium, if at all, at a considerably higher plateau. Some of the same effects could be achieved by administered price increases. Either way, the implications would be serious.

Consumer price increases, which would probably be intensely unpopular in the short run, would release some of the resources tied down in subsidies (which total over 50 billion rubles a year for food alone). They would sop up excess demand and shorten the queues at state stores. They would help curtail underground economy activities spawned by the gap between official and black market prices, which now invites warehouse and retailing employees to pull merchandise off the shelves, sell it on the side for the going price, and pocket the difference. Price increases could also give a shot in the arm to the legal private sector, if this were sought by the regime, by enabling legitimate entrepreneurs to get materials and supplies from state outlets, rather than by today's common ruses of pilfering and dealing under the table.

Andropov spoke, as Brezhnev never did, of the need to iron out "distortions and discrepancies" in the price structure. Big price increases were levied in 1983 on some consumer products and most construction materials, but the prices of other scarce goods were lowered later that year. Under Chernenko, the regime signaled a greater willingness to use price inducements by introducing seasonal sales of overstocked consumer goods. Gorbachev, while complaining of the burden of price subsidies and acknowledging that artificially low prices produce lineups, has waffled on remedy. In his interview with *Humanité,* he defended the past practice of freezing consumer prices, but seemed to be lumping this together with other economic "shortcomings" that could now properly be re-examined. At the Twenty-seventh Congress he was more venturesome, presenting prices as an "active instrument of economic and social policy." There had to be, he declared, an orderly restructuring of the price system, with prices somehow to be correlated both with production cost (the traditional Soviet method) and with consumer demand. Time will reveal if he means business.[65]

Overhaul of planning and management. The most ambitious of the moderate reforms in the economic realm, and therefore the least likely to materialize quickly, would be comprehensive overhaul of the structures by which industry and the rest of the command economy is planned and managed. A Western market economist might submit that the only way to bring about industrial efficiency in the Soviet Union would be to do away holus-bolus with state ownership and planning—in short, to restore capitalism. This can be excluded from the present discussion as highly radical or even revolutionary, no more likely to come to pass in the USSR under Gorbachev than communism is to be instituted in the United States after the 1988 presidential election. Comprehensive economic reform under Soviet conditions would have to be moderate change carried out within the frame of reference of the existing system, not with the aim of abolishing the system. Such a shift has been attempted by other communist regimes, most recently in China under Deng Xiaoping. The Chinese reforms have of late been praised by some Soviets, but closer at hand, and harder for conservatives to dismiss, is the experience of the USSR's small East European ally, Hungary.[66]

That nation's New Economic Mechanism, put in place in 1968 by leader János Kádár, sought to overcome the numbing overcentralization of the command economy by administrative decentralization and partial reliance on markets.[67] Macroeconomic planning—setting rough targets for growth, proportions among end-uses, interest rates, income and wealth distribution, and the like—was retained, but microeconomic planning was scaled down. For many products, the NEM replaced obligatory physical plans and central interference in the firm—the crude "thumbs" of the classic Soviet model—with the "fingers" of indirect, decentralized controls. Although Hungarian factories remained the property of the state, their relations with one another and with planners were now mediated in large part by the market. It was a highly regulated market, but a market all the same, with autonomous buyers and sellers arriving at agreements on the basis of price. Plant directors were far more independent than before, and profit maximization, tied to bonuses and other incentives, served as the main operational goal. Rewards were given for developing new products and conserving capital, labor, and materials.

Visiting Budapest in June 1986, Gorbachev declared that the Soviet leadership was following developments in Hungary with "attention and respect," and that it would feel free "to borrow whatever is useful, whatever is suitable for our country" from the Hungarians and other allies.[68] It was the most he is likely to say about emulation, for there are many reasons why the Hungarian model cannot be transplanted root and branch to Soviet soil. Most basic is that the political dynamics of the two countries are so different. Even if the USSR, the world's first socialist state and the imperial power in Eastern Europe, wanted to copy the economic institutions of a client state, it would never admit to doing so. Nor can the Soviet leaders feel as free as Kádár to experiment with far-reaching reform. Political upheaval in Hungary, had that resulted from economic change, could have been quelled by Soviet tanks, but there would be no external force to rescue the Soviet regime if it lost control.

Kádár's formula, the Soviets are well aware, has not been an economic cure-all. Old habits have lingered tenaciously, Hungarian growth rates have been disappointing to some, and the reform has gone through a number of course corrections, most recently in 1980. As Soviet conservatives point out, the Soviet economy is also dissimilar in structure to that of Hungary. Decentralization, they say, would be much harder to achieve and control in a country of 280 million people (to Hungary's 10 million), sprawled over eleven time zones and with economic priorities that include provisioning and arming a huge military establishment. Decentralization and marketization are also frightening to many in the Soviet establishment because, to work well, they would at some point require a greater leap into the unknown than other reform projects. In Poland, where Edward Gierek's regime tried to mimic Hungary while leaving intact much of the old, top-heavy apparatus, "the result of following such a policy was the gradual suffocation of the new system," giving rise to the economic and political fiasco of the late 1970s.[69]

None of these considerations, however, rules out *a priori* a Soviet structural reform that, if not a duplicate of Hungary's, at least would draw on some of the same principles. Hungary's NEM, while admittedly no panacea, has produced results in terms of economic quality and balance that are gratifying to most Hungarians and certainly impress the visiting Soviets who load up their shopping bags in the stores of Budapest. The very bigness of the Soviet economy, though often cited as a deterrent to decentralization, could be seen in a way as making it a better candidate for controlled marketization. The transition to decentralized operations might be bumpier, but overcentralization is also less workable in the continent-wide Soviet Union than it was in Hungary before

1968. As for the risk of getting the worst of both worlds by undertaking halfway and contradictory reforms, it is possible that enough Soviets have learned something from the Polish debacle. They may also remember their own lack of success with partial decentralization after the Kosygin reform of 1965. Indeed, the failure of the 1965 measures, given too little room to work, rather resembles earlier experiences that led the Hungarians to embrace a deeper reform.

It was Yuri Andropov, a former ambassador to Hungary and the top Soviet authority on Eastern Europe when the Kádár reforms were being hammered out, who made economic restructuring a subject of urgent debate. Ten days after becoming General Secretary, he said discussion had to begin on ways "to expand the independence" of lower-level management, which, he insisted, could be "combined with greater accountability and with concern for national interests." In later statements, Andropov pressed for wider use of "economic levers and stimuli," including prices, credit, and ample rewards for innovation.[70] In late 1982 a working group headed by Nikolai Ryzhkov, then a newly appointed secretary of the Central Committee, took the issue up. One of the contributions to the intramural debate was the "Novosibirsk Report," prepared in the spring of 1983 by a team of pro-reform advisers headed by Tat'yana Zaslavskaya and later obtained by Western journalists. It perceptively argued that economic restructuring was an intensely political question that "cannot but produce conflict." Progress, the document maintained, would be possible only "on the basis of a well-conceived strategy aimed at galvanizing those groups that are interested in the change and immobilizing those groups that might hamper it." Zaslavskaya identified the industrial ministries, "less qualified and more inert" personnel at the plant level, and conservative officials in Gosplan as those most opposed to decentralizing change.[71]

The first concrete decision, a joint party-government resolution promulgated at Andropov's urging on July 26, 1983, reflected a standoff. Beginning January 1, 1984, a large-scale experiment in streamlined management was to be conducted in five industrial ministries, two of them at the national level and three in the republics. A watered-down version of the 1965 Kosygin reform, it assigned plant directors added leeway to decide on output, operations, and disposal of profits, gave them stable norms for input use, and made contract fulfillment the chief criterion for attaining bonuses. The experiment was applied to additional ministries in 1985 and 1986, and, under the terms of a July 1985 resolution under Gorbachev, it will be mandatory for all industry in 1987.

The scheme's main utility has been as a wedge opening the way for further debate, which it does because, unlike the localized experiments of the Brezhnev era, it is highly visible and has the Politburo's imprimatur. Taken as a decentralizing device, it does not go terribly far. As the Minister of Instrument Building, Mikhail Shkabardnya, exclaimed at the Twenty-seventh Congress, "No matter how much is said about the positive results of the . . . experiment, and there indeed are some, unfortunately even hard working enterprises have received practically no serious stimulus for taking on taut plans and no real independence. There is a whole mass of narrow-minded factors constraining healthy initiative." Shkabardnya pleaded with academic economists to come forward with new ideas, because "one gets the impression that the planning organs, imprisoned by existing methods of administration and management, are essentially more occupied with polemicizing about improving the economic mechanism than with really changing it."[72]

If Gorbachev is sincere about the "radical reform" of management that he touted at the congress, he and colleagues like Ryzhkov (now head of government) and Nikolai Talyzin (Nikolai Baibakov's replacement in Gosplan) eventually will have to go beyond polemics and beyond the Andropov experiment. If Gorbachev's words at the congress were a mere smoke screen for inaction, the experiment may be the sum total of his management reform. This is less than likely, if for no other reason than that it would not be in character for so shrewd a politician to make promises he had no intention of keeping—especially after he had made rapid headway in consolidating his power and was under no pressure to promise anything in particular.

Whatever its content, planning and management reform will not be revealed tomorrow. What with Gorbachev's commitment at the congress to proceed "step by step" and the fact that the Andropov experiment will become universal only in 1987, we should not expect a coherent design to crystallize until the end of the decade. A new Council of Ministers Commission on the Improvement of the Economic Mechanism, formed in early 1986, will be examining many of the minutiae of economic structure. The big picture, it is hoped, will be provided by a Council for the Study of Productive Forces under the Academy of Sciences, chaired by Abel Aganbegyan (for years Zaslavskaya's boss in Novosibirsk), which is believed to have direct access to the Kremlin.

A few contours of the grand design are already visible through the fog. It is abundantly clear that, flexible or not about property relationships in areas such as agriculture and small services, Gorbachev is totally committed to state ownership of industry. No less certain is that he will not disassemble central planning and institute a pure form of market socialism. He is a believer, as he noted in his Togliatti speech, in "the enormous advantages of the planned economy" and in the desirability "of even strengthening the principle of centralization where that is necessary."[73] Gorbachev and his allies aspire to make central planning more effective by training a new generation of more skilled planners and by computerization under the aegis of the State Committee for Computer Technology and Informatics, established in March 1986 under Nikolai Gorshkov, a former defense industry executive. Equally important, they want to lighten the coordination load by riveting the attention of Gosplan and other central bodies onto what Gorbachev defines as "strategic tasks," that is, questions of the economy's long-term direction and shape. Gosplan is to become "the true economic research headquarters of the country, relieved of routine management questions."[74] The dozens of economic ministries are to be superseded, apparently, by a much smaller set of super-ministries, the first of which, Gosagroprom (the State Agro-Industrial Committee), headed by Vsevolod Murakhovskii, came into being in November 1985. Embryos for two other super-ministries have been formed in the "bureaus of the Council of Ministers" for civilian machine-building and energy, and the next to appear will probably be for construction.

Below this streamlined center, economic policy is to be implemented by "economic levers." These would be indirect controls, as distinct from the "administrative levers" involving the issuance of detailed commands directly to the firm. Managers are to have greater operational independence and be relieved, or so it is hoped, of the "petty tutelage" of Gosplan, the State Bank, the Ministry of Finance, and a myriad of other nursemaids. Prime among the economic levers to be emphasized, if Gorbachev's statements are read side by side with other fragments, will be prices and profits. More profits will be retained by managers for use on bonuses and worker benefits, and managers will have a greater incentive than now to cut costs and produce quality goods. If profitability (rate of profit per unit of capital or economic input) can successfully be instituted as a parameter of the whole economic system, it theoretically can be used to compare enterprises with one another and to make political decisions about their viability. Depending on the degree to which prices are allowed to find their own level—and this is one of the haziest things about the Gorbachev vision to date—Soviet enterprises operating under the revised rules would be confronted with at least some of the same uncertainties, and hence spurs to efficiency, as firms operating in a Western-type market.

The new Soviet leadership will not marketize the economy, but it is perhaps prepared to consider some utilization of the market mechanism under terms where, to use a metaphor of the Soviet 1920s, the economic and political "commanding heights" remain in state hands. This is indicated by the March 1986 decision on agricultural procurement, the glimmerings of a more permissive attitude toward small private enterprise, the idea of forcing factories to be more responsive to consumers by having them market their own products, and the bold statements about the "socialist market" of Murakhovskii and others. The Murakhovskii plea virtually coincided with the removal from the editorship of the party's theoretical journal, *Kommunist*, of Richard Kosolapov, one of the most doctrinaire opponents of market principles in the establishment. Time and again, reform-minded Soviets, in propounding administrative decentralization and limited use of the market, highlight the point that there are Kosolapovs by the thousand throughout the elite. They are far from scarce even in the economics profession. "It is well known," one pro-reform economist explains in an essay on the possible use of profit as the main success indicator in industry, "that certain economists disapprove of this concept and find in it 'a bad after-taste' reminding them of how the basic goal of capitalist production is the race after profit."[75]

Surveying the preliminary results of his first, modest efforts at economic restructuring in June 1986, Gorbachev stated the obvious by saying that "the reconstruction to this point is going slowly."

There was perhaps an iota of self-criticism in the remark that some officials, while grasping the necessity of changes, "simply do not know how to achieve them in practice." For them, presumably, clearer guidance would suffice. In other quarters, however, Gorbachev saw hoodwinking of the leadership and real defiance of its plans. Some managers were content with "the illusion of restructuring: in words everything goes smoothly, while there are no real changes." Worse, within the Moscow ministries and planning organs, decentralization was being obstructed because it would lessen central power. "Under contemporary conditions," Gorbachev asserted, "it is impermissible to decide all questions from the center, and in fact it is a practical impossibility." But others deny this truth, displaying "blind faith in the omnipotence of the apparat" and, snubbing party policy, "trying through whatever means to retain their command rights."[76] It is against them and the mentality that sustains them that Gorbachev must make progress before his vaunted restructuring becomes more than a slogan.

Opening up the media and the arts. By and large, the post-Brezhnev leaders have been most fixated on issues bearing directly on the performance of the economy. The main variation on this rule, and an extremely important one, is the shift toward greater frankness in public communication by officials, intellectuals, and artists. This political change could affect all spheres of Soviet society.

Although "discipline and order" were Yuri Andropov's watchwords, he did display an interest in information and opinion about national problems circulating more freely. The party and government would do better, he told the Central Committee in 1983, "if there were greater publicity in their work and regular accountability of leading officials before the population." Andropov also called for a removal of taboos in the social sciences, but without doing the same for Soviet culture, where he argued the party still had to "direct the development of art so that it serves the people's interests."[77]

Mikhail Gorbachev's policy on this score has so outdistanced Andropov's that it merits recognition as a distinct element of the emerging program of moderate reform. Gorbachev brought up *glasnost'*—derived from the word for voice, *golos*, and translatable as "publicity," "openness," or "accessibility"—in his maiden speech as General Secretary. "The better people are informed," he averred, "the more consciously they will act, the more actively they will support the party, its plans, and its programmatic goals."[78] His emphasis was less on the right to know than on the utility of an informed and involved citizenry to the regime, but either way he was pointing to more unfettered and realistic political communication.

Key Gorbachev appointees in the information realm are individuals whose careers were set back under Brezhnev and who seem inclined toward plain speaking.[79] Under them, factual coverage of sensitive issues, including the working of decision bodies, has been noticeably improved in both the print and the electronic media. Weekly press bulletins on Politburo meetings, an Andropov innovation, are now more detailed and, for the first time, give the precise date of the meeting. As concerns policy advocacy, it is not so much that heterodox ideas are being vented for the first time, for qualified experts and consultants already had latitude under Brezhnev, as that the ideas can be put more argumentatively and with less recourse to aesopian language, and appear in the central press and not only in specialized journals. When fault is assigned, it is now easier to name names and demand explanations.

In culture, Gorbachev moved more circumspectly, yet by the winter of 1985-86 there were many small clues of a thaw in the making. These included calls for an easing of censorship, the most ringing by the poet Yevgeni Yevtushenko at the congress of RSFSR writers in December 1985 (in a speech then heavily censored in print!).[80] Whether out of Gorbachev's (and his wife's) reputed interest in drama or for some other reason, several plays probing the dark side of Soviet life appeared unexpectedly on Moscow and Leningrad stages and were given favorable reviews. One of the most iconoclastic, *Dictatorship of Conscience,* by Mikhail Shatrov, depicted a mock trial, set in 1920, of the hallowed Lenin and put anti-Stalin prophecies into the mouths of its characters. As early steps, government commissions were set up to examine the work of the great poet Osip Mandel'shtam, who died in Gulag under Stalin, and of Vladimir Vysotskii, the irreverent pop balladeer who become a cult figure before his death in 1980 but was shunned by the cultural establishment.

The issue of public communication flared several times at the Twenty-seventh Congress. In a confessional speech on the second day, Boris Yel'tsin of Moscow demanded a sharper confrontation with the party's recent failures. "Why does . . . the demand for radical changes get stuck in the inert stratum of time-servers carrying a party ticket?" he asked. "One of the chief reasons is that a number of party leaders lack the courage to appraise in a timely and objective way the situation and their personal roles in it, to speak the bitter truth." There could be no room for "zones immune from criticism," Yel'tsin claimed, or for bosses who "put themselves forward as miracle-workers, denigrating the collective wisdom" of the party. "The indisputability of authorities, the infallibility of the leader, 'double morality'—these are intolerable and impermissible in today's circumstances." One of Yel'tsin's recommendations was for "a system of periodic accountability of all leaders and at all ranks," including regular reports by Kremlin leaders to representative party bodies.[81]

Speaking the day after Yel'tsin's outburst, Yegor Ligachev reminded the congress that in the past, "as is well known, comrades, we have had in these matters [of expression] 'freezes' and 'thaws.'" Ligachev called for "a stable atmosphere of sincerity" and promised preparation of better party histories and ideological materials, but only a moment later berated editors, *Pravda's* among them, who had signed off on politically suspect articles during the runup to the congress.[82] Ligachev was stung, it would appear, by the comments in *Pravda* about elite privilege and the desirability of a party purge. His statement, sided with by several other speakers, showed how little unanimity there is within the Soviet elite on the limits of openness. Yel'tsin had concurred in the *Pravda* article and, for good measure, had taken a poke at Ligachev personally by disparaging the Central Committee department that Ligachev headed in 1983–85.[83]

Gorbachev at the congress was closer in tone to Yel'tsin than to Ligachev. "You sometimes hear it said that we should speak more carefully about our shortcomings. . . . There can be only one, Leninist answer to this: communists always and in all circumstances need the truth." He took issue with the "not a few officials" who had "persecuted" critics, a comment that was followed up after the congress by measures to protect critics from reprisal from superiors. Gorbachev championed "calling things by their proper name," though he diluted the appeal's impact by neglecting even to mention the name of Brezhnev or of Khrushchev, whose 1961 party program the congress was in the midst of revising.[84]

The Chernobyl' incident two months after the congress showed at once how much Soviet practice has changed and how far it has to go. The pig-headed refusal to make public acknowledgment of the reactor blaze until almost three days after the April 26, 1986, explosion, and Gorbachev's silence until eighteen days afterward, mirrored the most archaic of Soviet attitudes. Bad news was first withheld by local and ministerial officials from their superiors, who then acted instinctively to cover up the tragedy. Evacuation was needlessly delayed, and the Ukrainian capital of Kiev, we are told, was swept by near-hysteria because of the information vacuum.

To their credit, the Soviets did eventually own up to the magnitude of the disaster, concede that it was caused by negligence, and agree that those affected should have been told more. Once the initial blackout was lifted, press coverage was incomparably more revealing than for any like incident in Soviet history. The Politburo, while accepting no blame itself and standing by the nuclear power program, has permitted a reprint of a Moscow writer's statement that Chernobyl' "sprouted . . . from the same root system from which [literary] hack-works, incompetence, money-grubbing, servility, corruption, and bad personnel policy also branch out."[85] Permitted, too, has been criticism of the blackout and of the make-believe nature of some of the first stories:

> One of the stern lessons of the first month of the "Chernobyl' era" has been given to our mass information media. Certain of them have still not reformed their work in the spirit of the decisions of the Twenty-seventh Congress. The headlong pace of events sharply reduced the time for gearing up and for the various kinds of clearance and coordination. I am speaking here of the quality and not the quantity of information. After the first several days, when information was extremely scarce, numerous articles did come out in the newspapers, and television began to carry announcements by specialists. There was much that was veracious and sensible in these articles and programs. But in certain of them there appeared notes that were so falsely cheerful and cap-throwing that it was as if we were hearing not about a shared misfortune but about an alarm exercise or a mock competition of fire brigades.[86]

An intimation that something was gained from Chernobyl' is that it was followed by the most strident attacks yet on official suppression of information and debate. *Pravda,* for example, insisted that members of the party and the population hereafter be told the reasons for the transfer or dismissal of leaders, information that is rarely provided in the Soviet Union: "After all, publicly significant information cannot be the privilege of only a narrow circle of 'the elect,' or of 'the ordained' among us." An article in *Izvestiya*, one of many on the future of the city of Moscow since the fall of Grishin, pointed out that "we all need to learn more about living in conditions of publicity and openness." Like *Pravda*, it identified privileged control of information as the crux of the matter: "Far from all of those who are used to merely acquainting public opinion with decisions that they have already taken in isolation are prepared to lose this prestigious, in their eyes, privilege of unaccountability."[87]

The other major post-Chernobyl' development was the quickening of the thaw in official culture. The Union of Cinematographers held its five-year convention in mid-May and elected a new slate of officers. One of the first actions of the new union head, Elem Klimov, who as a director is said to have tangled repeatedly with the censors, was to set up a committee to review films held back from showing under Brezhnev. Gorbachev on June 19 made his first personal intervention in cultural politics. Receiving a group of writers in the Kremlin, he exhorted them to participate in the "psychological and moral reshaping" of society. The authors were urged to write "bold and non-clichéd" works, and the government-sponsored artistic unions, in which membership is virtually obligatory, were derided for "inertia, complacency, and bureaucratism."[88] That same day the veteran Minister of Culture, Petr Demichev, was removed from his post, without immediate announcement of a replacement.

In late June the convention of the USSR Union of Writers was the scene of heated verbal duels between orthodox and more liberal-minded literary figures. Georgi Markov, first secretary of the union since 1971, was displaced by a less intolerant literary bureaucrat, Vladimir Karpov, and a number of respected authors were named to the union leadership. The poet Andrei Voznesenskii, proclaiming that "The people want publicity" and "Our readers are mature enough to read everything," proposed creation of a commission to see long-suppressed works into publication and even of a cooperative publishing house managed by the writers themselves. Yevtushenko offered an impromptu resolution (adopted unanimously) to declare the former house of Boris Pasternak a permanent memorial, while several speakers called for the publication at last of *Doctor Zhivago*, the Nobel Prize-winning Pasternak novel about the Russian Revolution (which has never been published in the Soviet Union) and the formal revocation of an infamous Stalin-era decree anathematizing the poet Anna Akhmatova and the humorist Mikhail Zoshchenko. Western correspondents were told by writers present that they were notified in closed session of a pending curtailment of the powers of Glavlit, the state censorship agency.[89]

It remains to be seen how deeply the incipient thaw will penetrate. Gorbachev's interest in the arts, in particular, has increased apace with his frustration at bureaucratic resistance to his economic program. What is not evident is how closely he will expect writers and others to hew to his own agenda, with its emphasis on the present and the economy. In his June 19 audience, he underlined the importance of exploring "contemporary conflicts and real collisions," and this may have been his way of cooling the ardor of the now middle-aged "angry young poets" of the Khrushchev era—Yevtushenko, Voznesenskii, and others—for a reckoning with the sins of Soviet history. Many of the writers with the reputations that would make them the most useful allies do not share Gorbachev's faith in technology and economic growth.

After many years of guardianship, all but the bravest Soviet intellectuals will wait to see what the new boundaries on expression will be and for evidence that yet another freeze is not around the corner. Some may take heart from the fact that it is now possible to read in the country's second most important newspaper a nostalgic call for a return, not, as in a million essays under Brezhnev, to the spirit of the Great Patriotic War, but to the temper of 1956, the year that Nikita Khrushchev exposed Stalin's tyranny: "Our society had just entered a new phase of its development, it was carrying out a break from the severe epoch of the 'personality cult' and toward new conditions of public life. Fresh ideas and voices were arising in literature, painting, music. A battle was going on with routine, regimentation, fear, stupidity, and especially with lies. 'Rust eats iron,' the proverb says, 'but lies eat the soul.'"[90]

The Strategy and Politics of Moderate Reform

It was predicted in Chapter 3 that Gorbachev would face a crucial decision by the turn of the 1990s on political personnel—either to stay with the team cobbled together during the succession, which by then will be aging and declining in vigor, or to promote a younger group. A similar moment of truth is bound to arrive on policy matters. Gorbachev to this point, while making some headway, has skirted or barely anticipated the most problematic of the decisions bound up in the economic "acceleration" and "restructuring" that is central to his program. A perfect example would be the refusal to look in the face the immense problem of setting realistic prices, which most Western specialists believe cannot be done without marketization.[91]

Gorbachev has sometimes seemed to want to promise all things to all people, and this can easily degenerate into wishful thinking or hollow rhetoric. "If the people are with the party," he intoned in April 1986, "then we can move mountains."[92] It does not hurt to aspire to move mountains, but the movers must have a policy fulcrum powerful enough to do the job. Such a fulcrum does not yet exist in Gorbachev's case, and this will be ever more apparent by the next scheduled party congress in 1991. The easier decisions on moderate reform will then all have been made and digested. On the thornier issues, debates, advisory groups, and experiments will have dragged on long enough to have clarified the problems. Preliminary economic moves will either have to be affirmed and deepened or will suffer the fate of the Kosygin industrial reform of the 1960s.

Decisions about policy will in point of fact interlock with decisions about personnel. The coalition that took shape under Andropov, then backed Gorbachev during his grab for power, yokes together individuals with quite disparate policy views, united mainly by an antipathy to Brezhnevism. It was much easier to get these strange bedfellows to agree on blitzes against corruption and alcohol than it will be on, say, encouraging private enterprise or decentralizing industrial administration. As the reform agenda shifts toward more daunting problems, centrifugal forces can only build within the leadership, requiring Gorbachev to declare himself by leaning left or right. He may well part ways in the process with figures like Yegor Ligachev, his lieutenant in the party apparatus, who seems quite orthodox on economic questions and clearly harbors reservations about the open style of debate that Gorbachev and some of his younger colleagues favor. That Ligachev turns seventy in 1990 may force the issue, for to keep him in place Gorbachev would have to accept a chief deputy who not only is more conservative than he but is failing in stamina to boot.

It would probably be a mistake to overdramatize or overpersonalize the choices ahead. There is a tendency in Western discussions to cast the maker of reforms in the mold of the citizen politician in a Frank Capra movie of the 1930s—the outsider who speaks from the heart and does open battle with corruption, cigar-chomping bosses, and injustice. In the real world, the reformer, at least the moderate reformer, is more likely to be a man with a dilemma than a man with a cause. He usually is a product of the very system that needs revamping, not a Cincinnatus operating at its margins. He is undecided on how far to push change and leery of damaging institutions with which he identifies. Typically, he is the last person to be fully open about what he is doing. "It is of the essence of the reformer," Samuel Huntington reminds us, "that he must employ ambiguity, concealment, and deception concerning his goals."[93] Fox as much lion, he has to be no less nimble at disarming conservatives than at rallying those in his own camp. Rarely does he shout his ideas from a soapbox or provoke a single, climactic encounter with the foe. Instead, to quote a landmark study, the reformer must pull off "extraordinary feats of contriving" in the course of which some hostile groups are won over, others are outsmarted, and the die-hards are "barely overcome by a coalition of highly heterogeneous forces."[94]

Whatever the machinations within the Politburo, moderate reform in the Soviet Union can be expected to obey a similar dialectic. If Gorbachev indeed forges ahead with it, he will have to continue covering his right flank by placating establishment conservatives and reactionaries. Some can be shoved out of the way, as Grigori Romanov and Viktor Grishin were in 1985–86, but others will have to be bought off with side payments and concessions. The trick will be not how to strike compromises but how to prevent them from gutting the reform program. Kosygin's modest economic reforms were ground down in the 1960s by opposition, including opposition by Brezhnev, but one difference this time should be that the political arsenal of the General Secretary will be deployed on behalf of innovation. This will have to be done skillfully. Strategic deception as to the ultimate results of reform may be needed, although with the danger of so obfuscating reformist goals that their adherents lose sight of them and hope in their attainment.

At least as important, moderate reformers in the contemporary Soviet Union, Gorbachev included, will not want to reform everything. To the extent that there is momentum today toward policy innovation, it is mainly on economic and socioeconomic issues. Even here the reformers want to proceed carefully. In many other areas, Gorbachev is like most others in the Soviet elite in being conservative—not wanting, as Andropov said in 1983, to lose "a single valuable grain" of cherished experience. Liberalization in the media and the arts has been tentative, selective, and by all indications of less moment to the General Secretary than his personnel and economic decisions. The drives against corruption, inefficiency, and alcoholism have at times been highly peremptory in tenor. More than one errant official has been pilloried in the media without a semblance of due process, and drinkers have been held up to public ridicule in high-handed ways that have alarmed Soviet jurists.[95]

Political expediency and personal conviction thus should unite to make moderate reform as much an amalgam as was the predominantly conservative approach of the Brezhnev years. It will mingle reformism, conservatism, and maybe reaction as well. There will be considerably more of the first element, but nothing like a disappearance of the others. Lending additional ambiguity ought to be the different points of origin of the policies pursued. After several decades in which sundry reform proposals and minor experiments have been floated, as much effort is apt to go into implementing familiar solutions as into inventing novel ones. Many of the ideas now percolating in Soviet debates have been around for a long time—a temperance campaign, inducements for technological modernization, an increase in cooperative housing construction, better coordination of services by local governments, the brigade and link systems, and even decentralization of industry. Most of these date back to Khrushchev, and many were endorsed to some degree by the Brezhnev administration without being translated into action. To complicate matters, today's moderate reformers may see as one of their missions the reversal of some earlier reforms. Wages and labor discipline are cases in point. Thirty years ago it was considered a forward-looking step to mitigate the extreme inequality of earnings and the quasi-military factory discipline bequeathed by Stalin; today, wage leveling and worker indiscipline have long since been seen as a brake on growth.

Moderate reform may also lack a certain clarity because its advocates do not have master plans. In the absence of competitive elections, visionary factions within the ruling party, and periodic mass insurrections, Soviet politics does not generate grand visions for change. With the agony of earlier revolutions imposed from above still fresh in their minds, many Soviet reform advocates have made plain that they prefer eclectic changes: "After all, we are not talking here [on improving Soviet life] of a designer's studio, but about a historical process, during which the forms of our life take shape under the influence of a multitude of subjective and objective factors impossible of precise measurement. Consequently, the ambitious intent to create a detailed blueprint and construct according to it an ideal way of life is doomed to failure."[96] Andropov's confession that he had no "ready-made recipes" was fully in accord with this position, and Gorbachev, who has spoken several times of not having a magician's wand to wave, has been of like mind.

Of the several contradictions imbedded in moderate reform, Soviet-style, the most important is probably between ends and means. Without a radical change in the political system, which neither Gorbachev nor any other reformer of similar stripe is likely to want, the reformist leader is not infrequently driven to use unreformed, largely authoritarian methods in pursuit of his goals. There may be some calculated loosening of constraints on individual behavior, but no comprehensive relaxation seems likely. The leaders will still assign a strong role to central instruments of control, among them the party's hegemony over staffing decisions through the *nomenklatura* (confirmation list) system, the KGB, and limitations on expression. They may, indeed, want to strengthen some of these mechanisms, as Gorbachev has by resurrecting traditional techniques of scrutiny and rotation of key officials by the party command. When necessary, as Gorbachev's actions show, stern and even ruthless measures will be applied to push modernization, contain conflict within the establishment, and keep wider social frictions from degenerating into open strife.

It will be no easy thing to combine economic and social reformism with political authoritarianism. Gorbachev speaks glowingly of publicity and openness, and many seem to be aware that the computer technology on which such great hopes are being heaped will not accomplish much if it is not fed high-quality information. At the same time, the chief of the KGB, Viktor Chebrikov, can tell delegates to the party congress to beware of foreign spies seeking to buy up Soviet secrets and warn that video-cassettes, "in themselves, a good and progressive thing, are being used by certain people to propagate ideas foreign to us."[97] Needless to say, a country in which the video-cassette or the photocopying machine is considered a tool of subversion will lumber slowly, if at all, into the computer age. Managing this contradiction will probably become more important in the years to come.

Within the economic bureaucracy, some degree of decentralization would seem to be in the offing, but there are many in the regime who cannot resist the urge to give orders and who seem to think that they can issue commands even about decentralization. Referring to industrial managers involved in Andropov's five-ministry experiment who might not attain high efficiency quickly enough, one early review argued the need "to seriously reeducate such executives, to force them to think creatively and display initiative."[98] The observation betrays a certain obtuseness—how, after all, can someone be forced to display initiative?—but it also points up a serious shortcoming with many paper schemes for reform in a state-dominated society.

Pravda recently concluded that emerging opportunities for farm autonomy were not being fully utilized because many agrarian officials preferred the old ways: "Punctually executing commands given from above, they often see in managerial independence not a relief but an exam that intimidates them because it is so unknown."[99] In a country where nearly everyone is a civil servant, there is no entrepreneurial class whose energies are there simply for the uncorking. The new "economic levers" may eventually get the creative juices to flow, but in the meantime other means will be used as well—propaganda, personnel controls, inspections from the center—which, if overdone, will asphyxiate the very behavior they are supposed to be inducing. It is one of the ironies of the situation, therefore, that Soviet decentralization is seen to require prodding and nurturing from the center. As one commentator put it before Brezhnev's death, in a bureaucratic milieu in which centralization is as natural as gravity, decentralizing impulses have no chance without "constant, purposive regulation on the part of the state."[100]

Another minefield for moderate reformers in the USSR, like reformers everywhere, is that of popular expectations. If these puff up, the reformers may be forced to make unwanted concessions to mass opinion while at the same time fending off counter-reformers who think things are getting out of hand. In Hungary, the lid was kept on by memories of the repression following the defeated 1956 revolution and by the shadow of a watchful Soviet Union. Poland in the 1970s imposed no limit and, in fact, borrowed heavily abroad to begin a revolution of rising consumer expectations that could not be satisfied. Reform-minded Soviet politicians clearly intend to avoid this snare. Whether by puritanical sermons and calls for belt-tightening or by raw coercion and restriction of foreign contacts, they will do their utmost to prevent popular aspirations from outstripping the likely returns from policy innovation.

Social inequalities, which will grow sharper if the Soviet incentive structure is reformed and private enterprise expanded, constitute a further source of grief. Sheer envy will be a factor, and resentment will be especially strong among those whose incomes are hit hardest. In Poland, the introduction of merit-based pay under Edward Gierek "made sense in purely economic terms . . . [but] challenged the prevalent ethos of egalitarianism." Many in Solidarity nursed grievances over the perceived injustice of the new wage policy.[101] In Hungary, the fear of worker reaction convinced the government to soft-pedal its plan to diversify earnings. The attitude of most workers in the Soviet Union would be no different, at least initially, as every Soviet discussion of incomes policy illustrates. "Everyone is always for justice," Zaslavskaya has observed, but it will take a struggle (*bor'ba*) to get individuals and groups to accept any reallocation that disadvantages them. "A certain psychological tension is inevitable, even when punishment by the ruble is just. We are all too used to economic impunity."[102] While the Soviet leadership, with its stronger power position, might be thought better able than its East European confederates to ramrod through changes in incentives, its confidence is not unlimited.

Much as moderate reformers are able to defend them on rational grounds, other of the actual and foreseeable moves in the quest for economic productivity and efficiency—tighter supervision on the job, curbs on alcohol sales, expansion of enterprise autonomy, displacement of redundant workers, pricing goods and services to reflect scarcity, to name a few—promise to be equally unpopular with specific segments of the population. Lifelong drinkers will be afraid of running out of vodka, consumers of the unaffordability of goods, wage earners of the devaluation of savings, and workers of the loss of jobs. As with income distribution, even members of these groups who accept reform in principle will want to limit its applicability to their own case. Far-reaching industrial decentralization, the most extreme economic therapy under consideration, would be the most disruptive, particularly if it led to large-scale plant closings and mounting unemployment (as it might if profit were made the main criterion of survival). Some of the worst shocks can be cushioned (by, for example, wage increases to offset higher food prices), but there will nonetheless be material and psychological insecurity and deprivation for many social groups before the putative benefits begin to flow. That a factory manager, a local power center, or an impersonal market may do the collecting will not make the costs less onerous. Again, there are lessons for the Soviets in Eastern Europe. Squeamishness about raising Polish workers' food prices hamstrung Gierek's reforms, and in Hungary anxiety over a social explosion if too much were done too soon diminished the effect of the 1968 reform. "It is the alliance of conservative forces [in the bureaucracy] with the populace," one economist observes about Hungary, ". . . which represents a truly formidable threat to the reformers."[103] In the Soviet Union, such an alliance would be no less a menace to the reform coalition. Reformers may plan that eventually education and success will sell the changes, but in the short run they may be tempted to use stronger-armed methods.

In the final analysis, moderate reform in the Soviet Union will stand or fall on the political skill of the reformers, be they Gorbachev and his present associates or a reconstituted leadership. "The reform leader," as Huntington says, must be able "to inspire confidence and provide some measure of charismatic leadership, while at the same time having the political ability and adaptability to engage in log-rolling and back-scratching, to shift allies and enemies from one issue to the next, to convey different messages to different audiences, to sense the eddies and tides of public opinion and time his actions accordingly, and to hide his ultimate purpose behind his immediate rhetoric."[104] The Soviet reformer must do all this while maintaining precarious balances. He must lead and lean on officials and the public, but without trampling on them or losing their cooperation. He must be responsive without seeming weak-kneed, flexible but not directionless. He must sell inequality to socialists and computers to organizations in which clerks still tote up accounts with abacuses. He must use central power to promote decentralization and a gargantuan state to stimulate individual initiative.

Moderate reform, in keeping with its purpose, would not transform Soviet society or revolutionize political institutions and ideology. It would, however, retard the rot of those institutions and swing ideology, at the level of operating assumptions if not propagandists' manuals, more into line with reality. It would put a perceptible dent in the Soviet Union's problems, which is all that most of its backers expect of it. Properly executed, it would counteract negative economic and social trends that worry the population and the regime alike. Its makers, as will be discussed in Chapter 5, could look for certain roundabout benefits in terms of foreign policy. They could reduce corruption and improve the quality and availability of consumer goods and services. They could realistically hope to add a percentage point or two to annual economic performance—not a spectacular result, but enough to reverse the decline in growth rates, resume the gradual improvement in living standards and the equally slow closing of the economic gap with the West, and increase the surplus available for dealing with social problems such as the deterioration of the health care system. They could hope also to stem the unfavorable drift in popular attitudes, the boredom and cynicism about all things political and the belief, which waxed in the late Brezhnev period, that the regime cannot satisfy mass aspirations and that individuals are best advised to seek fulfillment in private pursuits.

If no reforms are seriously attempted, or if bungled reforms come to naught, none of these things will be achieved and pressing problems will go unrectified. All bets would then be off for the

Soviet 1990s. The likelihood would be high that, with another leader growing old in office toward the end of the decade and another program unfulfilled, the regime could not long postpone a crisis of legitimacy posing far more searching dilemmas than today. Some of the drastic departures from the status quo—radical reform, re-Stalinization, and maybe even revolution—might then look less outlandish than they do now. If moderate reform achieves some measure of success, the Soviet system will have won at least the chance to undertake further and perhaps deeper reforms. To paraphrase what Yevgeni Zamyatin, the great Russian writer in exile of the 1920s, said about revolution in his anti-utopian novel *We*: there is no such thing as the last reform.

5

The Changing Soviet Union and the World

Some degree of linkage between domestic politics and foreign relations has existed in every modern nation-state. The same politicians make and answer for decisions in the two realms, the same ultimate values find expression in policy, and the same finite pool of resources is apportioned. In the formative years of the Soviet system, these irreducibles aside, the international environment was connected to domestic strategy mainly through one special channel. That was Stalin's adamant belief that the Soviet Union needed to be secured from invasion and subversion, at the hands equally of new ideological foes and of Russia's traditional enemies. Security became a transcendent priority, to which many economic and other development decisions were single-mindedly subordinated. So intense, however, was the sense of external menace and the related one of Soviet exclusivism—captured in the dictator's teaching of "socialism in one country"—that the USSR in the high Stalin era was without qualification the most isolationist of all major states in the twentieth century. The acquisition of an East European empire after World War II affected this insularity hardly at all, superseding socialism in one country with the no less Manichean theory of "two camps," one headquartered in Moscow and the other in Washington.

De-Stalinization made possible the easing of this sequestration and fuller Soviet participation in international life. The world beyond Soviet borders came to be seen less as a uniformly alien environment and more as a mixed field, offering dangers but also positive opportunities for extending influence and realizing geopolitical and ideological goals. Related to this was the tendency under both Khrushchev and Brezhnev for foreign policy, as Alexander Dallin has put it, to be brought "home to the USSR."[1] Though not without wavering and not without disagreement over how far to go, the leadership spliced foreign policy to a wider band of domestic concerns and exposed the country more to currents in the world economy and culture. Yuri Andropov in the 1970s, while still chief of the KGB, phrased the post-Stalin consensus well: "We do not live behind a fence shutting us off from the external world. The internal development of the Soviet Union is firmly tied to the state of affairs in the world arena. We must take precise account of what happens there in drawing up our plans and defining the articles of expenditure in our budget. By the same token, the achievements of the Soviet Union . . . now exert a powerful influence on the development of the entire world."[2]

If reciprocal foreign-domestic effects are certain to figure in Soviet politics in the years ahead, the perplexing question is on what scale and with what significance. In the industrial democracies, domestic and foreign issues have interpenetrated much more than they have in the Soviet Union. The causes are many: new means of communication that spill information and ideas across state frontiers; vulnerability to joint ecological, public health, and demographic problems; the scramble for economic markets, the increase in technological cross-fertilization, and the globalization of capitalist finance and manufacturing; the calculus of modern warfare and military deterrence, which draws on the knowledge and resources of society as a whole; and the growth of international organizations and sociopolitical movements. Where does the USSR after Brezhnev fit into this picture? How, in concrete terms, will external events impinge on internal politics and on the prospects for moderate reform? In turn, what practical differences will the domestic Soviet situation spell for Soviet foreign activity? And what, finally, are the implications for Western policy?

Foreign and Domestic Policy in Interaction: Political Succession and Policy Choice

International relations during the political succession of the 1980s have presented the Kremlin with puzzles and daunting choices. As in domestic affairs, there was good reason by the end of the Brezhnev era for concern about an unfavorable tide of events and shrivelling dividends to established policy. The economic and political troubles of the allied governments of Eastern Europe in many ways reflected the Soviets' own, and the 1980–81 crisis in Poland imperiled Soviet interests as much as any episode in the region since 1945. Communist China, meanwhile, was building bridges to the West and Japan and introducing economic reforms, which face many of the same domestic obstacles as do reforms in the USSR but may eventually make China a more formidable rival.

In the Third World, where Soviet activism in the second half of the 1970s, directly and through proxies, had lengthened Moscow's client list, the costs of doing so were starting to hit home by the time of Brezhnev's death. The December 1979 invasion of Afghanistan, which the Politburo seems to have expected to be a quick campaign, proved to be the opening shot in an anti-guerrilla war of indefinite duration. The Soviet Union, long a proponent of "wars of national liberation," found itself in the unfamiliar spot of having to fight or help fight broadly based insurgencies in Afghanistan, Ethiopia, Angola, Mozambique, Cambodia, and Nicaragua.

Most disconcerting was the new cold war with the West, and foremost with the United States. Jimmy Carter, who campaigned in 1976 on a platform of deepening U.S.-Soviet détente and reducing the defense budget, finished his term presiding over American rearmament, preparing to introduce U.S. intermediate-range missiles into Western Europe, withdrawing the SALT II treaty from Senate ratification, and taking the lead in angry sanctions over Afghanistan. The inauguration of Ronald Reagan twenty months before Brezhnev's death took things from bad to worse. In both preceding Soviet successions, a new American leader, Dwight Eisenhower in 1953 and Lyndon Johnson in 1964, had headed American policy in what Moscow soon saw as a markedly more bellicose direction. This time, the new occupant of the White House was, out of deep conviction, the most anti-Soviet chief executive since the 1940s and the most committed to building and flexing American military muscle. Unlike Eisenhower and Johnson, he did not mellow his tone after taking office. Brezhnev was not far wide of the mark in alleging in October 1982, at one of his final public appearances, that the United States had "deployed a political, ideological, and economic offensive" against the Soviet Union.[3] The point was underscored in March 1983, four months into Andropov's reign, when President Reagan announced the Strategic Defense Initiative (SDI), the plan for space-based anti-missile defense that, if successful, would rewrite the entire strategic equation. In October 1983 came the invasion of Grenada, the harbinger of the "Reagan Doctrine" of Reagan's second term that would see mounting American support for anti-Soviet movements in the Third World.

Political succession and the foreign policy establishment. The charged international atmosphere may have made the process of leadership selection in Moscow tenser and more secretive than it would have been otherwise. It may also explain why the members of the oligarchy, even as they intrigued among themselves, took unusual pains to preserve outward unanimity. Conceivably (though unprovably), a desire to close ranks in the face of the Reagan challenge contributed to the way the losers in the early rounds of the succession were treated—to Andropov's failure, for example, to dispose of Konstantin Chernenko. Such an urge was evident when Foreign Minister Gromyko nominated Mikhail Gorbachev for General Secretary in March 1985. Gromyko directed a barb at foreigners who "long to see disagreements within the Soviet leadership." The Politburo vote in favor of Gorbachev had been unanimous, he insisted, and the leadership "will not give satisfaction to our political enemies on this account."[4]

There is no evidence, however, that foreign relations shaded the succession outcome. Andropov, it is true, had better foreign policy credentials than any of the other contenders in 1982, or indeed than any incoming General Secretary previously. And yet, it was Chernenko, a man with negligible involvement with external affairs and few if any qualifications to be the leader of a superpower, who took his place in 1984. The individuals who then battled to replace Chernenko—Gorbachev, Grigori Romanov, and probably Viktor Grishin—were provincial politicians with no more exposure to world affairs than he. Gromyko, laboring unconvincingly in his nomination speech to fit Gorbachev with the halo of a statesman, had to settle for holding him up as a good learner and apprentice ("He very quickly grasps the essence of the processes taking place outside our country"). And Gorbachev, appearing little worried about maintaining the façade of unity for foreign consumption, promptly sent Romanov, Grishin, Nikolai Tikhonov, and scores of lesser figures into retirement.

What of the reverse influence of the succession process on Soviet foreign policy? One direct and pronounced effect in domestic politics has been to reshuffle leading personnel. In foreign policy, this was avoided under both Andropov and Chernenko, during whose administrations Andrei Gromyko continued to function as Moscow's chief diplomat even as the General Secretaries became head of state and Chairman of the Defense Council. If Gromyko thought, as his March 1985 remarks insinuated, that Gorbachev, too, would leave him be, he was soon disillusioned. On July 2, 1985, it was Gromyko who became titular head of state—a position that, after twenty-eight years as Minister of Foreign Affairs, signified his graceful relegation to semi-active status. Gorbachev, already head of the party and Chairman of the Defense Council, acquired his own Foreign Minister in the Georgian party first secretary, Eduard Shevardnadze. Nineteen years younger than Gromyko, personally more engaging, and, like Gorbachev, a career regional politician, Shevardnadze had not a stitch of foreign policy experience and had never even worked in Moscow.

In the party apparatus, the key appointment was that of Anatoli Dobrynin as Central Committee secretary and head of the international department in March 1986. Dobrynin, the Soviet ambassador to the United States, displaced Boris Ponomarev, whose career stretched back to the Communist International in the 1930s and who had been department head for thirty-one years and secretary for twenty-five. Dobrynin quickly established himself as a counterweight to Shevardnadze and involved the international department more directly than before in East-West relations. Simultaneously with Dobrynin's elevation, Vadim Medvedev, Andropov's designate as head of the Secretariat's science and education department, took over as Central Committee secretary for relations with other communist countries from Konstantin Rusakov, the secretary since 1977. Another new secretary, Aleksandr Yakovlev, formerly ambassador to Canada and director of the Institute of World Economics and International Relations, also carved out a major foreign policy role, gaining control over external as well as internal propaganda.[5] Within the General Secretary's office, Andrei Aleksandrov-Agentov, the principal assistant for foreign relations since 1966, was retired in favor of Anatoli Chernyayev, a deputy head of the international department.

On the government side, a new Foreign Trade Minister, Boris Aristov, was named in October 1985 in the stead of Nikolai Patolichev, the minister since 1958. In the Ministry of Foreign Affairs, changes affecting ambassadors and middle management began in earnest around this time, then occurred at higher echelons in rapidfire sequence after the party congress. Both first deputy ministers were replaced in May 1986 (the new men are Anatoli Kovalev, moved up from deputy minister, and Yuli Vorontsov, who had been ambassador to France). Of the deputy ministers, two newcomers having been appointed in the autumn of 1985 (Vadim Loginov and Valentin Nikiforov), four more were named in May 1986 (Anatoli Adamishin, Aleksandr Bessmertnykh, Boris Chaplin, and Vladimir Petrovskii). Vorontsov, Bessmertnykh, and Petrovskii had all done substantial tours of duty under Dobrynin in Washington, and another former Dobrynin subordinate, the Americanist Georgi Korniyenko, was transferred into the international department as one of the two first deputy heads.

After a slow start, it has not taken long for the foreign policy establishment under Gorbachev to be handed over to men fresh to their jobs, indebted to some extent to the new head of the party, and far less accustomed to working together than the Brezhnev team, built around Gromyko, that Andropov and Chernenko did little to change. Within the Foreign Ministry, where high officials had the usual long terms in office under Brezhnev, only three of today's eleven deputy and first deputy ministers are pre-Gorbachev appointees, and just one of these (Leonid Il'ichev, appointed in 1965) is carried over from the Brezhnev era. Among the wider set of senior foreign policy managers in the party, government, KGB, and military, the same trend is evident. One Western study identified fifteen individuals as top foreign policy decision-makers in 1980. On average they had occupied their posts for fourteen years. On July 1, 1986, the seventeen persons holding analogous positions had been there for an average of only sixteen months.[6]

The staffing changes in foreign policy diverge somewhat from those in institutions dealing with domestic affairs in two ways. First, there has been less of a tendency than in the domestic party apparatus, at least, to import officials from outside the organization or functional area. Despite the fact that Shevardnadze is a rank outsider and the new Deputy Foreign Minister for personnel matters, Nikiforov, is from the Central Committee's organizational-party work department, nonspecialists from outside the foreign service and cognate agencies have not been mobilized on any scale. Of the new deputy ministers, only one other than Nikiforov (Chaplin) is not a professional from within the ministry, and Chaplin, originally a district-level party secretary in Moscow, had been ambassador to Vietnam since 1974.[7]

Another difference has been in the pace with which younger officials have been advanced. The very oldest members of the Brezhnev team are being pensioned off (the likes of Ponomarev, aged eighty-one at retirement, and Patolichev, seventy-seven). But Gorbachev has thus far been even more wary than he has been in domestic affairs of putting members of his own generation directly in their place. Although the new deputy foreign ministers have typically been in their mid-fifties, some of the other prime appointees have been a good deal older. Dobrynin, as an example, is sixty-seven and in questionable health, and Chernyayev, Gorbachev's closest foreign policy aide, is sixty-five. The fifteen top foreign policy officials in 1980, under Brezhnev, were on average seventy-two years old. Their opposite numbers in mid-1986, under Gorbachev, averaged sixty-six years of age. This is twelve years younger than the Brezhnev inner circle would have been in 1986, but the average year of birth (1920) shows that it is premature to speak of the full arrival of Gorbachev's age group. The latter's dominance will probably not be complete until the early 1990s, by which time many of them will be well into their sixties.

Assessment of the generational factor is further clouded by the fact that the evidence on inter-generational differences within the

Soviet foreign policy elite is largely based on the writings of scholars rather than diplomats and other officials. So far as the scholars go, the point has been made by Western analysts that the younger ones subscribe to "a less theological, increasingly pragmatic, and objective world outlook" and "endorse a more hopeful view of capitalist foreign policy than did their Stalinist predecessors." They are also thought on the whole to be more optimistic about the possibilities of coexistence and accommodation with the West and to have acquired in many cases "a particularly acute appreciation of the advantages which a relaxed international atmosphere holds for Soviet diplomacy."[8]

As concerns those with decision-making powers, it is safe to say that the middle-aged and younger among them are better educated and informed than their elders and have traveled and lived abroad more widely. Typically, they probably have fewer preconceptions about the iniquity of the West and the perfection of things Soviet. As in domestic politics, one should not imagine any of the generational groupings to be monolithic in attitude. The difference is that in foreign policy Gorbachev would appear to have taken deliberate care to surround himself with sources of differing and even contradictory advice. Among the older officials, for example, Anatoli Dobrynin is perceived as "a realistic promoter of rapprochement with the United States," whereas Aleksandr Yakovlev holds a harsher view (in his writings, which are quite extensive, he has repeatedly portrayed the United States as a totalitarian society bent on expansion).[9] Among the younger functionaries, Vadim Zagladin, associated for years with Ponomarev's hardline approach, has retained his position as a first deputy head of the international department, while Aleksandr Bessmertnykh, widely identified as closer to Dobrynin's pragmatism, has been given day-to-day responsibility for U.S.-Soviet relations in the Foreign Ministry.

A new look for Soviet foreign policy? Generational turnover has until now done less to shape Soviet foreign policy in the succession period than has the contest for power and position among individuals and cliques. Here, many of the same things that predispose the changing leadership toward moderate internal reform also goad it to try to break foreign policy logjams. Politburo successions shake up political alignments, shove new individuals into high office, and force bosses to compete for support from the intermediate and lower ranks. They make it easier than in normal times for old commitments to be reappraised and new ones debated. They produce a reaction against the less successful ideas of the previous leader and generally grease the machinery of policy change.

Some limited display of originality in foreign policy was made by Andropov. He held out an olive branch to Peking and showed restraint in the Third World, initiating none of the expensive interventions that marked the late Brezhnev period. Soviet proposals on arms control were sweetened, particularly concerning Intermediate-Range Nuclear Forces (INF) in Europe, and a rather clumsy campaign was waged to edge NATO publics over to the Soviet view. Several attempts were made to mollify the West on other points, such as the signing of the Madrid accord on European security and gestures on human rights. But relations with the United States, Andropov's main area of concern, degenerated rather than improved. They were brought to a new nadir by the Korean Air Lines incident in September 1983 and, following American installation of the first Pershing II and cruise missiles in Western Europe, the Soviet walkouts in November and December from the INF and strategic arms talks.

Chernenko inherited a dismal situation and, as in internal affairs, he made few and small moves to alter it. The Soviets drew into a kind of shell in 1984, vetoing further intra-German contacts, stalling negotiations with the Chinese, boycotting the Los Angeles Olympics, and unleashing a propaganda barrage against SDI. The June 1984 invitation of the United States to special negotiations over space weaponry was a glimmer of creativity, but it was withdrawn in confusion. Only in January 1985, two months before Chernenko's death—and at a time when Chernenko had dropped from public view and Mikhail Gorbachev, presumably, was already chairing Politburo meetings—did the agreement to return to comprehensive arms control negotiations with Washington show a less sullen cast of mind.

Since March 1985 Gorbachev, in both style and substance, has imparted an unaccustomed measure of vigor and flexibility to Soviet policy. He has held that changes in the international system "require a new approach, a fresh look at many things in foreign policy." He has acknowledged that the USSR is affected by "the closer interconnection and interdependency between countries and continents," and called for joint work on global ecological and energy problems and articulation of "civilized" norms of international conduct. He has paid a good deal of attention to Eastern Europe, as will be discussed below. He has flattered China by calling it a "great socialist neighbor" and has pushed economic and technical collaboration with this ex-ally. In a July 28, 1986, speech in the Pacific port of Vladivostok, he held out the possibility of negotiating a thinning-out of Soviet forces along the Sino-Soviet frontier and in Mongolia and elaborated on earlier calls for a conference on Asian security "in the mold of Helsinki" (to be held, he proposed, in Hiroshima). He also invited the Chinese to participate in joint space ventures and said that Moscow would consider opening foreign access to Vladivostok, hitherto a closed city, and making it a Soviet "window on the East."[10]

In the Third World, Gorbachev has moved to cultivate important, capitalist-oriented countries and refrained from getting entangled on the opposition side in the crises of pro-Western governments such as those of Haiti, the Phillipines (where he may actually have toyed with active support of President Marcos), and South Africa. Although he has stood by pro-Soviet governments beset by insurgencies (as in Nicaragua, where the United States is bankrolling the Contras, and in Angola, where UNITA has American and South African support), he has also advocated that local and regional conflicts be more effectively insulated from the East-West rivalry. Such clashes, he said in November 1985, are most often rooted in economic and social factors endemic to the region, and "to suppose that all these knots of contradiction are somehow an expression of the competition between East and West is not only incorrect but extremely dangerous."[11] The revised party program tones down the declarations of support for national liberation movements found in the 1961 program, and Gorbachev omitted reference to such aid in his speech to the Twenty-seventh Party Congress.

In relations with the United States, Gorbachev has displayed a tactical and public relations sense absent in recent Soviet behavior. He has kept the Reagan administration off balance by declaring and extending a unilateral moratorium on nuclear weapons testing, agreeing to the November 1985 Geneva summit and using it as a platform for expounding Soviet views, and issuing a volley of public disarmament proposals. Some of these—the January 15, 1986, summons to eliminate all nuclear weapons by the year 2000 is the best illustration—have had as much to do with grandstanding as with diplomacy.

At the same time, Gorbachev has introduced changes of substance into Moscow's American policy. Perhaps most important, he has subscribed to the concept of "mutual security" and indicated some understanding that Soviet restraint is necessary to sustain American attitudes and behavior that, in the final analysis, importantly affect the Soviets' own security. He shared with President Reagan at Geneva, according to his statement at the post-summit press conference, his "profound conviction that less security for the United States of America compared to the Soviet Union would not be in our interests, since it would lead to mistrust and produce instability." The United States, he argued, should be prepared to grant the Soviet Union the same consideration, in which case the two countries could work toward equal security at lower levels of armament.[12] This was precisely the outcome that eluded them during the détente of the 1970s, partly though not entirely because of the Brezhnev leadership's perseverence with weapons programs and third-area activities that made the United States feel insecure.

Regardless of their high public relations content, Soviet arms control proposals under Gorbachev have been pressed more urgently than at any time since Khrushchev. The priority has gone to heading off American systems that will require restructuring of Soviet forces, and hence heavy new financial commitments (such as SDI, the Trident II, and the MX). Explicit Soviet offers, and implicit hints of further concessions, have been unusually forthcoming. They have addressed specific issues identified by the United States in previous discussions as obstacles to agreement. Thus Gorbachev has indicated firmer acceptance than earlier Soviet leaders of on-site verification as a principle of effective agreements. The terms offered for doing away with Soviet SS-20 missiles aimed at Western Europe, in exchange for scrapping of American Pershings and cruise missiles, are a substantial turn toward the Reagan "zero option" of 1983, which Andropov rejected. Successive Soviet offers on strategic weapons, beginning with that brought to Washington by Shevardnadze in September 1985, have taken fuller account than in the past of the American contention that the large Soviet force of heavy ICBMs is a major source of instability. And, most indicative of a wish to cut a deal, the Gorbachev Politburo has consented to the continuation of laboratory research on the "Star Wars" SDI project, provided that (in the Soviet position forwarded in June 1986) the United States agrees to compliance with the Anti-Ballistic Missile (ABM) Treaty of 1972 for fifteen to twenty years or to some other safeguard against early deployment.

Another hallmark of Soviet policy under Gorbachev has been the interest declared in improving ties with advanced capitalist countries apart from the United States. Following the lead of Aleksandr Yakovlev, Soviet spokesmen have been elaborating a doctrine of multipolarity in international relations, as against the bipolar, U.S.-centered approach adhered to since World War II: "The Soviet Union decisively repudiates the model of so-called 'bipolarity' and the distorted conception of 'two superpowers.' . . . The USSR is significantly activating its relations with capitalist countries other than the U.S., with their regional groupings and organizations."[13] Gorbachev's address to the party congress, picking up on a pet theme of Yakovlev's, enumerated "three basic centers" of contemporary capitalism—the United States, Western Europe, and Japan—and predicted that other centers, and priority targets for Soviet diplomacy, might soon emerge.

As concerns Japan, Shevardnadze's visit to Tokyo in January 1986 was a first attempt to melt the deep freeze in relations. In the more assiduous wooing of the West Europeans, Gorbachev has engaged himself personally. He has emphasized that the Soviet Union is itself a European state sharing a cultural heritage and current interests with its neighbors. "We live in a single house," he said on the occasion of his October 1985 visit to France, his first outside the Soviet bloc as leader, "although some of us come into the house by one entrance and others through another entrance. We need to cooperate and lay down communications in this house." In an April 1986 address in East Berlin, and again during President François Mitterrand's return visit to Moscow in July 1986, Gorbachev spoke of a Europe disarmed and in political harmony "from the Atlantic to the Urals"—a transparent act of homage to the late French leader, Charles de Gaulle.[14] The Soviets have been unexpectedly solicitous of the British, agreeing during Shevardnadze's trip to London in July 1986 to the cancellation of mutual claims arising from the Russian Revolution and to a visit to Moscow by Margaret Thatcher. Nor have the West Europeans' multilateral organizations been ignored. The Warsaw Pact has issued a murky proposal for balanced reductions in forces. Of more interest, the Soviets have expressed an interest in establishing formal relations with the European Economic Community, which they have always refused to deal with as an entity.

It is only sensible to postpone judgment on Gorbachev's foreign program until he has had time to develop it more fully. Glancing at results to date, however, one would probably have to say that the post-Brezhnev initiatives have been more tepid in foreign than in domestic policy. There has been no overt repudiation of Brezhnevism in foreign relations, and one authoritative review of the Twenty-seventh Congress, the main forum of domestic de-Brezhnevization, saw fit to observe that the congress "demonstrates continuity with the decisions of the preceding [congresses] in the foreign policy sphere."[15]

Under Gorbachev, the Soviets remain in Afghanistan, where by 1987 they will have fought twice as long as they did against Nazi Germany. In U.S.-Soviet relations, it is mostly atmospherics that have changed, with practical agreements confined to such secondary matters as scientific and cultural exchanges, consulates, and resumption of direct air travel. The Soviets have not budged on any of the "three obstacles" that the Chinese see in the way of rapprochement (Afghanistan, Cambodia, and forces on the Sino-Soviet border), although Gorbachev's Vladivostok speech indicates some pliability on the last point. Vis-à-vis Japan, Moscow has shrunk from the one concession that would warm up relations in an instant, namely, parting with the four islands in the Kurile chain seized by Stalin in 1945. In the "European house," the other inhabitants have not yet seen enough in Soviet security proposals to make major reassessments, and they were justifiably offended by Moscow's original stonewalling on the Chernobyl' reactor accident, which spewed radioactive particles over much of the continent.

Why has political succession not produced swifter movement in Soviet foreign policy? The simplest answer is that foreign relations have had a lower priority than domestic issues. Frightening though many external problems may be, they probably distress the regime less than its difficulties at home. The Gorbachev coalition has been put together around internal issues, and this might have been harder to do if questions of external strategy were allowed to intrude. Furthermore, the process whereby Soviet foreign policy is made differs from that for domestic policy. State secrecy and censorship make the debate over foreign policy more stilted and abstract than the give-and-take over domestic issues. It is also harder for a new leader like Gorbachev to criticize his predecessor's foreign policy, because, in Soviet political culture, to do so openly is to give comfort to the foreign adversary.

More important, the objective opportunities for innovation are simply poorer in foreign than in domestic affairs. The system of states, lacking a common law or culture, is by its very nature less malleable than civil society—which grates on Soviet politicians accustomed to an internal politics that may be imperfectly controlled but is less volatile by comparison. The world seen from Moscow looks to be, as Gorbachev portrayed it at the Twenty-seventh Congress, "fraught with antagonistic tendencies, full of contradictions . . . a world of the most difficult possible alternatives and worries."[16] Because the international environment is so unpredictable, those arguing for constancy and caution have an easier time than in domestic policy. The reformist impulse is weaker here than in internal affairs, the grip of inertia solider, and the difference between reformist and conservative perspectives slighter.

Thirty years ago, Nikita Khrushchev and his adherents in the Stalin succession were able to exploit unusual circumstances to push through important and fruitful modifications to foreign policy (the Korean armistice, the Austrian peace treaty, the reconciliation with Tito's Yugoslavia, and overtures to the developing countries). It is easy to forget how foreign policy crises and failures like those surrounding the Hungarian Revolution, the rift with China, and the Cuban missile crisis eventually helped deflate Khrushchev's domestic authority. While gains like those of the mid-1950s could in principle be realized today, in practice it will be an uphill struggle.

In the Third World, for example, the anti-colonial revolution in Asia and Africa, the font of so many earlier successes, has nearly spent itself. The most dynamic forces in the developing nations, those fueled by ethnicity and religious belief, lend themselves poorly to mobilization and even, as in Afghanistan and Angola, to accommodation by Marxists. The United States, the Soviet Union's global adversary, has a popular and ardently anti-Soviet president with a constitutional mandate until January 1989. The Reagan administration, moreover, is deeply divided on the issue of negotiations with the USSR, as President Carter's was before it, and therefore sure to be a difficult bargaining partner under the best of circumstances.

Japan and Western Europe are not easy picking for Gorbachev and other Soviet statesmen, either. For the Japanese, the issue of the islands remains paramount. The Soviets have technical concerns about egress out of the Sea of Okhotsk for their Pacific Fleet, but their main fear surely is that negotiating over these clumps of rock may reawaken dormant territorial quarrels with other countries, including China. For the big countries of Western Europe, recent Soviet proposals on INF and other security issues, while welcome as a change of style, reopen security dilemmas that, at the very least, will require time to sort out. For the British and the French, the modified Soviet position on INF stipulates that they refrain from modernizing their independent deterrent forces, which flies in the face of fifteen years of government policy. For the West Germans, the prospect of a "zero option" being implemented and removing all American intermediate-range missiles from the continent revisits the conundrum of the late 1970s (the perceived strategic "uncoupling" of Western Europe from the United States) that motivated the original request for American missiles by then Chancellor Helmut Schmidt.[17]

In sum, foreign policy choices will tax the ingenuity and patience of the new Soviet leadership at least as much as domestic problems will. The outcome is not preordained, but the complexity of the choices is.

The big choices, domestic and foreign. Is there some organic connection between the Kremlin's grand choices over war, peace, and security and those with which it must grapple at home? According to students of Soviet history, the regime's domestic strategy has never absolutely determined its foreign orientation, or vice versa.[18] The best we can do for the 1980s and 1990s, therefore, is to sketch congruities of several sorts, showing probabilities but not certainties.

One coupling propounded by the occasional Western commentator, but easily refuted, is the notion that the regime will seek out adventures in external relations to distract public attention from internal troubles. Much as this has been done by insecure regimes elsewhere—the Argentine junta's attack on the Falkland Islands in 1982 being a classic example—this has never been the Soviet way. Risky undertakings abroad have been been neither timed nor publicized so as to stir up nationalism at home and thereby ease the mood of the Soviet populace. When they have been mounted—for instance, the sending of Soviet pilots and air defense batteries to Egypt in 1969–70 or the occupation of Afghanistan in 1979—military secrecy has meant that they have been hushed up rather than played up in the Soviet media. The conflict in Afghanistan has been getting fuller newspaper and television coverage under Gorbachev, but this is because the Politburo has reckoned that it loses by concealing the viciousness of the fighting from a population that hears about it through other channels, not because it expects to derive popular acclaim from its involvement in the war.

For the evolving Soviet regime, the most important nexus between domestic and foreign strategy would seem to lie in the agreed-upon primacy of the former over the latter. Each of the post-1982 General Secretaries, and Gorbachev with the most emphasis, has made reference to this imperative. Gorbachev declared during his visit to France that Soviet foreign policy "is called forth in the first instance by [Soviet] internal needs." In May 1986 he addressed an unusual two-day meeting of diplomats and other Soviet foreign policy personnel and, according to the brief communiqué provided by TASS, hinged his remarks on the necessity that external relations be conducted "in organic coordination with the internal tasks the party is dealing with today—economic, social, political, defense, ideological, and moral—and which are connected with major changes in socialist society and in the world as a whole."[19]

Not only do domestic needs, and especially economic needs, take precedence because they are more critical. There is also a growing realization in the Soviet elite that domestic modernization is a prerequisite for an effective foreign policy. Although this predates March 1985, Gorbachev has stated the thought most forthrightly. Soviet-style socialism, he maintained in one statement, "does not develop within the confines of some kind of isolated island. There is a competition between two social systems, the socialist and the capitalist, [and] this competition . . . in and of itself obliges us to concern ourselves with accelerating our socioeconomic development."[20]

It is difficult at this early date to say what this shift in orientation portends in practical terms. Common sense, and the brief record since November 1982, suggest that the preoccupation with the internal base, while it will not compel any particular action, will generally incline the Soviets toward moderation. Speaking in Paris about the needs of Soviet development, Gorbachev asserted that "among the most important conditions for achieving these [domestic] goals are not only a reliable peace but also a quiet, normal international situation."[21]

Beneath the bluster of statements like this lies an uncomplicated truth. International peace and quiet would indeed maximize the leadership time, creative energy, and material resources available for domestic needs. Inasmuch as it depends on Moscow, such a propitious climate would best be facilitated by a foreign policy that extends the country less than the Brezhnev regime's did. For this to happen, revolutionary ideology would not be abandoned, but it would have to take a back seat to geopolitics and the claims of domestic development. It was Andropov, borrowing the words of a Lenin speech given at the end of the Russian Civil War in 1921, who said shortly after his accession that the Soviet Union has to be "guided by the Leninist dictum that we have our main influence on the world revolutionary process through our [domestic] economic policy."[22] An economically moribund Soviet Union, by this reasoning, will be neither a beacon for others nor an efficient fomenter of progressive change over the long haul. The Andropov statement, clearly with Gorbachev's full backing, was written into the 1986 party program.

An obvious priority with this end in mind would be to achieve a less confrontational relationship with the United States. The Soviets have said repeatedly that this is their intention and that they are ready to arrive at compromises to realize it. However, the impasse over arms control and President Reagan's fervent commitment to SDI dim the chances of this happening before the swearing in of a new U.S. leader in 1989. If a second Reagan-Gorbachev summit in the United States cannot be arranged, or if Gorbachev comes back empty-handed from it, the Politburo will in all likelihood end its adherence to "the spirit of Geneva." We may yet see a return to the U.S.-Soviet shouting match of the early 1980s, though the advice of Dobrynin and other senior advisers with greater knowledge of the American scene will probably be to display forebearance until Reagan's departure.

The worse relations with Washington get, the more overtures the Soviets are likely to make to Western Europe and Japan. Progress here would not come at a bargain price either. Painful concessions will be needed to convert a Europe-first (or a Europe-and-Japan-first) policy from words to deeds, and we have yet to see if Gorbachev will be willing to make them. With the Europeans, it will require unprecedented Soviet flexibility on INF, French and British nuclear modernization, conventional force levels, and probably human rights issues (which are discussed below). With the Japanese, the sticking point will continue to be the northern territories.

The most noticeable shift in Soviet foreign policy in an era of moderate domestic reform should be one that is already apparent—a less forward posture, and a greater selectivity in picking friends and allies, in the Third World. The Brezhnev Politburo put most stock in radical regimes, usually in smaller, economically backward countries, that it helped install in some cases and to prop up in others. Well before 1982, some specialists and middle-level officials were pointing up the drawbacks of such a policy: in alienating larger, more moderate Third World states and powerful industrial powers; in saddling Moscow with financial subsidies and, in some areas, military liabilities as well; in imposing socialist economics on societies just entering the capitalist stage; and in associating the Soviet model with poverty and economic decay. Since Brezhnev's death, the critics have been given greater license to press their reservations and the leadership has moved a long way toward embracing them.[23]

Andropov's position was that "the social progress of these [developing] countries can . . . only be the result of the labor of their peoples and the correct policy of their leaderships," thereby absolving the Soviet Union of the main responsibility.[24] Gorbachev obviously concurs, and a clause to this effect, lifted almost verbatim from Andropov, was inscribed in the party program at the Twenty-seventh Congress. The appointment as secretary and head of the Central Committee's international department of Dobrynin, with his reputation for level-headedness and his dearth of experience with radical movements, is symptomatic of the go-slow strategy. The Soviet Union would now seem to see revolutionary prospects in the Third World and elsewhere, as Vadim Zagladin wrote shortly after the party congress, as being of a "long-term character" and as resting largely on the future attractiveness of socialist ways. "Special significance from this point of view is possessed by the acceleration of socioeconomic development and the perfection of socialism in the Soviet Union."[25]

It should be emphasized that the prognosis of Soviet discretion applies mainly to new commitments. When it comes to standing commitments, the attitude figures to change much less. In Indochina, for example, the Soviets, while probably restraining Vietnam from trying to expand its domain further, would concurrently support the continuing Vietnamese occupation of Cambodia and the settlement of the conflict there, if ever, on terms acceptable to Hanoi. The same would apply in the Middle East, where Gorbachev could be expected to stand by Syria, with which a friendship treaty and extensive military cooperation exist, while resisting bids from Libya or others for closer relations or risky undertakings on their behalf. With the Syrians, one guesses that the Kremlin under Gorbachev will counsel against an unprovoked aggression against Israel, but at the same time would resupply the Syrians in the event of a clash initiated by Israel, or of ambiguous origin, as vigorously as Brezhnev would have.

An especially onerous standing commitment is in Afghanistan, where Soviet forces are more heavily involved in fighting the Mujahedin than ever. If, as the U.S. government has estimated, the war cost the USSR 10,000 lives by of the end of 1985, and perhaps $18 billion to $36 billion worth of resources (to say nothing of the appalling damage done to Afghanistan), this is a strong disincentive to getting embroiled in similar conflicts in future.[26] Nor is there any lack of incentive to get out of this particular war, as Gorbachev's description of it at the Twenty-seventh Congress as a "running sore" made plain. Unfortunately, Moscow also sees past sacrifices as an investment on which it is entitled to a return. The result has been a policy of standing firm while probing for a dignified exit.

Gorbachev's July 1986 announcement in Vladivostok of the withdrawal by the end of the year of six regiments, coming to perhaps 7,000 of the approximately 120,000 Soviet troops in Afghanistan, is a token of flexibility and Soviet impatience but not yet of a breakthrough. Gorbachev made favorable reference to the "proximity talks" in Geneva between the Kabul government and Pakistan and stated that "as soon as a political settlement is finally worked out, the return of all Soviet troops from Afghanistan can be speeded up." He also endorsed the efforts of the new Afghan government of Mohammed Najib at "national reconciliation," saying these should include efforts to reach out to groups based in the refugee camps in Pakistan and Iran that are "prepared to participate sincerely" in the building of a new Afghanistan.[27] But the Geneva talks, under United Nations sponsorship, have limped along without resolution under Andropov, Chernenko, and Gorbachev, and, barring surprises, they are fated to continue for some time, with a timetable for Soviet evacuation remaining the main bone of contention. Nor is there any indication that Gorbachev has modified the more aggressive tactics adopted by Soviet commanders in 1984, which have included increased air and ground attacks on civilians. And the May 1986 replacement of Babrak Karmal by the younger Najib, previously the chief of state security, seems to have stemmed from a Soviet desire for more effective prosecution of the war and building of the regime's infrastructure, hand in hand with the indirect bargaining with Pakistan and the rebels.

There are good psychological reasons for the Soviet resolve to stand by inherited commitments. The same feeling of vulnerability that prompts the regime to weigh internal reforms and balk at added foreign burdens also puts it on guard against concessions on foreign policy giving the appearance (to either external or internal audiences) of lack of strength or will. A prickliness on this point is evident in many recent Soviet statements remonstrating, as Gorbachev has, about foreigners who misinterpret Soviet reasonableness "as a sign of weakness."[28] As a new General Secretary, Gorbachev also has to avoid creating the impression, not least among his colleagues in Moscow, that he is personally weak. It follows that Soviet cave-ins to pressure will be few and that there will be no pullbacks, in Afghanistan or anywhere else, unless face-saving formulas are found.

If domestic factors and exigencies help within limits to mold foreign policy, will foreign developments beyond the regime's control similarly influence domestic decisions? The confrontation with the United States of the first half of the 1980s was one such development, and on balance it in all likelihood enhanced the position of moderate reformers within the Soviet leadership. It gave them ammunition for the contention, found repeatedly in Gorbachev's speeches, that internal changes are mandatory for external competitiveness. Past a certain threshhold, however, a further worsening of the international climate would probably redound to the advantage of more conservative and even reactionary elements. Acute tension with foreign adversaries would reinforce the garrison mentality so closely associated in the Stalinist past with political and economic overcentralization. As a Soviet observer once argued, Stalin used foreign threat to serve "an obvious political goal—to justify theoretically . . . mass repression and severe infringements of socialist legality. In essence, Stalin often began from the proposition, as they say: if you live with wolves, then you must act like a wolf."[29] In an environment of total foreign policy crisis, certain moderately reformist decisions would probably be ruled out entirely (such as cutting the defense budget), some changes would be deferred, others would be attenuated for lack of adequate political and material resources, and generally the authoritarian aspects of the changes would be accentuated. Were the external disturbance pressing enough, it might conceivably drive the regime completely away from moderate reform.

Specific Effects: Five Hybrid Domestic/Foreign Issues

Beyond the interplay of domestic priorities and the grand foreign policy problems of war and peace, Soviet decision-makers must deal with a similar phenomenon on less momentous issues that can be thought of as hybrids, affecting both internal and external interests. Five of the more important of these mixed issues will be touched on here: ethnic and regional problems; defense spending; foreign economic ties; change in Eastern Europe; and human rights. In each case we want to know how the internal and external aspects of the issue interlock and how they bear on moderate domestic reform.

Ethnic and regional questions. One cluster of internal problems that arguably reverberate in foreign policy has to do with relations among the Soviet Union's numerous ethnic and geographic components. Illustrative examples are Siberian resource projects, Jewish emigration, and concern over Islamic fundamentalism.

It is probably the case that the ambitious Siberian development plans of the 1960s and 1970s were struck in part to fortify the area east of the Urals against possible Chinese encroachment and to pave the way for Soviet-Japanese cooperation in extracting the region's mineral and energy riches. Foreign policy considerations have thus had the effect of favoring the budgetary claims of Siberia, populated mainly by Russians, over those of such non-Russian areas as the Ukraine and Central Asia. Similarly, relations with foreign governments have swayed Soviet treatment of those ethnic communities in which the desire to emigrate is widespread, Jews and Germans being the main ones. Many have thought that the 1979 decision to invade Afghanistan was inspired to some extent by the Politburo's anxiety over the Islamic revival in Iran and Afghanistan spreading to Soviet republics like Uzbekistan and Tadzhikistan. Similarly, some have attributed the fierce condemnation of the rise of Solidarity to a fear of Polish events polluting the nearby Baltic republics, one of which (Lithuania) has religious and cultural ties to Poland and another (Estonia) experienced a few Solidarity-like strikes in the early 1980s.

In actuality, the interweaving of foreign and domestic concerns of this sort has not been particularly strong in the recent Soviet past. It is not apt to be so in the immediate future, whether or not the Kremlin perseveres with moderate internal reform. Concerning regional development projects, including those in Siberia, the bottom line in Soviet decisions has always been the domestic economic payoff rather than national security. The second trans-Siberian railway, the Baikal-Amur Mainline (BAM), begun in 1974 as the centerpiece of Siberian modernization, was built principally because Soviet planners thought it made good economic sense to do so. It would be open to Chinese interdiction in the event of an Asian war. While certain areas would profit disproportionately from massive foreign investment in Soviet fuel and raw materials—of the type with which the Japanese declined involvement in the 1970s but which they and others continue to explore—precedent indicates that the Soviet authorities will approach such plans with an eye to maximizing the total returns to the USSR, not to any individual region.[30]

For the most part, relations between the Russian majority and the national minorities also are but weakly connected to Soviet foreign policy appraisals. Policy toward Soviet Jews, an atypical group in the Soviet context (because of its small size, unique history, and lack of a territorial base), is an exception. Jewish emigration will assuredly be influenced by progress in U.S.-Soviet relations, and it will also be a bargaining chip in negotiations with Israel and attempts to reassert the Soviet presence in the Middle East. As party leader in Soviet Georgia, Eduard Shevardnadze is known to have facilitated the exodus of Jews from his own republic, and his appointment as Foreign Minister seems to have activated Soviet discussions of the problem with Israel, the World Jewish Congress, and a number of Western governments, including the United States and France.

When one surveys larger ethnic groups more pivotal to Soviet nationality policy, the correlation is not nearly so strong. Soviet hostility to Solidarity was amply fanned by Solidarity itself and owed little to ethnic developments on the Soviet side of the border (which, in any event, have a robust life of their own in the Baltic region). The intervention in Afghanistan is impossible to explain by any single factor. But the most reasonable interpretation is that Soviet troops were dispatched mostly to prevent a newly established satellite regime from escaping the Soviet orbit, and that Kremlin willingness to do so was increased by inaccurate military and intelligence information about the ease of pacifying the situation. Apprehensions about contamination of nearby Moslem areas in the Soviet Union appear to have had scant weight in the decision, and the Soviets' eagerness to involve themselves actively in Afghanistan, as opposed to sealing themselves off from it, probably reflects a confidence about Russian-Moslem relations within the USSR rather than a lack of it. The war, and the upsurge in religious feeling in the surrounding area, eventually provoked an increase in Soviet propaganda directed against militant Islam, but this should not obscure the fact that most of the Moslems of Soviet Central Asia have to date found little if anything to emulate in Khomeini-style fundamentalism.[31]

All things considered, external threats to the Soviet ethnic balance will be manageable in the decade to come, so long as Moscow's indigenous controls over the non-Russian communities remain as sturdy as they have been. Moderate, economic-centered reform should not have much direct effect on either the Soviet ethnic problem—which would be greatly aggravated only by Yugoslav-style decentralization to territorial units, which the Soviets are not actively considering—or its relevance for foreign policy.

Defense spending. It is self-evident that defense policy, at once a claimant on national treasure and a means of projecting Soviet power abroad, straddles the demarcation line between domestic and foreign issues. A modern military establishment never comes cheap, but for the USSR, with its nervousness about invasion, its global ambitions, and its resolve to compete militarily with an American colossus with almost double the economic capacity, the costs have been exorbitant. Soviet military expenditures stand at anywhere from 12 or 13 percent of total GNP to as much as 15 to 17 percent, depending on the methodology used in calculation. As a proportion of the national economy, they have for five decades surpassed the military spending of all other industrial countries, including the United States (where the ratio to GNP is some 7 percent). It is generally believed by Western specialists that the rate of increase of Soviet military spending was dampened after 1976 to the vicinity of 2 percent a year, about half the pace of the previous decade. The decision to do so was taken, one has to assume, for two reasons: economic stringency, and the relatively relaxed state of East-West relations in the mid-1970s. While the volume of resources devoted to military-related research and development kept growing at 4 to 5 percent a year, procurement of military hardware expanded either marginally or not at all.[32]

Developments since that time have tugged Soviet military policy in differing directions. Pointing one way is the sharpening of Soviet economic difficulties, which now stretch the country's resources more thinly than ever. Pointing the other way is the worsening of relations with the United States and the ambitious U.S. program of force modernization and expansion, begun under President Carter and accelerated by Ronald Reagan. A complicating factor is the evolution of Soviet military doctrine since 1977 or so, in good measure because of somber rethinking of the implications of nuclear weapons for war-fighting. Soviet military thought has deemphasized the practicality of using nuclear armaments in an all-out conflict with the West and placed steadily greater emphasis on the importance of preparing for a "general conventional war" waged in numerous theaters. Marshal Nikolai Ogarkov, appointed Chief of General Staff in 1977, reformed Soviet force structure (by creating unified theater commands for ground, sea, and air forces over huge areas) and publicly importuned civilians for improvement of non-nuclear weapons, of the mobilizational infrastructure, and of stockpiles of war matériel.[33]

Ogarkov's downgrading in September 1984 (to head of the new Western theater command) was apparently due more than anything to weariness among party politicians over his shrill claims about the short-term danger of war at American instigation. The Ogarkov demotion made it clear that, much as their advice is respected, the armed forces do not unilaterally determine defense policy. The point has been further underscored by Marshal Sergei Sokolov, the new Defense Minister named in December 1984 (and in 1979 the officer directly responsible for organizing the occupation of Afghanistan), being accorded no more than candidate membership in the Politburo, a large notch down from the full membership given Marshals Grechko and Ustinov from 1973 to 1984. While the generals continue in the main to take a more alarmist view of American intentions, the tendency among many civilians has been to accept certain points of the military diagnosis of Soviet strategic needs but to argue that they can be implemented only in the long run, not immediately. Most in the party hierarchy have also been considerably more willing than the military to explore the possibility of a negotiated accommodation with Soviet adversaries, even if this means trading away hardware assets such as the SS-20s trained on Western Europe, some ICBMs, and perhaps even some of the multiple-warheaded heavy ICBMs that are a priority target of American negotiators. These the Brezhnev regime, bowing to military wishes, tended to see as sacrosanct.

Gorbachev assuredly intends to maintain "strategic parity" with the United States, one of the few of Brezhnev's accomplishments that he has unstintingly praised, and roughly the current military balance with the West. He knows that the price tag for this will be high. He has at no time indicated, however, that Soviet military spending ought to rise in the short run, and on several occasions he has described President Reagan's SDI as a plot to force the Soviet Union into bankruptcy.[34] The phrase he has used to describe the appropriate level of Soviet military effort is that which will "maintain the defense capability of the country at the necessary level," a relatively restrained formulation among those used in the abstruse Soviet debates over the issue. Acknowledging pressure from Soviet hawks to accelerate military programs, he has insisted time and again that the only guarantee of security over the years will be a sound economic and social base, dynamic enough to give Soviet forces the latest technology and ready for prompt response to an enemy provocation.

Gorbachev stated his position most clearly in his April 1986 speech in Togliatti, where he claimed that "numerous letters" had been reaching the Central Committee from citizens concerned that under the cover of negotiations the West was preparing "a breakthrough in armaments to which we would not be able to react." This would never happen, he said, for a vigilant Soviet leadership would know when an urgent response was needed. For now, the Soviet Union could safely concentrate on underlying problems: "The main front in the struggle for peace lies in the resolution of the problems of improving socialist society," including Soviet science, technology, productivity, and "moral potential." Summarizing, he sounded his by now familiar refrain about the centrality of the economy: "In a word, a strong and healthy economy is what will bring success in our peace policy."[35] The most appropriate response to the external security challenge was thus long-term modernization, with an emphasis on the quality of the instruments available for military purposes, rather than short-term mobilization stressing quantity.

Will the Soviets therefore reduce their mammoth military budget and be more willing as a result to make concessions in disarmament negotiations? We cannot say for certain, and one has to doubt if the Politburo itself knows what it will do. The Brezhnev leadership in the mid-1970s trimmed the rate of increase of defense spending, if not the actual defense budget, in order to shunt resources into mass consumption. Gorbachev, to judge by his public statements, would probably jump at the chance to go further in this direction, though more for the sake of economic investment than for consumption. He and his allies in the civilian leadership may find some in the military high command to be receptive to such a policy shift on professional grounds. "Many Soviet military leaders," a recent U.S. government report concludes, "appear to realize . . . that the military will be the ultimate beneficiary of successful industrial modernization and have voiced their support for it. Soviet military authors are aware that economic improvements will ease resource constraints and accelerate the introduction of new technology, thus setting the stage for more rapid military modernization in the 1990s."[36] Many of the weapons on the drawing boards for five or ten years hence will incorporate more sophisticated features and components that in turn will require advanced microelectronics, computer-aided design, and new fabricating and testing techniques—all of them benefits that Gorbachev promises to deliver through economic modernization, and through innovation in the economy as a whole and not just in the nine defense-production ministries.

Conversely, Gorbachev is not buffeted by economic forces so overwhelming that they will compel him to retreat on defense spending no matter what. It is well to remember that the Soviet leaders have consistently been prepared, even at moments of great domestic strain, to make formidable sacrifices to keep Soviet military readiness at the level ordained by perceived national security needs, however inflated these may look to the outsider. There will be no deep cuts in the defense budget unless the Politburo comes to believe that external conditions, and above all relations with the United States, permit them.

As a practical matter, the regime would not get a particularly quick economic boost from saving on defense. Long lead-times in converting military assembly lines, supply and transport bottlenecks, and other organizational problems would restrict the impact—so much so that one U.S. government study estimated in the early 1980s that, if military spending were not to grow at all for the rest of the decade, Soviet economic growth would improve as a result by only one-tenth to one-fifth of a percent a year.[37] Moreover, the Soviet defense industry provides more spin-offs to the civilian economy than it used to, and abruptly squeezing it might interfere with this flow.[38] In sum, slashing the defense budget will be no economic cure-all. It will make a contribution to balanced growth only if it is part of a concerted and forward-looking strategy.

This is not to say that a marked increase in military spending could easily be enacted, either. To step up armaments production in the current five-year plan would clash directly with Gorbachev's prized industrial modernization. Conflict would be greatest in the machinery sector, where military and civilian plants would compete for scarce machine tools, automated manufacturing systems, basic materials (metals and chemicals), intermediate products (including engineering plastics, microprocessors, and advanced composite materials), laboratory space and instrumentation, and skilled labor.[39] A large increase in military spending would probably have a deleterious effect on consumption levels as well. One study several years ago by Western economists predicted that the Soviet standard of living would drop by roughly one-third of a percentage point for every one percent of acceleration in military spending.[40]

Gorbachev's preferred course will probably be to leave military research, development, and production at essentially current levels, grant civilian and general-purpose industrial plant priority in investment, and defer the difficult decisions on allocation of the eventual results of investment until the beginning of the 1990s. Defense plants quite likely will be forced to devote somewhat more resources than before to production for the consumer and for other civilian uses and, conceivably, for export, without giving up production capacity.[41]

As far as manufacture of military hardware is concerned, Gorbachev could take advantage for the time being of the huge investment bequeathed him by the Brezhnev regime—one of the few Brezhnev legacies for which he can be truly grateful. According to a recent analysis by U.S. intelligence agencies, almost all of the production capacity needed to support Soviet force modernization for the rest of the 1980s is in place today. Assembly lines are already rolling for key weapons systems such as the Blackjack bomber, the SU-27 fighter, the SS-25 ICBM, and the T-80 heavy tank. "Our calculations suggest that virtually no additional investment in the plant and equipment is needed to manufacture the military hardware that we believe will be in production in 1986–88 and that most of the capacity required to turn out the military equipment projected to be in production in the early 1990s is already available. . . . Gorbachev can 'coast' for a few years on the strength of the USSR's past investment in its military-industrial complex."[42] Only after this, once the results of his first half-decade in power are in and it is clear whether arms control negotiations are going anywhere, will he and his colleagues be in a position to set their subsequent course.

Foreign economic ties. A drift away from economic autarchy was one distinguishing feature of the Soviet 1960s and 1970s. The ratio of imports to GNP, which was less than 1 percent by the end of the isolationist 1930s (when the volume of the USSR's foreign trade was no greater than tiny Finland's) and about 3 percent in the mid-1960s, climbed to roughly 5 percent at the beginning of the 1980s, low by world but high by Russian standards. Fastest was the spurt in trade with the industrialized capitalist countries. Imports from OECD members rose from 20 percent of the Soviet total in 1965 to a high of 36 percent in 1975, during which time imports from Eastern Europe slid from 58 to 41 percent of the whole. Procurements were massive of Western grain and of machinery and equipment for the automotive, fertilizer, petroleum, and other industries embodying a higher level of technology than that prevalent in the USSR. Particular attention was paid after the mid-1970s to acquisition through overt and covert channels of Western technology with military significance, notably in the areas of computers and electronics.

Although precise documentation is difficult, it is agreed that increased trade has been of substantial benefit to the Soviet economy. It has been said, to take one estimate, that the $7 billion the Soviets spent on grain imports in 1982 was $32 billion less than it would have cost them to produce the extra grain themselves. The Pentagon maintains that acquisition of Western technology saved Moscow $640 million in 1980 in major military projects. According to a British economist, imports of advanced Western equipment netted the Soviet economy about one-half a percent a year in additional growth in the 1970s, and some Western experts put it higher than that.[43]

There has been abundant discord within the Soviet elite about the desirability of expanding foreign economic ties. Prominent among the opponents of expansion have been the military, the KGB, the Ministry of Finance (which tends to disapprove of increases in foreign indebtedness), and elements in the scientific establishment (led by the eighty-three-old president of the Academy of Sciences, Anatoli Aleksandrov). Nationalism, veiled or open, is an important glue in the skeptics' argument. "Unfortunately," one critic recently wrote, "certain of the leaders of our industry and scientific organizations still consider the adoption of foreign experience as a disparagement of the prestige not only of the given agency but of indigenous [Soviet] science and technology in general. . . . Some of these people are convinced that our social system automatically compensates for every shortcoming in knowledge and experience."[44]

Pitted against them have been a coalition of foreign trade officials, academic specialists, planners, and economic executives, who have advocated closer integration of the Soviet Union into the global economy as a means of spurring Soviet economic growth and, as a byproduct, of easing international tensions. Many pro-integrationists have propounded an export-led trade strategy, as distinct from the more passive, import-driven approach typical of the regime in the past and favored by Brezhnev. In orthodox Soviet practice, foreign purchases are used chiefly to substitute for specific Soviet shortfalls or to aid production for domestic needs, and they are made up to a ceiling set by earnings from the sale of raw materials and fuels—a strategy not greatly different from that of many Third World countries. The Soviets are able to ship embarrassingly few complex manufactured goods to the world market: machinery and equipment sold to the developed capitalist countries at the present time make up only 4 percent of Soviet exports.[45] The critics have urged that aggressive export of manufactured goods set the pace in trade, and that the traditional "foreign trade monopoly" of the Ministry of Foreign Trade be lifted or amended so that industrial producers have the liberty to seek out foreign markets directly. Innovation in foreign trade has often been joined to an appeal for moderate reforms in the domestic economy—the link being the assertion that the discipline of foreign competition will force greater internal efficiency, including efficiency in the assimilation of foreign technology. Soviet experts on the Third World have been engaged in the same sort of controversy, with a growing subset of them favoring greater participation by developing nations in the world economy, and perforce greater reliance on the capitalist countries.[46]

In high circles, it was the anti-integrationist outlook that gained ground in the late Brezhnev period and throughout the Andropov-Chernenko interregnum. Yuri Andropov, perhaps for tactical reasons, was cooler toward economic intercourse with the West than his rival Chernenko, and the latter as General Secretary seemed less supportive of expanded commerce than he had been earlier. Even pro-reform advisers long sold on greater trade were allowing in 1983 that the Soviet Union was being "forced to approach collaboration with the West more selectively."[47]

This greater caution was in part a straightforward backlash against the perceived perfidy of the West on trade issues. In the Soviet opinion, the U.S. Congress acted in bad faith in 1974 by passing the Jackson-Vanik amendment to the Trade Reform Act, tying most-favored-nation status for tariffs to changes in Soviet emigration policy. When the Politburo rejected this as unacceptable interference in Soviet internal affairs, the normalization of U.S.-Soviet commercial relations agreed to by Brezhnev and Richard Nixon in 1972 failed to materialize. Later in the 1970s and under the Reagan administration after 1980, the United States imposed economic sanctions, and encouraged its allies to do likewise, in retaliation for Soviet treatment of dissidents, intervention in Afghanistan, and policy toward Poland. The sanctions included the post-Afghanistan embargo on U.S. grain exports to the Soviet Union (rescinded by President Reagan in 1981), revoking of export licenses for oil and gas equipment, suspension of Soviet fishing and air landing rights, and tightening up of the multilateral COCOM controls on industrial exports. Many Soviets saw these measures as an affront and continue to do so today.

A second item in Soviet thinking in the early 1980s was a more deep-seated recalculation by some officials and specialists of the economic utility of foreign trade and technology transfer. By this line of reasoning, Western countries, insofar as they tried to use commerce to wage "economic warfare" against the Soviet Union, were unreliable partners. Access to foreign markets would not stimulate Soviet productivity if it could be cut off at a moment's notice. And undue reliance on imports, including cheap foreign food, could be a crutch, diverting the regime from tending to internally-generated problems. Imported technology, the argument ran, was no substitute for the indigeneous product, and it was often utilized poorly because of inadequate Soviet planning and management. Hence the Soviet Union would get better results by forgetting about bypassing its economic problems through the trade route and by getting its internal house in order, pushing integration with Eastern Europe, and learning to make effective use of current levels of trade.

A third and more tangible variable in the equation was the deterioration of the financial conditions that enabled the rapid expansion of inter-bloc trade in the 1960s and 1970s. Soviet hard currency earnings leapt with world oil and gold prices after 1973 (oil, natural gas, and gold account for the lion's share of these earnings), only to level off after 1980 when prices sagged. Net indebtedness to the West, which had been a paltry $600 million in 1971, swelled to $7.5 billion in 1975 and $12.4 billion in 1981—enough for the Kremlin's conservative money managers, under the impact of the Polish debt crisis, to decide to cap it. The net debt was pared to $10 billion in 1982-83, and trade with the OECD countries, which had soared by 31 percent a year in 1971–75 and 10 percent a year in 1976–80, was up by only 4 percent in 1983 and actually dropped marginally in 1984.

Here things stood when Mikhail Gorbachev took office. He in one sense immediately altered the picture by declaring in June 1985 what sounded like concurrence in the pro-integrationist and export-oriented thesis that had lately been battered by its opponents:

> The tasks of scientific and technological progress demand from us a new approach to all of our foreign economic activity. The country's foreign trade turnover has reached a large volume, 140 billion rubles, but we can and must accelerate the tempos of its growth. The main thing is to impart a more progressive character to both exports and imports.
>
> Our export of machinery and equipment has in recent years grown slowly. There are several reasons for this: the poor competitiveness of much of it, and the insufficient interest of our industrial enterprises in working at exports. It is impossible to tolerate this any longer. And in our import policy we must more effectively utilize the possibilities of the international division of labor.[48]

There was one jarring note in the speech. Speaking of imports, Gorbachev said that "in the first instance" the Soviet Union had to strengthen ties to its traditional East European partners in CMEA. Subsequent events showed that, whatever his commitment in theory to full Soviet participation in the global division of labor, his approach to implementation is evolutionary and not as far removed from historic Soviet concerns as the call for a "new approach" intimated. Gorbachev's choice as Foreign Trade Minister, Aristov, is in fact an East Europeanist (ambassador to Warsaw from 1978 to 1983, Deputy Foreign Minister in charge of bloc relations after that), and he has busied himself to a large extent with CMEA affairs. On the export front, a July 1985 decree announced modest measures to prod industrial enterprises and ministries to develop foreign sales of manufactured goods, including special bonuses for managers and the right to use a portion of the convertible currency income from export sales to upgrade export and domestic lines.[49] But no action has yet been taken on the sales monopoly of the Foreign Trade Ministry, which continues to interpose itself between Soviet sellers and foreign clients.

In his more recent remarks on trade, Gorbachev has sent out mixed signals. At his Geneva press conference, he said he favored expanded trade with the United States for political reasons, as "a material base for political relations, for their improvement, for the formation of an atmosphere of trust." He told visiting American businessmen in December 1985 that the Soviet government had taken "quite a critical attitude toward our foreign trade organizations," holding them responsible for some past failures, and also that the Soviets would welcome "new forms of production and scientific-technical collaboration." Yet, in the same address, he distinguished between the economic integration (*integratsiya*) sought with Eastern Europe and the less intense economic collaboration (*sotrudnichestvo*) to which the USSR aspired with capitalist countries.[50]

Foreign economic ties, touched on desultorily in Gorbachev's speech to the Twenty-seventh Party Congress, were left for Premier Nikolai Ryzhkov to cover. Affirming Gorbachev's avowed policy of boosting Soviet exports and reorienting them toward machinery and modern manufactures, Ryzhkov also stated plainly that closing in on this goal would be slow: "It is understandable that this demands time, but it is necessary that work be under way already in the Twelfth [1986–90] Five-Year Plan." Foreign commerce may be one of the few economic issues on which Ryzhkov is as committed to change as Gorbachev, for in later statements he has expressed support for "a change in the entire system of management" in the foreign trade sphere, and especially for increases in enterprise independence and incentives "to heighten their [material] interest in export."[51]

The regime's gradualism on foreign economic relations reflects enduring insecurities, activated perhaps by the sense that internal economic modernization through moderate reform is too crucial a task to be left open to interference by ideological adversaries. "We will not," as Gorbachev has phrased it, "let our plans depend on the intentions of other states in relation to our country."[52] A more immediate impediment to trade liberalization lies in the continued short supply of hard currency earnings. The tumble in world oil prices has hit the Soviet Union hard, accounting more than any single factor for the 7 percent drop in Soviet-OECD trade registered in 1985, Gorbachev's first year. Soviet imports from the developed Western countries have fallen from their 1975 high of 36 percent of total imports to 27 percent, whereas East European imports have risen sharply from 41 to 62 percent. The only way to counter the trend would be to borrow more heavily from Western banks. This the Soviets have grudgingly done—net indebtedness by the end of 1985 is estimated to have risen to an all-time high of $14.8 billion—but this has not been enough even to sustain previous rates of trade with the capitalist countries. There are conflicting signs at present on the attitude toward raising Western loans. On the one hand, the Soviets have put out feelers about following Hungary, Poland, and Rumania into the World Bank and International Monetary Fund, which would ease their access to capital pools. On the other hand, when the conservative chairman of the State Bank, Vladimir Alkhimov, was retired in January 1986, his replacement was Viktor Dementsev, one year older than he (born in 1918) and a product of the Ministry of Finance, an organization long opposed to enlarging the Soviet debt.

The prospect of static or reduced trade with the West for some years to come, if that is the reality, does not help the chances of internal Soviet innovation in the form envisioned by the present leadership, but it should not irreparably harm them either. Import-led Soviet-Western trade flourished under a Brezhnev regime that refused to make more than minimal changes at home and seemed often to see imports as a way of avoiding more systematic improvements. Brezhnev's heirs, with less access to the implicit short-term subsidies provided by expanded imports, now have greater reason to direct their main energies to internal improvements. Export-oriented trade linked to such improvements would be a major departure from traditional practice. It is not yet apparent whether the Soviet leaders will act on their statements about moving in this direction.

Eastern Europe. The politics, economics, military organization, and culture of the six allied states in Eastern Europe are inextricably bound up with those of their Soviet patron and master. So intimate is the association, springing out of occupation by the Red Army and coerced Sovietization after World War II, that forty years later many Soviet politicians still conceive of their policies toward Eastern Europe, and even the internal affairs of the six countries, as an extension of Soviet domestic policy. This creates a standing conflict of interest with the East European societies and indeed with their governments, for whom the only reliable basis for legitimation has been identification with local aspirations and nationalism.

Political successions in the Soviet Union have always had a destabilizing effect on Eastern Europe, as they bring turnover of leaders, political infighting, and a preoccupation with internal Soviet problems. The resultant absence of consistent policy guidance, it has been argued, helped bring about the local miscalculations that provoked the 1956 Soviet invasion of Hungary and the Warsaw Pact intervention in Czechoslovakia in 1968.[53] The succession of the 1980s has introduced a similar note of uncertainty. Soviet policy has wavered since the Solidarity rebellion in Poland inaugurated the decade, and the new Central Committee secretary in charge of liaison with Eastern Europe, Vadim Medvedev, was appointed only in March 1986 (replacing a Brezhnev crony, Konstantin Rusakov) and has no prior administrative experience with bloc issues. If Yuri Andropov had a good deal of acquaintance with Eastern Europe, having served four years in Budapest and held Medvedev's current position for a decade, this has been true for neither Chernenko or Gorbachev.

Several circumstances differentiate the present transition from previous ones. For one, political succession is not only a dominant fact in the Soviet Union but is imminent in five of the six allied countries—in Rumania because of the poor health of President Nicolae Ceauşescu and in East Germany, Czechoslovakia, Hungary, and

Bulgaria because the present leaders are over seventy years of age (and in Hungary and Bulgaria have been in power for three decades). These changes will take place, moreover, in political systems that in terms of makeup and policy are more divergent from one another and from the Soviet prototype than ever before. Eastern Europe thus presents the Kremlin not with a single problem but with a tangle of problems, defying any quick fix or uniform solution. In Poland it must contend first and foremost with the shakiness of the regime, in East Germany with pacifism and the attraction to West Germany, in Czechoslovakia with a pervasive ossification under Gustav Husak exceeding even that of the Brezhnev regime in the USSR, in Hungary with economic revisionism and a desire to trade more freely with the West, in Bulgaria with a dozen small defiances of Soviet wishes, and in Rumania with a maverick foreign policy and a mix of Balkan inefficiency and Stalinist repressiveness that may yet spark another Solidarity.

The one generalization that holds for all the USSR's partners, from the Baltic to the Black Sea, is that each is bogged down today in severe economic difficulties. They range from incredible depression and disorganization in Poland (where planners do not expect to regain 1978 production levels until 1990 and are speaking of the loss of a whole generation of economic development), through a growth deceleration of Soviet dimensions in most of the other countries, to a relatively mild slowdown in East Germany (buoyed by its special relationship with West Germany). In each case, the regime artificially stimulated economic growth in the 1970s by heavy borrowing in the West, proved unable to sell enough in the world market to service its debt, and then had by the early 1980s to slash imports and consumption to cope with a balance-of-payments crisis. Net hard-currency indebtedness, which had been only $6 billion in 1970, increased tenfold by 1981 and was still in excess of $55 billion in 1985, or approximately nine times the Soviet level per capita.

The economic woes of Eastern Europe converge on Soviet policy in three principal ways. First, they can be traced in substantial measure to postwar copying of Stalinist economic institutions and to maintenance of these under Soviet pressure. To the extent that reformers in the bloc regimes contemplate changes in economic arrangements, they are calling into question aspects of the Soviet archetype. Second, both continuation of the economic status quo and attempts to reform it carry the potential of destabilizing the regimes, and thereby of prompting Soviet military intervention. Such an act would have grievous feedback effects on the USSR itself. Third is the simmering issue of Soviet economic subsidization of the East European countries, or the lack thereof. Western economists generally accept that there has been some degree of implicit subsidy by the Soviet Union since the early 1970s—due mainly to Soviet marketings of petroleum at prices below world par—but there is no unanimity on its magnitude or how to weigh it against other manifestations of political and economic influence. In the countries concerned, the sense of grievance is mutual. The Soviet rulers feel, rightly or wrongly, that they help keep their dependent states afloat, whereas many in Eastern Europe believe that Soviet magnanimity is less than is claimed and even that it is they who are doing the subsidizing.[54]

The Soviet leadership immediately after Brezhnev's death was mainly concerned with political normalization in Poland and with reducing what they saw as the East European drag on the Soviet economy. Andropov, at the same time, seemed not to foreclose political, economic, and social adaptation within the bloc. He stressed that "big differences in economics, in culture, and in the ways and methods of developing socialism" are inescapable within the bloc. "This is natural, even if at times it seemed to us that [the development of communism] would be more uniform."[55] Other Soviet spokesmen described East European economic reforms as essential, spoke approvingly of how "these reforms are taking on a more radical character," and emphasized that "each country [in the alliance] has its particularities" and that reforms can be expected to "differ in terms of depth, tempo of implementation, complexity, and many concrete features."[56]

Gorbachev's line toward Eastern Europe has built on Andropov's but has been rather sterner in tone. In April 1985 the Warsaw Pact at Soviet insistence was renewed for an additional thirty years, despite the preference of some signatories for a shorter term. That summer the Soviet press printed several articles sharply attacking East European deviance in a variety of areas, and from time to time this has been repeated. Visiting Warsaw for the congress of the Polish Workers' Party in June 1986, Gorbachev made it clear that Solidarity-type democratization would be intolerable to Moscow in future. He praised General Jaruzelski to the skies and, by highlighting that the Polish regime had defeated Solidarity "with its own forces," he prompted none too subtly the conclusion that Soviet forces would be used in future if indigenous communists were to lose control.[57]

Predictably, priority has been given under Gorbachev to economic issues. Bulgaria, politically loyal but economically derelict, was singled out for opprobrium in the fall of 1985, particularly for delivering substandard goods to the Soviet Union. CMEA has been promoted as a framework for bloc economic integration and an alternative to dependence on the capitalist market. Gorbachev in December 1985 hosted a CMEA summit that ratified a grandiose plan for economic and scientific coordination up to the year 2000. He has called for development of direct ties between Soviet and East European enterprises, creation of joint firms, and, without giving specifics, for establishment of "a new economic mechanism for our collaboration."[58]

Gorbachev has not been unaware of the need for adaptability within the bloc. Barely had the sinister-sounding calls for East European conformity been printed in mid-1985 than softer and seemingly more authoritative pronouncements appeared. The interests of the communist states, said the most detailed of these, could never coincide completely, as each partner "has its own specific interests, its own main problems." Economic and other forms of integration could be pursued "only with the voluntary assent of each and all."[59] Gorbachev at the Twenty-seventh Congress, while lauding economic coordination, also stated Moscow's willingness to live with diversity among its allies: "Unity has nothing in common with uniformity, with hierarchy, with interference by some parties in the affairs of others, with the striving by any party to monopolize the truth." And in his Warsaw speech, after saying in effect that there could be no more Solidarities, he went on to underline the importance of the national parties making pragmatic responses to their societies' needs.[60]

Soviet-East European relations in the immediate future will be dominated by bread-and-butter economic issues, chief among them haggling over terms of trade. Since the price of Soviet oil shipments to the region lags by formula behind world prices, it will take some time before the drop in world oil prices is passed on to the bloc countries, and this is bound to stir resentment. Over the next decade, however, two larger issues will be predominant.

The first is whether political instability will erupt in the form of a mass insurrection against a client regime, or of capture of a regime by radical reformers bent on redefining their relationship with Moscow. Soviet economic pressure, if excessive or oafishly managed, could conceivably set off such an explosion, which would be most threatening to the Soviets if it involved—as it never has in the past—local insubordination followed by Soviet military intervention in more than one country in the region. Mayhem in the East European empire might have important effects at home, for it could play into the hands of Soviet hard-liners and superpatriots or, to the same effect, activate the survival instincts of middle-of-the-roaders in the regime. The leadership could then wind up declaring a bloc-wide state of siege, delegating new control powers to the army and KGB, and stifling for a time even whispers of reform.

The second unanswerable question is whether Gorbachev and his colleagues will tolerate, or even encourage, reforms within the East European systems. If tolerance is the line, Moscow will have to decide whether to approve technocratic economic reforms only or wider-reaching social change and political liberalization—a dilemma that has its counterpart within the Soviet Union. Most Soviet conservatives, and some of more reformist bent as well, fearing that another Prague Spring or Solidarity could be the surprise result of national experimentation, might see merit in keeping Eastern Europe on a tight leash. But the result of such a policy would sooner or later be the delegitimation of most of the client regimes and either their reliance on brute force to stay in power—a generalization, in a way, of the current Polish situation—or their adoption of ever more strident forms of nationalism (inevitably anti-Russian nationalism), along the lines of present-day Rumania. Moscow's role in Eastern Europe would then be reduced to that of gendarme and the task of the internal Soviet reformer made simultaneously more imperative and more difficult.

Human rights. No Soviet domestic issue was more internationalized in the Brezhnev years than policy vis-à-vis what Western liberals conceive of as "human rights"—individual entitlements to freedom of the person not normally recognized by authoritarian governments. The Soviets lay emphasis in their own definition of human rights on issues of social and economic equality rather than individual liberty, but I shall follow Western terminology here, for it has been over human rights as they are understood in the West that the worst conflict has taken place.

Two sides of this multifaceted matter acquired particular salience in the 1960s and 1970s. The first was official treatment of political dissidents, individuals willing to make a public statement of discontent with the Soviet system, which rendered them subject to prosecution under clauses of the Soviet criminal code prohibiting "anti-Soviet agitation and propaganda." Western intercession at times mitigated Soviet repression of political dissent and may well have saved some of the dissidents' lives. The second prominent subissue was mass emigration of Soviet citizens, something that had been practically impossible for most of Soviet history but in the 1970s was allowed some 400,000 persons, about two-thirds of them Jews. Along with dissent and emigration, a number of other human rights questions cropped up in bilateral and multilateral dealings with Western countries: reunification of family members not part of a group seeking wholesale emigration, flow of information, journalists' working conditions, and the like.

Human rights problems were raised during the European security negotiations leading to the 1975 Helsinki accord, "Basket Three" of which dealt with political and civil rights, and have since that time been taken up by most of the West European countries. The impact was greatest on relations with the United States, where initially Congress and private groups took the lead but eventually Presidents Carter and Reagan, too, espoused the cause. American elite and mass attitudes toward the Soviet Union were greatly affected by such Soviet behavior as the denial of exit permits (which often received more media attention than the issuance of up to 50,000 visas a year in the late 1970s), the brutal suppression of the Helsinki Watch Group (set up to monitor Soviet compliance with the 1975 agreement), and the treatment of Andrei Sakharov and other prominent dissidents. Also affected were the course of U.S.-Soviet economic relations and the timing if not the substance of American arms control proposals. The Soviets, for their part, reluctantly swallowed the need to bargain over aspects of individual rights as a condition of dealing with Washington, and used carefully rationed concessions to secure American favor and doses of repression to get across displeasure with American policy.

The limited East-West dialogue over human rights all but ceased after the Soviet intervention in Afghanistan. Western sanctions and condemnation of the invasion, coming at a time when the Soviet authorities were particularly thin-skinned about criticism from within, seem to have convinced them that they had nothing to lose by taking a harsher line. They were confirmed in this belief by the new round of sanctions following the imposition of martial law in Poland in 1981. Jewish emigration fell sharply to fewer than a hundred a month, prominent dissidents were jailed and the best known civil rights advocate in Moscow, Academician Sakharov, exiled to the city of Gorky, and new restrictions were slapped on postal, telephone, and radio communication.

Under Yuri Andropov, who as KGB chief was responsible for implementation of the post-Afghanistan crackdown, the hard line was continued but some flexibility was hinted at. Criminal code amendments broadened the definition of ideological subversion, simplified the resentencing of political prisoners, and made transmission of an "official secret" a crime. The Andropov Politburo in the spring of 1983 withdrew the Soviet Union from the World Psychiatric Association, mostly, it seems, to prevent investigation of the use of mental clinics and prisons against political dissidents. Later that year, however, it signaled publicly and privately that Jewish emigration might be resumed and prominent dissidents allowed to leave, and it granted visas to a family of Siberian Pentacostalists who had lived in the U.S. embassy in Moscow for years awaiting exit permission. It also made slight concessions at the Madrid review of the Helsinki agreement, giving paper assurances on family reunification and foreign journalists' rights and consenting to a new round of discussion at experts' meetings on human rights and human contacts. Chernenko showed the odd flash of compassion as General Secretary, but this was outweighed by retrogressive decisions such as the dismissal of Yuri Lyubimov, the brilliant director of Moscow's Taganka Theater, after he criticized the Soviet cultural bureaucracy while on a visit to Britain.

Mikhail Gorbachev became party leader accompanied by few hopes of a turnabout on human rights. The issue undoubtedly has been of far less interest to him than changes in economic management and, in foreign policy, arms control. He has, nonetheless, paid more than a little attention to it. At the Twenty-seventh Party Congress, he rather surprisingly listed the "humanitarian" as one of the four main spheres of Soviet foreign policy. He spoke evasively in one passage of the Soviet interest in the broadening of political and personal rights, "in conformity with the laws of each country," but in a more forthcoming vein in the next sentence of a commitment to "the resolution in a humane and positive spirit of problems of family reunification, marriage, and development of contacts among people and organizations." Gorbachev reiterated the commitment to President Mitterrand in July 1986, insisting that it was "not only words."[61]

The Gorbachev leadership has from the outset allowed rumors to circulate of a possible reopening of the emigration door for Soviet Jews. It released Anatoli Shcharanskii, after seven years of confinement for leading the agitation for Jewish emigration, and permitted Yelena Bonner, Sakharov's wife, to travel abroad for medical treatment. It promptly granted the request by Joseph Stalin's daughter, Svetlana Alliluyeva, who had voluntarily returned to the USSR under Chernenko after seventeen years in the West, for permission to move back to the United States with her daughter Olga. Alliluyeva told a Western interviewer afterward that the decision was made by Gorbachev personally and that she thought he wanted to show that he was "a modern, civilized ruler" and that the Soviet system was becoming more humane.[62] In May 1986, after the Berne forum on human contacts agreed to at Madrid, Moscow announced settlement of 150 family reunification cases of interest to the United States.

The Chernobyl' disaster, in that it touched on individuals' and groups' right to know about a common danger, was also in a fashion a case in human rights. The dilatory Soviet response properly infuriated many of Gorbachev's countrymen and millions of other Europeans. This may be less significant in the long run than that a combination of domestic and international pressure—pulled together by an information loop running through satellite photographs, short-wave radio broadcasts, and word of mouth—eventually persuaded the Soviets to go public. Gorbachev's televised address of May 14, 1986, took the predictable swipes at the U.S. government and the Western media, but also proposed creation of an international early-warning system on nuclear accidents. The acceptance of emergency help from Dr. Robert Gale and other American specialists, and the plan for joint monitoring of the more than 100,000 residents of the Ukraine and Belorussia who may have delayed effects from radiation, was highly unusual in terms of Soviet national pride.

Chernobyl', Gorbachev's obviously heartfelt belief in *glasnost'*, and the still fragile thaw in Soviet culture provide grounds for some optimism about a gradual expansion of the boundaries of acceptable commentary and criticism in the Soviet Union. Developments in this area should be watched closely and with an awareness of how deeply ingrained is the resistance to change. This is a far cry, however, from saying that there is going to be a dismantling of controls or that the Soviet system's basis of legitimacy—the doctrinally sanctioned right of the Communist Party to rule—is going to be tampered with. The moderate reform forecast in this book has to do primarily with economic and social policy, and it holds out but a slender prospect of the systematic democratization advocated by more radical reformers. There seems to be not the ghost of a chance, for example, that the Soviet people will any day soon gain the right to form autonomous trade unions or interest associations, vote in competitive elections, or purchase and read whatever foreign publications they please. Gorbachev and some of his colleagues may well have concluded that economic and social modernization cannot succeed without a freer atmosphere for the exchange of ideas and information. But, as suggested in Chapter 4, they also seem convinced that the divisions and stresses attendant on their economic program require that certain key individual freedoms remain restricted.

When it comes to dissent and emigration, the human rights issues that have garnered so much Western interest, the outlook is uneven. Soviet dissent has lost the philosophical unity, and the overriding concern with the individual's right to stand apart from the collective and the state, that it had ten or fifteen years ago. Soviet dissenters today are attracted to a greater variety of causes, including anti-Russian nationalism and several kinds of anti-democratic ideology, than they were when the phenomenon first came to the attention of the West.[63] The trend toward unmuzzling the state media may make it easier to voice within-system criticism of Soviet failings, and I would venture to say that it has already done so. Once the line out of the approved channels and into the world of protest and dissent has been crossed, however, the dissenter is not likely to be much more leniently treated under Gorbachev than he was under Brezhnev.

Emigration, and in particular Jewish emigration, remains a question mark so long as East-West relations remain as hostile as they are. If that enmity is defused, it may be easier for Soviet conservatives and reactionaries to accept emigration on humanitarian grounds, of which the most acceptable will continue to be family reunification. For Jewish emigration to resume, the Soviets can be expected to insist on nonobstruction by Jewish groups in the United States of trade liberalization and other legislative measures of interest to Moscow—a commitment that Jewish leaders may not be able to make. If emigration does begin again, Moscow will surely demand more strenuously than it did in the 1970s that the emigrants have close relatives abroad and that they relocate in Israel, not in the United States or Canada.

On both dissent and emigration, the most to be anticipated—and it is nothing to be sneezed at—is gradual and selective improvement. The regime may be persuaded by outsiders to bend its rules in particular instances, usually for persons fortunate enough to have articulate defenders in the Western democracies, but redrafting of the rules is something it will tend to by its own lights and at its own pace, if it does so at all. It is a delusion to imagine that Western leaders could negotiate a wholesale liberalization of the Soviet system even in the sunniest East-West climate.

Implications for Western Policy

Coping with the Soviet fact has always been difficult for Western societies and governments, and it will not be less so in the coming decade. While sensitivity to the domestic agenda facing Soviet leaders may not tell us all we need to know in defining U.S. and allied policy, it does inform policy in important respects. Several insights flow from a hard look at the Soviet system as it is and as it is likely to evolve.

First, we owe it to ourselves to be realistic about internal conditions in the Soviet Union. Too many Western decision makers, especially in Washington, have been attracted of late to crude and inaccurate images of the Soviet regime. Two of these stand out. One treats the Soviet Union as a country of almost supernatural strength, a monolith ruled by true believers who pay no heed to public wants and are at liberty to proceed with foreign adventures and conquests. In the second and pretty well opposite image, the USSR is, as President Reagan said of it in his June 1982 address to the British Parliament, "inherently unstable," a society riddled with conflicts and tensions and experiencing a "great revolutionary crisis," which before long will issue in the downfall of its institutions.[64]

Neither impression is realistic, and neither forms a reliable foundation for Western policy. The Soviet system, though it has no more prospect of eternal life than any other human construct, is at the present time stable in its fundamentals. The USSR is not Poland—its homegrown regime is far older, stronger, and ornerier, and the average citizen is more stoically acceptive of its continuance. There is no revolutionary crisis in the Soviet Union today. Nor is there the obverse, a static regime in total command of events and oblivious to the population's every demand. Enough has happened since Brezhnev's death for us to say with some confidence that major changes are occurring in the Soviet elite and that the regime is trying to retool economic and other public policies so as to revive economic growth, better meet its welfare objectives, and enhance Soviet international competitiveness. The authoritarian Soviet system is responding in its own way to problems that have been brewing for some time, reflecting a capacity for change—the outer limits of which have not yet been sharply defined—and for averting a breakdown in which everything will change.

Western observers ought to use multiple criteria, depending on the purpose, for assaying the significance of change in the Soviet Union. If the objective is to reflect on the lessons of developments there for analogous problems in our own kind of society, the best touchstone would probably be that of the consensus values of Western liberal culture. But if the aim is to understand how the Soviet people themselves are affected by regime decisions, or to consider how these actions relate to the current policy agenda of Western governments, then the most instructive comparisons are historical—with how the Soviets have behaved in the recent past, not with our idealized vision of how a government should behave. Whether the issue is Chernobyl', economic reform, or dissent, more will be learned about Mikhail Gorbachev by comparing him to Leonid Brezhnev than to Thomas Jefferson.

Second, we have a limited though not nonexistent capacity to influence the Soviet domestic system. Among observers who reject the simplistic notions that the Soviet Union is either wholly static or on the verge of falling apart, numerous schemes for rehabilitating its system of government have found favor over the years. It would take a small library to house them, but what they have in common is the premise that the West can through deliberate policy influence the evolution of Soviet society in ways congenial to Western values and interests. At various times, and with special conviction during the détente of the 1970s, it has been asserted that the Soviet Union can be helped along the path to social and political pluralism by conciliatory Western policies and expanded commerce, scientific contacts, and so forth. Recently, in the climate of strained relations of the 1980s, it has been proposed that the best way to hasten the advent of reforms is through severe Western pressure on security, trade, human rights, and other issues.[65]

Negative sanctions, as proposed by the latter group and practised by the last two U.S. administrations, may from time to time be necessary as an expression of moral outrage or, if well designed and implemented, may raise the cost to Moscow of taking foreign policy decisions inimical to the West. When aimed at internal Soviet problems, they may extract an ad hoc concession favorable to a particular individual, faction, or cause with which a Western government or interest group sympathizes. But this is not the same as promoting systemic reform. If moderate reforms occur within the system, as predicted in this essay, this will be essentially the result of trends and pressures internal to Soviet society. The most important external pressure has been the one underscored by the challenge from the Reagan administration, that is, the general pressure to compete with societies organized on the basis of capitalist economics and democratic politics.

When it comes to concrete issues such as those considered in the present chapter, Western leverage, at least in the short term, is not great. Foreign governments are in no position today to dictate Soviet domestic policy on questions like human rights, as American legislators tried futilely to do with the Jackson-Vanik amendment. Nor have they any right to ignore the unintended consequences of trying to intervene in this fashion. In the case of Soviet Jews, the United States, while helping some to get exit visas, has in effect made the rest of those wishing to leave hostage to changes in U.S.-Soviet relations over which they have even less control than they originally had over Kremlin decisions. On a cultural issue like the current controversy among Soviet writers and literary bureaucrats over whether to fully recognize the work of Boris Pasternak, one can hardly think of anything that would be of less help to those working for change in Moscow than Western threats of punitive measures unless Pasternak is rehabilitated.

The outlook for creative use of affirmative rather than punitive measures on the part of the West is somewhat better. Hard but necessary to accept is the reality that system changes of deep significance gestate over long periods. To alter attitudes and values takes generations; they cannot be reformed from year to year or from one Western election campaign to another. It must also be realized that carrots from the West can sometimes be as helpful to Soviet counter-reformers as to reformers. While Gorbachev is probably as reform-minded a General Secretary as we are likely to get, the fact remains that we have no direct control over the internal politics of which he is a part and little indirect influence over decisions about how to use benefits taken from negotiations with foreign governments.

The ultimate Western resource for influencing Soviet society is not integrated circuits, Iowa corn, or gas turbines but the slow-acting magnet of Western culture, based on a belief in the sovereignty of the individual. It is a tool that by its very nature resists positive manipulation by governments. The state, to be sure, can take negative action against it. Every Russian government from Peter the Great in the early eighteenth century to Brezhnev in the 1970s has sought to do so, drawing on Western science and industry while guarding against value transfer. We simply do not know whether the present Soviet leadership, and the ones that follow, can successfully prolong the effort. What we can infer from experience is that it is conditions of political and military détente that give the greatest advantage to the individual. A less polarized East-West climate gives freer play to those irreverent forces—in literature, modern music, sport, the laboratory, and elsewhere—that celebrate the person's right to think and act for himself.

Third, we should accept that addressing Soviet foreign behavior directly is more important than doing so indirectly by way of Soviet society. No Western government will want to renounce completely attempting in specific cases to restrain Soviet foreign conduct by angling incentives at carefully targeted sections of the Soviet bureaucracy or society. But this must be done without emotion and with only the soberest expectations of success.

The point can be illustrated by the much-discussed area of foreign trade. Here the starting point for Western policy calculations must be the fact that imports come to a mere 5 percent of Soviet GNP, with those from the developed Western nations accounting for a declining share, only about 1.4 percent in 1985. Imports from the United States, by far the most militant Western country when it comes to economic sanctions, represent little more than one-tenth of a percentage point of the Soviet total. The problems are not confined to the low Soviet dependence on external trade, for economic penalties turn out to be a two-edged sword. One study has concluded that the 1980–81 U.S. grain embargo caused a loss of $11.4 billion in output of goods and services on the American side, and it has been estimated that even the relatively small volume of U.S. commerce with the Soviet Union keeps approximately 60,000 Americans employed.[66] As the 1981–82 attempt to deny the Soviets equipment for oil and gas transmission and refining showed, it is enormously difficult to get the members of an uncoerced alliance to agree on concerted sanctions. And Western actions, finally, can have unanticipated and disagreeable effects on the Soviets themselves. "Rather than force changes in Soviet foreign-policy behavior, the economic sanctions of the 1980s have aroused Soviet anxieties about the security implications of East-West commerce, and may have slowed the expansion of Soviet reliance on Western goods and technology."[67]

The more sweeping the projected effect on the Soviet system, the less likely that effect is to be achieved by deliberate Western policy. Whatever our admiration for those who oppose the Soviet regime from within, our interests give us no alternative to dealing sensibly with it as it exists. George Kennan, the dean of American Sovietologists, speaks the truth with his usual eloquence:

> American sympathies are, of course, engaged in behalf of people who fall afoul of any great political police system. This neither requires nor deserves any concealment. But, if what we are talking about is the official interrelationship of great governments, a choice must be made between the interests of democratization in Russia and the interests of world peace. In the face of this choice, there can be only one answer. Democracy is a matter of tradition, of custom, of what people are used to, of what they understand and respect. It is not something that can be suddenly grafted onto an unprepared people—particularly not from outside, and particularly not by precept, preaching, and pressure rather than by example. It is not a concept familiar to the mass of the Russian people; and whoever subordinates the interests of world peace to the chimera of an early democratization of the Soviet Union will assuredly sacrifice the first of those values without promoting the second. By the nature of things, democratization not only can but must wait; world peace cannot.[68]

Fourth, internal factors make moderation in Soviet foreign behavior more likely but not absolutely necessary. The political succession of the 1980s has helped prompt a preliminary Soviet reevaluation of certain of the more unsuccessful and self-defeating external policies followed by the Brezhnev leadership. Elite competition and the continuation of generational change, combined with economic difficulties, greater openness about systemic problems, and the demands of effecting even limited domestic reform, add to the attractiveness from the Politburo's point of view of a less assertive and confrontational foreign policy in the years ahead. There are sound and logical reasons for the Soviets to be more accommodating in dealings with the industrial democracies and to resist new undertakings abroad that might divert scarce resources from more pressing domestic tasks.

Western leaders would be fooling themselves, however, were they to take the extra step of thinking that no concessions were required on their part. For one thing, the Politburo, in seeking to improve Soviet foreign relations, has more than one option to choose from and is under no compulsion to go for that preferred by any one foreign country, be it the United States or a lesser power. Gorbachev seems more conscious than previous Soviet leaders of the possibilities of courting Western Europe and Japan in preference to the Americans. The recoil against Maoist dogma in China also gives him more scope for maneuver in relations with that country than any Soviet boss has had in a quarter-century. Financially, the Soviets could recoup at least a decent fraction of what they stand to gain from détente with the United States by mending fences with the Chinese and demobilizing some of the fifty lavishly equiped divisions stationed along their mutual border since the late 1960s. It was this that Gorbachev dangled before Peking in his July 1986 Vladivostok speech.

By the same token, there is no iron requirement for the Soviets to modify their foreign policy for domestic reasons. Partial domestic reform, while making certain shifts in foreign conduct attractive, could at least be attempted without them. Failure to chop the military budget, to take that one example, would make economic reform more difficult but not impossible, and by keeping resource use taut it arguably would make some other aspects of economic reform more imperative. Further to the same point, a steady-state or even a leaner military establishment, were that to be accomplished, would not dictate a more conciliatory foreign policy. In the Third World, at least, the Kremlin (like the White House) could find ways to use stable or smaller forces more efficiently and aggressively. I am not predicting that this will happen, merely pointing out the possibility.

The USSR is not strong enough to keep on piling up costly foreign commitments or to want to speed up the arms race, but it is strong enough to persevere with most of its existing commitments. Awareness of Soviet liabilities must not blind us to Soviet assets. The USSR is still the largest country on the globe and ranks first in the size of its army, second or third in economic strength (depending on how the Japanese economy is measured), and third in population. The Soviet bear may have an ache in its belly and a limp in its gait. This still leaves it a very big bear, with teeth and claws and a tough hide to match. It is far from being crippled, and, if cornered, it will be dangerous.

Fifth, we should realize the enormity of the domestic and foreign policy choices Moscow has to make by five years from now. The regime's shift in domestic strategy has been incomplete and tentative. Gorbachev faces, among other things, intertwined dilemmas about personnel and policy that cannot be postponed much beyond the turn of the 1990s. The inconsistencies in his program as initially enunciated will have come out into the open by then. He will have to decide whether to try to renew the leadership group that cohered around him during the succession struggle, to move ahead with deeper and more daring economic reforms, to allow the opening up of the media to continue, and to embark on a new and costly phase of modernization of Soviet military forces. These choices cannot help but be entangled with foreign policy decisions. While policy toward the Soviets' volatile East European empire and toward the developing countries will not be unimportant, the most momentous decisions will concern relations with the West and arms control.

These imminent Soviet choices intersect with events in the United States, where the presidential and congressional elections of 1988 will set a general framework for a post-Reagan foreign policy. Of the many specifics that concern the Soviet Union, the most urgent by far is security and arms control, where SDI, with its prospect of putting directed energy weapons in space, has assumed a special place in Soviet fears since its announcement in 1983. Soviet concern about SDI is well-founded, not because in the version now foreseen it will soon negate their nuclear deterrent, but because it embodies already advanced but rapidly developing technologies that may have a significant impact on the superpower balance either singly or in combination. The Soviet government would be foolish were it not to be alarmed at the prospect of a defense system being put in orbit over their territory, though a variety of countermeasures to this (decoys, reduction of burn-time of ICBM boosters, and so forth) are within their technical means. Probably more worrisome to them is the possibility that SDI research will issue in laser and other weaponry capable of offensive use in and from space, and thereby induce an enormous new spiral in the arms race.[69]

If American politics and American-Soviet negotiations have not between them brought about at least an interim deal on nuclear armaments by the end of the 1980s, Gorbachev will be in an unenviable and perhaps untenable predicament. Having bought a breathing space in the mid-1980s for negotiations and internal "acceleration," using the argument that the U.S. threat is long-range and qualitative, he will not have as easy a time with his military establishment and civilian hard-liners during the bargaining over the Thirteenth Five-Year Plan, covering 1991–95, if no easing of tensions is in sight. This will be especially so if American development of SDI and related technologies continues unabated, and worst of all if the United States proceeds with preliminary deployments over Soviet objections and pulls out of the ABM Treaty in order to do so.

If all-out mobilization against the United States is ordered, the consequences for Soviet internal affairs will be profound. The political and cultural climate will surely harden, and even limited economic reform may go down the drain. In this case there is a real chance that Mikhail Gorbachev, too, will go down the drain, replaced by a hawk—or, as it was said of Stalin, a wolf—more suited to the times.

Sixth, we should take advantage of current circumstances that are highly favorable to developing a less dangerous relationship with the Soviet Union. The relationship between the USSR and the Western countries has always contained elements of both competition and collaboration. Both were present during the détente of the 1970s, and the coexistence of the two is inescapable in future. It is the blend and balance of the two ingredients that is all-important.

The West is probably in a better position today than at any time since Nikita Khrushchev was leader to work toward safer and more satisfying relations. The accession of new Soviet leaders, their evident determination to make internal modernization their highest priority, and their stated desire for some kind of modus vivendi with the West provide the opening. The Soviet regime is responding in part to unfavorable changes in the international "correlation of forces," as they call it. But it is also acutely mindful of domestic needs. It is not in our interest to ignore these Soviet perceptions or to try, in what surely would be an act of hubris, to exploit Soviet internal difficulties to force Moscow to beat a wide retreat abroad.

While our main concern has to be with Soviet external behavior, Western moderates should be willing to discuss cooperative measures that play to encouraging trends within the Soviet system. One such area is trade. Here it is the Soviets who must take the initiative by following up on Gorbachev's hints of greater integration into the world economy. If they do so, and back up verbal declarations by a willingness to go after new export markets and seek foreign credits, the OECD countries should take the Soviets up on the offer. They should seek means of cushioning economic cooperation from the inescapable ups and downs of political relations.

While the nonmarket nature of the Soviet economy makes adherence to GATT problematic, participation in the World Bank and IMF, as the Soviets are already allowing their East European allies to do, is worth at least exploring with an open mind. Western conservatives in the past spoke wisely, if perhaps prematurely, about the restraining effect of economic interdependence. It is not out of character for Western liberals to wager on the civilizing effect of economic exchange. In both cases, the bet may bring substantial winnings, but only if stuck with through thick and thin.

In a second field, information and knowledge exchange, technology and Gorbachev's policy of relative internal openness already give the West an opportunity. Aside from foreign radio broadcasting to the USSR, to which the Kremlin is not likely to give official assent, and such traditional vehicles as reciprocal stays by scholars and students, a good number of innovative proposals for mutually agreeable interchange have recently been floated. The Soviets seem receptive, for instance, to cooperative research on global problems such as pollution, the "greenhouse effect," urban and regional planning, and energy. Soviet scientists have applauded the American astronomer Carl Sagan's proposal of a joint U.S.-Soviet manned expedition to Mars. Gorbachev suggested after Chernobyl' that the International Atomic Energy Agency be upgraded and given the right to inspect nuclear power plants for safety hazards and that more demanding standards for prompt reporting of accidents be agreed on. All these possibilities deserve investigation, for their practical benefits but also for their symbolic value in diminishing Russian and Soviet insularity.

The West's most important means for addressing Soviet power are the same today as they have always been: economic strength, sufficient military power, and intelligent use of the traditional instruments of statecraft and balance of power. Neither the United States nor any of the other Western democracies has any objective reason to fear that it cannot compete with the Soviet Union. Opposing Soviet aggression and balancing Soviet strength are necessary elements of Western strategy, and they should be undertaken calmly and honestly, in a spirit that neither trivializes the Soviet challenge nor fantasizes it to be the source of all that ails the world. Equally vital as a component of a reasoned policy toward the USSR are negotiations, with the give-and-take that characterize all politics. This is all the more so today, when the possibilities of agreement have improved.

In the 1970s it was the Soviets who were more open than the United States to the charge of seeking short-term competitive advantage at the expense of long-term cooperation. It was Russian leaders who at times seemed to see individual weapons systems as ends in themselves, who mistook America's post-Vietnam malaise for evidence of an irreversible decline, and who applied outmoded concepts to a changing world. Today it is the duty of the leadership of the United States to see to it that their actions do not expose them to the same indictment, with results that would be equally damaging to the interests of their own country and every other.

Appendix: A Soviet Leadership Chronology, 1976–86

The Politburo, or Political Bureau of the Central Committee of the Communist Party of the Soviet Union, is the dominant policy-setting body in the Soviet system. Charged under the party rules with "leadership of the party's work" in between plenary sessions of the Central Committee, it in fact makes or confirms all major decisions at its weekly meetings. The members of the Politburo, who have numbered anywhere from ten to sixteen over the last decade, all hold full-time executive positions in the party or state bureaucracies, most of them in Moscow but a few in the provinces. In addition to members, the Politburo has several candidate or non-voting members, some of whom eventually get promoted to full membership. The much larger Central Committee (the 1986 version has 307 voting members), elected at five-year intervals by a party congress packed with supporters of the leadership, meets only several times a year. It normally acts more as a sounding board than as a maker of decisions, but the fact that it must pass on all changes in the top leadership gives it considerable potential power.

The Central Committee Secretariat ranks next to the Politburo in political status. The rules assign it the function of "leadership of routine work, mainly in personnel selection and organizing the verification of implementation." Its members, called "secretaries of the Central Committee," have ranged between nine and twelve in total since 1976, and they are all full-time employees of the party based in Moscow. They meet as a group once a week, and between times each heads or supervises one or more of the Secretariat's twenty-odd administrative departments. Several of the secretaries—three at the present time—are simultaneously members of the Politburo, which gives them unique double-standing.

The most powerful individual by far is the General Secretary, who is the party's chief executive and spokesman and chairs meetings of both the Politburo and the Secretariat. He is also, by convention if not legal right, Chairman of the Defense Council, a state body responsible for national security. Finally, General Secretaries Brezhnev (in 1977), Andropov, and Chernenko—but not, so far, Gorbachev—have had themselves named titular head of state, or Chairman of the Presidium of the Supreme Soviet. This job, which involves signing decrees, receiving foreign statesmen, and the like, is currently performed by Andrei Gromyko, who is also a member of the party's Politburo.

The Starting Point: the Leadership Selected after the Twenty-fifth Party Congress, March 5, 1976

Politburo Members

L. I. Brezhnev (b. 1906)—General Secretary
Yu. V. Andropov (b. 1914)—Chief of KGB
A. A. Grechko (b. 1902)—Defense Minister
V. V. Grishin (b. 1914)—First secretary of Moscow city party committee
A. A. Gromyko (b. 1909)—Foreign Minister
A. P. Kirilenko (b. 1906)—Central Committee (CC) secretary, responsible for general economic coordination
A. N. Kosygin (b. 1904)—Chairman of Council of Ministers
F. D. Kulakov (b. 1918)—CC secretary, responsible for agriculture
D. A. Kunayev (b. 1912)—First secretary of Kazakhstan party committee
K. T. Mazurov (b. 1914)—First Deputy Chairman of Council of Ministers
A. Ya. Pel'she (b. 1899)—Chairman of Party Control Committee
N. V. Podgornyi (b. 1903)—Chairman of Presidium of Supreme Soviet
G. V. Romanov (b. 1923)—First secretary of Leningrad oblast party committee
V. V. Shcherbitskii (b. 1918)—First secretary of Ukrainian party committee
M. A. Suslov (b. 1902)—CC secretary, responsible for ideology
D. F. Ustinov (b. 1908)—CC secretary, responsible for military and police sector

Politburo Candidate Members

G. A. Aliyev (b. 1923)—First secretary of Azerbaidzhan party committee
P. N. Demichev (b. 1918)—Culture Minister

P. M. Masherov (b. 1918)—First secretary of Belorussian party committee

B. N. Ponomarev (b. 1905)—CC secretary, responsible for relations with non-ruling communist parties

Sh. R. Rashidov (b. 1917)—First secretary of Uzbekistan party committee

M. S. Solomentsev (b. 1913)—Chairman of RSFSR Council of Ministers

Secretariat

Brezhnev

Kirilenko

Kulakov

Suslov

Ustinov

Ponomarev

K. U. Chernenko (b. 1911)—responsible for Brezhnev's office, some personnel matters

V. I. Dolgikh (b. 1924)—responsible for heavy industry

I. V. Kapitonov (b. 1915)—responsible for party organization

K. F. Katushev (b. 1927)—responsible for relations with ruling communist parties

M. V. Zimyanin (b. 1914)—responsible for internal propaganda, culture, science and education

April 26, 1976 Defense Minister Grechko dies. Replaced April 29 by CC secretary Ustinov.

October 26, 1976 Ya. P. Ryabov (b. 1928), party first secretary in Sverdlovsk oblast, replaces Ustinov as CC secretary for military and police sector.

March 16, 1977 Katushev demoted to Deputy Chairman of Council of Ministers and Soviet representative on CMEA.

May 24, 1977 Podgornyi removed from Politburo. Katushev formally removed from Secretariat. K.V. Rusakov (b. 1909), Brezhnev's assistant, replaces Katushev as CC secretary for relations with ruling parties.

June 16, 1977 Brezhnev replaces Podgornyi as Chairman of Presidium of Supreme Soviet.

October 3, 1977 Chernenko and V. V. Kuznetsov, First Deputy Chairman of Presidium of Supreme Soviet (b. 1901), made candidate members of Politburo.

July 17, 1978 Kulakov dies.

November 27, 1978 Chernenko made full member of Politburo. Mazurov removed from Politburo. M. S. Gorbachev (b. 1931), party first secretary of Stavropol' krai, succeeds Kulakov as CC secretary for agriculture. E. A. Shevardnadze (b. 1928), party first secretary of Georgian republic, and N.

A. Tikhonov (b. 1905), a First Deputy Chairman of Council of Ministers, made candidate members of Politburo. Mazurov removed from Council of Ministers November 28, making Tikhonov Kosygin's top deputy.

April 17, 1979 Ryabov removed from Secretariat, demoted to first deputy chairman of Gosplan (State Planning Committee).

November 27, 1979 Tikhonov made full member of Politburo. Gorbachev made candidate member of Politburo.

October 4, 1980 Masherov dies. Succeeded October 16 as first secretary of Belorussian party committee by T. Ya. Kiselev (b. 1917), a Deputy Chairman of Council of Ministers.

October 21, 1980 Gorbachev made full member of Politburo. Kiselev made candidate member of Politburo.

October 23, 1980 Tikhonov replaces Kosygin as Chairman of Council of Ministers. Kosygin resigns from Politburo for health reasons.

December 18, 1980 Kosygin dies.

March 3, 1981 Twenty-sixth Party Congress is first since 1927 to close without any change in Politburo or Secretariat.

January 25, 1982 Suslov dies.

May 24, 1982 Andropov replaces Suslov as CC Secretary for ideology. CC secretary Dolgikh made candidate member of Politburo.

May 26, 1982 V. V. Fedorchuk (b. 1918), head of Ukrainian branch of KGB, replaces Andropov as chief of KGB.

November 10, 1982 Brezhnev dies.

November 12, 1982 Andropov appointed General Secretary.

November 22, 1982 Kirilenko retired from Politburo and Secretariat. Aliyev made full member of Politburo. N. I. Ryzhkov (b. 1929), a first deputy chairman of Gosplan, made CC secretary for economic coordination.

November 23, 1982 Aliyev made First Deputy Chairman of Council of Ministers.

November 29, 1982 Transportation Minister I. G. Pavlovskii (b. 1922) is first government minister to be dismissed by Andropov.

December 17, 1982 N. A. Shchelokov (b. 1910) removed as Interior Minister, replaced by KGB chief Fedorchuk. Fedorchuk replaced in KGB by V. M. Chebrikov (b. 1923), a deputy chief of KGB since 1968.

January 12, 1983 Kiselev dies. Succeeded as first secretary of Belorussian party committee by N. N. Slyun'kov (b. 1929), a deputy chairman of Gosplan.

March 24, 1983 Foreign Minister Gromyko acquires additional title of First Deputy Chairman of Council of Ministers.

March 28, 1983 N. V. Bannikov (b. 1914) of Irkutsk oblast is first major provincial party leader to be retired by Andropov.

April 1983 (exact date unknown) Ye. K. Ligachev (b. 1920), first secretary of Tomsk oblast party committee, named head of Central Committee Secretariat's organizational-party work department, replacing Kapitonov.

May 29, 1983 Pel'she dies.

June 15, 1983 Romanov moved from Leningrad and added to Secretariat, responsible for military and police sector. V. I. Vorotnikov (b. 1926), first secretary of Krasnodar krai party committee, made candidate member of Politburo. Solomentsev succeeds Pel'she as chairman of Party Control Commission.

June 16, 1983 Andropov named Chairman of Presidium of Supreme Soviet.

June 25, 1983 Vorotnikov replaces Solomentsev as Chairman of RSFSR Council of Ministers.

October 31, 1983 Rashidov dies. Succeeded as first secretary of Uzbekistan party committee by I. B. Usmankhodzhayev (b. 1930), an Uzbek functionary.

December 26, 1983 Solomentsev and Vorotnikov made full members of Politburo. KGB chief Chebrikov made candidate member of Politburo. Ligachev made CC secretary for party organization. CC secretary Kapitonov loses all responsibility for organization and personnel, assigned to light industry.

February 9, 1984 Andropov dies.

February 13, 1984 Chernenko appointed General Secretary.

April 11, 1984 Chernenko named Chairman of Presidium of Supreme Soviet.

December 20, 1984 Ustinov dies. Succeeded as Defense Minister December 22 by his long-time first deputy, Marshal S. L. Sokolov (b. 1911).

March 10, 1985 Chernenko dies.

March 11, 1985 Gorbachev appointed General Secretary.

April 23, 1985 Chebrikov, Ligachev, and Ryzhkov made full members of Politburo. Defense Minister Sokolov made candidate member of Politburo. RSFSR Agriculture Minister V. P. Nikonov (b. 1929) made CC secretary responsible for agriculture.

June 1985 (exact date unknown) G. P. Razumovskii (b. 1936), party first secretary of Krasnodar krai, succeeds Ligachev as head of CC department of organizational-party work.

July 1, 1985 Romanov removed from Politburo and Secretariat, retired. Shevardnadze made full member of Politburo. Regional party first secretaries B. N. Yel'tsin (b. 1931) of Sverdlovsk and L. N. Zaikov (b. 1923) of Leningrad made CC secretaries, responsible for construction and military and police sector respectively.

July 2, 1985 Gromyko named Chairman of Presidium of Supreme Soviet. Shevardnadze replaces Gromyko as Foreign Minister.

September 27, 1985 Ryzhkov replaces Tikhonov as Chairman of Council of Ministers.

October 15, 1985 Tikhonov removed from Politburo, retired. Ryzhkov released from Secretariat because of appointment to replace Tikhonov. N. F.

Talyzin (b. 1929), new First Deputy Chairman of Council of Ministers and chairman of Gosplan, named candidate member of Politburo.

December 24, 1985 Grishin replaced as first secretary of Moscow city party committee by Yel'tsin.

February 18, 1986 Grishin removed from Politburo, retired. Yel'tsin made a candidate member of Politburo, released from Secretariat because of appointment to replace Grishin. CC secretary Rusakov retired.

March 6, 1986 New Central Committee elected by Twenty-seventh Party Congress makes more changes. Zaikov added to Politburo. Belorussian party leader Slyun'kov and Leningrad's Yu. F. Solov'ev (b. 1925) made candidate members of Politburo. Politburo candidates Kuznetsov and Ponomarev (also a CC secretary) retired. Kapitonov removed from Secretariat, named chairman of Central Auditing Commission. Five new CC secretaries appointed: A. P. Biryukova (b. 1929), A. F. Dobrynin (b. 1919), V. A. Medvedev (b. 1929), A. N. Yakovlev (b. 1923), and Razumovskii.

June 19, 1986 Demichev removed as Culture Minister, succeeds Kuznetsov as First Deputy Chairman of Presidium of Supreme Soviet.

The End Point: The Leadership as of July 1, 1986

Politburo Members

M. S. Gorbachev (b. 1931)—General Secretary

G. A. Aliyev (b. 1923)—First Deputy Chairman of Council of Ministers

V. M. Chebrikov (b. 1923)—Chief of KGB

A. A. Gromyko (b. 1909)—Chairman of Presidium of Supreme Soviet

D. A. Kunayev (b. 1912)—First secretary of Kazakhstan party committee

Ye. K. Ligachev (b. 1920)—CC secretary, with oversight of ideology and party organization

N. I. Ryzhkov (b. 1929)—Chairman of Council of Ministers

E. A. Shevardnadze (b. 1928)—Foreign Minister

V. V. Shcherbitskii (b. 1918)—First secretary of Ukrainian party committee

M. S. Solomentsev (b. 1913)—Chairman of Party Control Commission

V. I. Vorotnikov (b. 1926)—Chairman of RSFSR Council of Ministers

L. N. Zaikov (b. 1923)—CC secretary, responsible for military and police sector and economic coordination

Politburo Candidate Members

P. N. Demichev (b. 1918)—First Deputy Chairman of Presidium of Supreme Soviet

V. I. Dolgikh (b. 1924)—CC secretary, responsible for heavy industry

N. N. Slyun'kov (b. 1929)—First secretary of Belorussian party committee

S. L. Sokolov (b. 1911)—Defense Minister

Yu. F. Solov'ev (b. 1925)—First secretary of Leningrad oblast party committee

N. F. Talyzin (b. 1929)—First Deputy Chairman of Council of Ministers, chairman of Gosplan

B. N. Yel'tsin (b. 1931)—First secretary of Moscow city party committee

Secretariat

Gorbachev

Ligachev

Zaikov

Dolgikh

A. P. Biryukova (b. 1929)—responsible for light industry and consumer services

A. F. Dobrynin (b. 1919)—responsible for relations with non-ruling communist parties and more generally for foreign policy

V. A. Medvedev (b. 1929)—responsible for relations with ruling communist parties

V. P. Nikonov (b. 1929)—responsible for agriculture

G. P. Razumovskii (b. 1936)—responsible for party organization

A. N. Yakovlev (b. 1923)—responsible for propaganda and culture

M. V. Zimyanin (b. 1914)—responsible for science and education

Notes

CHAPTER 1

1. The most explicit effort is in Chernenko's eulogy, in *Pravda*, November 13, 1982, p. 2.
2. L. I. Brezhnev, *Vospominaniya* (Memoirs) (Moscow: Politizdat, 1981), p. 16.
3. T. H. Rigby, "The Soviet Leadership: Towards a Self-Stabilizing Oligarchy?" *Soviet Studies*, 22 (October 1970), p. 175.
4. *XXV s'ezd Kommunisticheskoi partii Sovetskogo Soyuza: stenograficheskii otchet* (The 25th Congress of the Communist Party of the Soviet Union: Stenographic Record) (Moscow: Politizdat, 1976), I, 186–187.
5. *Pravda*, December 20, 1981, p. 1.
6. Vladimir Bukovsky, *To Build a Castle—My Life as a Dissenter* (New York: Viking, 1979), p. 228.
7. Bruce Parrott, *Politics and Technology in the Soviet Union* (Cambridge, Mass.: MIT Press, 1983), p. 211.
8. Quotation from Jerry F. Hough, *Soviet Leadership in Transition* (Washington, D.C.: Brookings Institution, 1980), p. 64. The calculation of Politburo turnover is my own (1.3 demotions a year under Khrushchev, 0.4 under Brezhnev).
9. L. I. Brezhnev, *Leninskim kursom: rechi i stat'i* (On the Leninist Course: Speeches and Articles) (Moscow: Politizdat, 1970–83), III, 307.
10. Robert Sharlet, "The New Soviet Constitution of 1977," in Erik P. Hoffmann and Robbin F. Laird, eds., *The Soviet Polity in the Modern Era* (New York: Aldine, 1984), p. 250.
11. Brezhnev, *Leninskim kursom*, I, 22.
12. A good summary is Stephen F. Cohen, "The Stalin Question Since Stalin," in his *Rethinking the Soviet Experience: Politics and History Since 1917* (New York: Oxford University Press, 1985), pp. 93–127.
13. See Amy W. Knight, "The Powers of the Soviet KGB," *Survey*, 25 (Summer 1980), pp. 138–155.
14. *Pravda*, May 10, 1981, p. 1.
15. I. Bagramyan, "Rol' traditsii v vospitanii molodezhi" (The Role of Tradition in the Upbringing of Youth), *Partiinaya zhizn'*, no. 24 (De-

cember 1981), p. 52.

16. Roy A. Medvedev, *On Stalin and Stalinism* (Oxford: Oxford University Press, 1979), pp. 178–182.
17. An account of the ideological debate over Russian nationalism can be found in John B. Dunlop, *The Faces of Contemporary Russian Nationalism* (Princeton: Princeton University Press, 1983), especially chaps. 9–10.
18. T. H. Rigby, "Forward From 'Who Gets What, When, How,'" *Slavic Review*, 39 (June 1979), p. 206.
19. Zhores A. Medvedev, *The Rise and Fall of T. D. Lysenko* (New York: Columbia University Press, 1969), chaps. 9–10.
20. On debates over domestic policy, see for instance Peter H. Solomon, Jr., *Soviet Criminologists and Criminal Policy: Specialists in Policy-Making* (New York: Columbia University Press, 1978); Ronald J. Hill, *Soviet Politics, Political Science and Reform* (Oxford: Martin Robertson, 1980); Thane Gustafson, *Reform in Soviet Politics: Lessons of Recent Policies on Land and Water* (Cambridge: Cambridge University Press, 1981); Peter A. Hauslohner, "Managing the Soviet Labor Market: Politics and Policymaking Under Brezhnev," Unpub. Ph.D. thesis, University of Michigan, 1984; Archie Brown, "Political Science in the Soviet Union: A New Stage of Development," *Soviet Studies*, 36 (July 1984), pp. 317–344.
21. As one respected analyst wrote midway through the Brezhnev period, "virtually no conceivable proposal for incremental change in party policy . . . has not been aired in the Soviet press." Jerry F. Hough, "The Soviet System: Petrifaction or Pluralism?" *Problems of Communism*, 21 (March–April 1972), p. 31.
22. Paul Cocks, "Rethinking the Organizational Weapon: The Soviet System in a Systems Age," *World Politics*, 32 (January 1980), p. 251.
23. The serious intentions of the 1965 reform, and the lengths to which Brezhnev had to go to undo it, are emphasized in Hauslohner, chaps. 3–4.
24. Richard J. Vidmer, "Soviet Studies of Organization and Management: A 'Jungle' of Competing Views," *Slavic Review*, 49 (Fall 1981), p. 409. Computerization is described in Martin Cave, *Computers and Economic Planning: The Soviet Experience* (Cambridge: Cambridge University Press, 1980).
25. The example of the agricultural links is recounted in Alexander Yanov, *The Drama of the Soviet 1960s: A Lost Reform*, Research Series, no. 56 (Berkeley: Institute of International Affairs, University of California, 1984). The link experiment's main spokesman, Ivan Khudenko, died in prison in 1974. His chief advocate within the Soviet elite was Gennadi Voronov, a Politburo member retired in 1973, but, by Yanov's account, he was also supported by Dinmukhammed Kunayev, a

Brezhnev protégé in the Politburo.

26. See especially Darrell L. Slider, "Social Experiments and Soviet Policy-Making," Unpub. Ph.D. thesis, Yale University, 1981.
27. Jane P. Shapiro, "Soviet Consumer Policy in the 1970s: Plan and Performance," in Donald R. Kelley, ed., *Soviet Politics in the Brezhnev Era* (New York: Praeger, 1980), p. 106.
28. Gertrude E. Schroeder, "Soviet Living Standards: Achievements and Prospects," in Joint Economic Committee, U. S. Congress, *Soviet Economy in the 1980s: Problems and Prospects* (Washington, D.C.: GPO, 1983), II, 370.
29. There is some controversy over this point. One commonly used index for the earnings distribution, the so-called decile ratio, shows greater inequality after 1968; comparison of the earnings of workers with white-collar personnel in industry, a better measure, shows greater equality. See Michael Ellman, "A Note on the Distribution of Earnings in the USSR Under Brezhnev," *Slavic Review*, 39 (December 1980), pp. 666–671; Alec Nove, "Income Distribution in the USSR: A Possible Explanation of Some Recent Data," *Soviet Studies*, 34 (April 1982), pp. 286–288; Jerry F. Hough, "Soviet Succession: Issues and Personalities," *Problems of Communism*, 31 (September-October 1982), pp. 25-26. A recent Soviet press account (*Pravda*, February 3, 1986, p. 3) refers matter-of-factly to how "in the 1970s the course was followed of leveling out and averaging pay."
30. Gustafson, *Reform in Soviet Politics*, p. 52.
31. Angel O. Bryne, James E. Cole, Thomas Brickerton, and Anton F. Malish, "U.S.-U.S.S.R. Grain Trade," in Joint Economic Committee, *Soviet Economy in the 1980s*, II, 64.
32. Brezhnev's change of heart and the related debate are traced in detail in Parrott, *Politics and Technology in the Soviet Union*, chaps. 5–6.
33. Even with respect to dissent, it could be argued that the Brezhnev approach was not much harsher than Khrushchev's and was more predictable. According to a historian formerly involved in the movement, the landmark Sinyavskii-Daniel trial of 1966 showed that "the authorities refrained from extrajudicial repressions, from torture or beatings during the investigation, from ascribing terrorist intentions to those they accused of 'anti-Soviet agitation,' and, consequently, from capital punishment for verbal 'anti-Sovietism.' In comparison with practices under Stalin, this restraint was a considerable improvement." When this and subsequent trials made clear the penalty to be exacted, "there were more than a few who were not deterred by this cost from their desire to speak the truth aloud." Ludmilla Alexeyeva, *Soviet Dissent: Contemporary Movements for National, Religious, and Human Rights* (Middletown, Connecticut: Wesleyan University Press, 1985), p. 277.

34. Maurice Friedberg, "Cultural and Intellectual Life," in Robert F. Byrnes, ed., *After Brezhnev: Sources of Soviet Conduct in the 1980s* (Bloomington: Indiana University Press, 1983), pp. 278–279.
35. S. Frederick Starr, *Red and Hot: The Fate of Jazz in the Soviet Union 1917–1980* (New York: Oxford University Press, 1983), pp. 318, 320.
36. This was the phrase used by Zbigniew Brzezinski in his influential article, "The Soviet Political System: Transformation or Degeneration?" *Problems of Communism*, 15 (January–February 1966), pp. 1–15.
37. Brezhnev, *Leninskim kursom*, VI, 245–246, 249.
38. Gertrude E. Schroeder, "The Slowdown in Soviet Industry, 1976–1982," *Soviet Economy*, 1 (January–March 1985), p. 46.
39. Yuri Brezhnev, born in 1933, spent most of the 1960s as a Soviet trade representative in Sweden, and was a Deputy Minister of Foreign Trade from 1976. Churbanov made his career in the political organs of the Interior Ministry, became a deputy minister in 1977, and was made First Deputy Minister of the Interior in February 1980, after his predecessor was killed in the Soviet invasion of Afghanistan.
40. In November 1978 Gorbachev, three years younger than Ryabov, was appointed to the Secretariat, thus displacing Ryabov as the youngest member of the leadership. Ryabov's demotion in April 1979 has been linked by some Kremlinologists to the declining fortunes of his apparent patron, Andrei Kirilenko. But Katushev, a Secretariat member since 1968, was not thought to be connected to any such figure. If Brezhnev so mistrusted younger men, it might have been only his death in 1982 that saved Gorbachev from following Katushev and Ryabov.
41. Brezhnev in his memoirs describes defending Tikhonov, then director of the Nikopol' Piping Works, from an irate ministerial superior. L. I. Brezhnev, *Vozrozhdeniye* (Rebirth) (Moscow: Politizdat, 1978), pp. 50–51.
42. For a well-documented example, see Thane Gustafson, "The Origins of the Soviet Oil Crisis, 1970–1985," *Soviet Economy,* 1 (April-June 1985), pp. 103–135.
43. Paul Cocks, "Administrative Reform and Soviet Politics," in Joint Economic Committee, *Soviet Economy in the 1980s*, I, 47.
44. A. G. Aganbegyan in *Literaturnaya gazeta*, May 4, 1977, p. 11.
45. Brezhnev, *Leninskim kursom*, V, 527, and VII, 254.
46. Ibid., VIII, 210.
47. Ibid., VII, 533; *XXVI s'ezd Kommunisticheskoi partii Sovetskogo Soyuza: stenograficheskii otchet* (The 26th Congress of the Communist Party of the Soviet Union: Stenographic Record) (Moscow: Politizdat, 1981), I, 67; *Pravda*, October 28, 1982, p. 1.
48. The most nuanced discussion of this is in Hauslohner, pp. 661–670.

49. All references to the revised party program are to the final edition as printed in *Pravda*, March 7, 1986.

CHAPTER 2

1. *Pravda*, April 23, 1982, p. 2.
2. Ibid., February 26, 1986, p. 10.
3. Ibid., February 14, 1986, p. 2.
4. Ibid., December 22, 1982, p. 2.
5. Murray Feshbach, "The Soviet Union: Population Trends and Dilemmas," *Population Bulletin*, 37 (August 1982), p. 30.
6. Statistics and background information in this paragraph taken from Stephen Rapawy and Godfrey Baldwin, "Demographic Trends in the Soviet Union: 1950–2000," in Joint Economic Committee, U.S. Congress, *Soviet Economy in the 1980s: Problems and Prospects* (Washington, D.C.: GPO, 1983), II, 265–296; Christopher Davis and Murray Feshbach, "Rising Infant Mortality in the U.S.S.R. in the 1970s," *International Population Reports*, series P-95, no. 74 (Washington, D.C.: U.S. Bureau of the Census, Foreign Demographic Analysis Division, 1980); John C. Dutton, Jr., "Causes of Soviet Adult Mortality Increases," *Soviet Studies*, 33 (October 1981), pp. 548–559; Ellen Jones and Fred W. Grupp, "Infant Mortality Trends in the Soviet Union," *Population and Development Review*, 9 (June 1983), pp. 213–246. On infant mortality, one new study argues that all of the rise may prove to be accounted for by a combination of improved registration and changes in Soviet definitions of live births and infant deaths. Barbara A. Anderson and Brian D. Silver, "Infant Mortality in the Soviet Union: Regional Differences and Measurement Issues," Paper presented at Annual Meeting of Population Association of America, San Francisco, April 1986.
7. Growth figures are taken from revised Central Intelligence Agency measures, based on 1982 prices, as given in Central Intelligence Agency and Defense Intelligence Agency, *The Soviet Economy Under a New Leader*, Paper submitted to Subcommittee on Economic Resources, Competitiveness, and Security Economics of the Joint Economic Committee, U.S. Congress (March 19, 1986). Earlier U.S. government statistics, based on 1970 prices, showed somewhat higher growth rates.
8. P. Pavlov, "Postizheniye istiny (razmyshleniya pered s'ezdom)" (Comprehending the Truth [Reflections Before the Congress]), *Planovoye khozyaistvo*, no. 11 (November 1985), p. 77.
9. Joint Economic Committee, U.S. Congress, *USSR: Measures of Economic Growth and Development, 1950–80* (Washington, D.C.:

GPO, 1982), pp. 20, 22; Gertrude E. Schroeder, *Consumption in the USSR: An International Comparison*, Study prepared for Joint Economic Committee, U.S. Congress (Washington, D.C.: GPO, 1981), p. 18. Schroeder rated the Soviet standard of living at 34 percent of the American level in 1976, up only 6 percent from 1955.

10. *Pravda*, February 26, 1986, p. 2.
11. See especially Janos Kornai, *Economics of Shortage* (Amsterdam: North Holland, 1980); and *Growth, Shortage and Efficiency* (Berkeley and Los Angeles: University of California Press, 1982).
12. G. Kh. Shakhnazarov, "Razvitiye lichnosti i sotsialisticheskii obraz zhizni" (Personal Development and the Socialist Way of Life), *Voprosy filosofii*, no. 11 (November 1977), p. 20.
13. Jones and Grupp, pp. 232–233.
14. Loren R. Graham, "Reasons for Studying Soviet Science: The Example of Genetic Engineering," in Linda L. Lubrano and Susan G. Solomon, eds., *The Social Context of Soviet Science* (Boulder, Colorado: Westview Press, 1980), pp. 235–236.
15. Timothy J. Colton, "Making Policy for Soviet Urban Development," Paper prepared for Annual Meeting of American Association for the Advancement of Slavic Studies, Monterey, California, September 1981.
16. This last point is made in S. Frederick Starr, *Red and Hot: The Fate of Jazz in the Soviet Union* (New York: Oxford University Press, 1983), pp. 318–319.
17. Charles E. Lindblom, *Politics and Markets: The World's Political-Economic Systems* (New York: Basic Books, 1977), chap. 5.
18. *Pravda*, April 12, 1985, p. 1.
19. Josef C. Brada, "Soviet-Western Trade and Technology Transfer: An Economic Overview," in Bruce Parrott, ed., *Trade, Technology, and Soviet-American Relations* (Bloomington: Indiana University Press, 1985), pp. 3–34.
20. Alex Beam, "Atari Bolsheviks," *Atlantic*, March 1986, p. 28.
21. *Sotsialisticheskaya industriya*, July 20, 1985, p. 2.
22. Joseph S. Berliner, *The Innovation Decision in Soviet Industry* (Cambridge, Mass.: MIT Press, 1976), p. 529.
23. A detailed analysis is in Ed A. Hewett, *Energy, Economics, and Foreign Policy in the Soviet Union* (Washington, D.C.: Brookings Institution, 1984), chap. 2.
24. Figures on working age population from V. I. Perevedentsev, "Vosproizvodstvo naseleniya i sem'ya" (Population Propagation and the Family), *Sotsiologicheskiye issledovaniya*, no. 2 (April-June 1982), p. 81. The accepted Western projections, based on somewhat different definitions, are in Murray Feshbach, "Population and Labor Force," in

Abram Bergson and Herbert S. Levine, eds., *The Soviet Economy: Toward the Year 2000* (London: George Allen & Unwin, 1983), pp. 92–101.

25. *Pravda*, February 26, 1986, p. 4.
26. Herbert S. Levine, "Possible Causes of the Deterioration of Soviet Productivity Growth in the Period 1976–80," in Joint Economic Committee, *Soviet Economy in the 1980s*, I, 154; CIA/DIA, *The Soviet Economy Under a New Leader*, Figure 3 (between p. 17 and p. 18).
27. Roman Solchanyk, "Russian Language and Soviet Politics," *Soviet Studies*, 34 (January 1982), pp. 23–42.
28. *Pravda*, December 22, 1982, p. 2.
29. Ibid., May 27, 1983, p. 1.
30. For a good example, see William Fierman, "Uzbek Feelings of Ethnicity: A Study of Attitudes Expressed in Recent Uzbek Literature," *Cahiers du Monde russe et sovietique*, 22 (April-September 1981), pp. 187–229.
31. S. Enders Wimbush, "The Russian Nationalist Backlash," *Survey*, 24 (Summer 1979), p. 37.
32. V. Z. Rogovin, "Sotsial'naya politika i yeye vliyaniye na obshchestvennye nravy" (Social Policy and its Influence on Public Mores), *Voprosy filosofii*, no. 8 (August 1978), p. 12.
33. Projections are in Feshbach, "The Soviet Union," p. 2; and same author, "Trends in the Soviet Muslim Population—Demographic Aspects," in Joint Economic Committee, *Soviet Economy in the 1980s*, II, 297–322.
34. Vera S. Dunham, *In Stalin's Time: Middleclass Values in Soviet Fiction* (Cambridge: Cambridge University Press, 1976).
35. Walter D. Connor, "Generations and Politics in the USSR," *Problems of Communism*, 24 (September–October 1975), p. 27.
36. The effect has been greatest on rural television viewers, for whom "the urban life they see portrayed on television throws into startling relief the tremendous disparities between town and country." Ellen Propper Mickiewicz, *Media and the Russian Public* (New York: Praeger Special Studies, 1980), p. 39.
37. *Pravda*, February 26, 1986, p. 4.
38. Murray Yanowitch, "Schooling and Inequalities," in Leonard Schapiro and Joseph Godson, eds., *The Soviet Worker: Illusions and Realities* (London: Macmillan, 1981), p. 134; and more generally Gail Warshofsky Lapidus, "Social Trends," in Robert Byrnes, ed., *After Brezhnev: Sources of Soviet Conduct in the 1980s* (Bloomington: Indiana University Press, 1983), pp. 200–210.
39. *Literaturnaya gazeta*, January 8, 1975, p. 11.
40. Ibid.

41. *Trud,* May 30, 1981, p. 2.
42. T. I. Zaslavskaya, "Ekonomicheskoye povedeniye i ekonomicheskoye razvitiye" (Economic Behavior and Economic Development), *Ekonomika i organizatsiya promyshlennogo proizvodstva,* no. 3 (March 1980), pp. 19–20.
43. T. I. Zaslavskaya and L. L. Rybakovskii, "Protsessy migratsii i ikh regulirovaniye v sotsialisticheskom obshchestve" (Migration Processes and their Regulation in a Socialist Society), *Sotsiologicheskiye issledovaniya,* no. 1 (January–March 1978), p. 62.
44. *Pravda,* May 17, 1985, p. 1.
45. Figures from Vladimir G. Treml, *Alcohol in the USSR: A Statistical Study* (Durham, N.C.: Duke Press Policy Studies, 1982).
46. Zaslavksaya, "Ekonomicheskoye povedeniye," pp. 28–29.
47. Igor Birman and Roger A. Clarke, "Inflation and the Money Supply in the Soviet Union," *Soviet Studies,* 37 (October 1985), pp. 494–504. See the earlier discussion in Igor Birman, "The Financial Crisis in the USSR," ibid., 32 (January 1980), pp. 84–105.
48. *Literaturnaya gazeta,* September 26, 1979, p. 10.
49. *Pravda,* June 16, 1983, p. 2. Valuable general accounts are Gregory Grossman, "The 'Second Economy' of the USSR," *Problems of Communism,* 26 (September-October 1977), pp. 25–40; Aron Katsenelinbogen, "Coloured Markets in the Soviet Union," *Soviet Studies,* 29 (January 1977), pp. 62–85; Dennis O'Hearn, "The Consumer Second Economy: Size and Effects," ibid., 32 (April 1980), pp. 218–234; Dimitri K. Simes, "The Soviet Parallel Market," *Survey,* 21 (Summer 1975), pp. 42–52.
50. *Trud,* June 6, 1985, p. 2.
51. *Sotsialisticheskaya industriya,* April 25, 1985, p. 2.
52. S. Kheinman, "XXVI s'ezd KPSS i strategiya intensifikatsii" (The 26th Congress of the CPSU and the Strategy of Intensification), *Kommunist,* no. 3 (February 1982), p. 27.
53. James R. Millar, "The Little Deal: Brezhnev's Contribution to Acquisitive Socialism," *Slavic Review,* 44 (Winter 1985), pp. 694–706.
54. *Pravda,* June 16, 1983, p. 2. There are dozens of revealing anecdotes about corruption in a book by a former Soviet lawyer: Konstantin M. Simis, *USSR: The Corrupt Society* (New York: Simon and Schuster, 1982).
55. Maurice Friedberg, "Soviet Letters Under Brezhnev," *Problems of Communism,* 29 (May–June 1980), p. 53.
56. Ludmilla Alexeyeva, *Soviet Dissent: Contemporary Movements for National, Religious, and Human Rights* (Middletown, Connecticut: Wesleyan University Press, 1985), p. 452.
57. Gertrude E. Schroeder, "The Soviet Economy on a Treadmill of 'Re-

forms,'" in Joint Economic Committee, U.S. Congress, *Soviet Economy in a Time of Change* (Washington, D.C.: GPO, 1979), I, 313.

58. S. E. Goodman, "Technology Transfer and the Development of the Soviet Computing Industry," in Parrott, *Trade, Technology, and Soviet-American Relations*, p. 132.
59. *Ekonomicheskaya gazeta*, no. 32 (August 1982), p. 7.
60. *Sotsialisticheskaya industriya*, April 26, 1985, p. 2.
61. *Sovetskaya torgovlya*, October 12, 1982, p. 2.
62. "No one in Soviet society espouses a violent revolution or *Putsch*. . . . No one wants war or a violent revolution; no one believes in the possibility of improving the present situation in this way." Alexeyeva, p. 455.
63. John Bushnell, "The 'New Soviet Man' Turns Pessimist," in Stephen F. Cohen, Alexander Rabinowitch, and Robert Sharlet, eds., *The Soviet Union since Stalin* (Bloomington: Indiana University Press, 1980), pp. 181–182, 187.
64. Brian D. Silver, "Political Beliefs of the Soviet Citizen: Sources of Support for Regime Norms," Michigan Working Papers in Soviet and East European Studies (Ann Arbor: University of Michigan, November 1985). This paper also reports unfavorable responses by the emigrants to other features of the Soviet system, such as collectivized agriculture.
65. Nancy Lubin, *Labour and Nationality in Soviet Central Asia* (Princeton: Princeton University Press, 1984), quotation at p. 226.
66. Barbara A. Anderson and Brian D. Silver, "Sex Differentials in Mortality in the Soviet Union: Regional Differences in Length of Working Life in Comparative Perspective," forthcoming in *Population Studies*, July 1986.
67. Lester C. Thurow, "A Useful Mirror," *Atlantic*, February 1983, p. 102.
68. K. Chernenko, "Leninskaya strategiya rukovodstva" (The Leninist Strategy of Leadership), *Kommunist*, no. 13 (September 1981), pp. 10–11; emphasis added.
69. *Pravda*, June 16, 1983, p. 2.
70. Jones and Grupp, pp. 233–237; Anderson and Silver, "Infant Mortality in the Soviet Union."
71. Martha Brill Olcott, "Soviet Islam and World Revolution," *World Politics*, 34 (July 1982), p. 499.
72. Ye. Goldberg, "Polneye udovletvoryat' zaprosy voinov" (To More Fully Satisfy the Troops' Concerns), *Kommunist vooruzhennykh sil*, no. 21 (November 1982), p. 32; Ye. Goldberg, "Vysokii dolg rabotnikov voyennoi torgovli" (The Lofty Duty of Military Trade Personnel), *Tyl i snabzheniye Sovetskikh Vooruzhennykh Sil*, no. 4 (April 1982), pp. 41–42.
73. See Boris Rumer, "Soviet Investment Policy: Unresolved Problems,"

Problems of Communism, 31 (September–October 1982), pp. 53–68. Actual investment did not fall as much as planned, partly because of the fear of disruptive consequences.

CHAPTER 3

1. L. I. Brezhnev, *Leninskim kursom: rechi i stat'i* (On the Leninist Course: Speeches and Articles) (Moscow: Politizdat, 1970–83), VIII, 115.
2. Burlatskii, Arbatov, and Bovin were successive heads in the 1960s of the "group of consultants" advising the Central Committee on foreign policy, with which Andropov was associated from the beginning and which worked under his direct supervision between 1964 and 1967. Burlatskii went on to senior positions in social science research and the media, acquiring somewhat of a maverick reputation. Arbatov became founding director of the Academy of Sciences' Institute of the United States and Canada, and Bovin political commentator for *Izvestiya*.
3. Arkady N. Shevchenko, *Breaking with Moscow* (New York: Ballantine, 1985), p. 315. Details of Andropov's career that reinforce this image can be found in Amy W. Knight, "Andropov: Myths and Realities," *Survey*, 28 (120) (Spring 1984), pp. 22–44.
4. Zhores Medvedev, *Ten Years After Ivan Denisovich* (London: Macmillan, 1973), p. 46.
5. *Pravda*, November 23, 1982, p. 1.
6. Among the obvious Brezhnev cronies retired or demoted under Andropov were Politburo member Kirilenko, the heads of two Central Committee departments (G. S. Pavlov and S. P. Trapeznikov), Interior Minister N. A. Shchelokov, and the head of the construction industry, I. T. Novikov.
7. "I am convinced, comrades, that it is possible without harm to business to cut the staffs of many establishments and organizations. We can always find a use for the people released in places where personnel are short." *Pravda*, June 16, 1983, p. 1.
8. Quotations from ibid., August 16, 1983, p. 1; and Yu. Andropov, "Ucheniye Karla Marksa i nekotorye voprosy sotsialisticheskogo stroitel'stva v SSSR" (Karl Marx's Teaching and Certain Problems of Socialist Development in the USSR), *Kommunist*, no. 3 (February 1983), p. 20.
9. *Pravda*, June 16, 1983, pp. 1–2, and November 23, 1982, p. 1.
10. Andropov, "Ucheniye Karla Marksa," p. 13; *Pravda*, November 23, 1982, p. 1.
11. Andropov, "Ucheniye Karla Marksa," p. 13; *Pravda*, August 16, 1983, p. 1, and December 27, 1983, p. 1.

12. Shevchenko, p. 242.
13. *Pravda*, September 25, 1981, p. 1.
14. Marc D. Zlotnik, "Chernenko's Platform," *Problems of Communism*, 31 (November–December 1982), p. 70.
15. Only nine members of the 1981 Central Committee had earlier worked reasonably closely with Chernenko, of whom one had died in early 1982. Of the remaining eight, three (P. F. Alekseyev, N. A. Shchelokov, and S. P. Trapeznikov) were demoted under Andropov and the other five (A. M. Aleksandrov-Agentov, I. I. Bodyul, K. M. Bogolyubov, K. V. Rusakov, and G. E. Tsukhanov) were demoted under Gorbachev.
16. L. I. Brezhnev, "Glavy iz knigi 'Vospominaniya'" (Chapters from the Book *Memoirs*), *Novyi mir*, no. 1 (January 1983), p. 21.
17. Quotations from *Pravda*, February 14, 1984, pp. 1–2, and March 3, 1984, pp. 1–2.
18. Ibid., February 14, 1984, p. 1.
19. All quotations from Gromyko's speech are from "Rech' tovarishcha A. A. Gromyko na plenume TsK KPSS 11 marta 1985 goda" (Speech of Comrade A. A. Gromyko at the Plenum of the CC of the CPSU, March 11, 1985), *Kommunist*, no. 5 (March 1985), pp. 6–7.
20. Blair A. Ruble, "Romanov's Leningrad," *Problems of Communism*, 33 (January-February 1984), pp. 36–48.
21. Kapitonov worked closely with Grishin in the party machine of Moscow city and oblast from 1950 to 1956 and, as first secretary of the oblast, was Grishin's immediate superior from 1954 to 1956. Kapitonov's first deputy, N. A. Petrovichev, was also out of the Moscow organization.
22. The best biographical sketch is Archie Brown, "Gorbachev: New Man in the Kremlin," *Problems of Communism*, 34 (May-June 1985), pp. 1–24. The only longer treatment of value is Zhores A. Medvedev, *Gorbachev* (New York: W. W. Norton, 1986).
23. Just how Gorbachev avoided the fate of the two other Central Committee secretaries from his age group who were demoted in 1977 and 1979, Katushev and Ryabov, remains unclear. One scholar has speculated that Gorbachev had a special relationship in the late 1970s with Chernenko, his eventual rival, based on their mutual connection with Kulakov, the Stavropol' man who preceded Gorbachev as national party secretary for agriculture and who in the 1940s served in Penza region with Chernenko. Jerry F. Hough, "Gorbachev's Strategy," *Foreign Affairs*, 64 (Fall 1985), pp. 35–36.
24. *Pravda*, April 24, 1985, pp. 1–2.
25. Ibid., June 27, 1985, p. 1.
26. Ibid., July 3, 1985, p. 1.

27. Quotations from *Pravda*, April 24, 1985, p. 2; "Nastoichivo dvigat'sya vpered" (Move Urgently Forward), *Kommunist*, no. 8 (May 1985), p. 32; *Pravda*, February 28, 1986, p. 4.
28. Kapitonov was not completely retired; he became chairman of the party's auditing commission.
29. The more prominent of the long-time Brezhnev clients retired under Gorbachev include, aside from Tikhonov and Rusakov from the inner leadership, A. M. Aleksandrov-Agentov (Brezhnev's assistant for foreign policy), V. E. Dymshits (Deputy Chairman of the Council of Ministers), G. K. Tsinev (first deputy head of the KGB), and P. A. Gorchakov (chief political officer in the Strategic Rocket Forces). After Kunayev and Shcherbitskii in the Politburo, the most important Brezhnev crony left is I. V. Arkhipov, who worked with Brezhnev in Dnepropetrovsk and is still one of four first deputy chairmen of the Council of Ministers.
30. G. Razumovskii, "Reshayushcheye zveno partiinogo rukovodstva" (The Decisive Link of Party Leadership), *Kommunist*, no. 4 (March 1985), p. 29.
31. One sop to the pride of veteran officials was the retention of a handful of retired leaders (including Tikhonov and former Politburo candidate members Kuznetsov and Ponomarev) on the 1986 Central Committee. The two ex-Politburo members who were retired in disfavor (Grishin and Romanov) were not given this honor.
32. *Pravda*, February 26, 1986, p. 2.
33. Frolov's early career and liberal views are described in Werner G. Hahn, *Postwar Soviet Politics* (Ithaca: Cornell University Press, 1982), pp. 169–181.
34. Quotations from "Nastoichivo dvigat'sya vpered," pp. 25–26; *Pravda*, April 24, 1985, p. 1.
35. Quotations from *Pravda*, June 27, 1985, p. 2, and July 12, 1985, p. 1.
36. Ibid., February 26, 1986, p. 5.
37. See Sidney I. Ploss, "A New Soviet Era?" *Foreign Policy*, 62 (Spring 1986), pp. 50–54. Zdenek Mlynar, an architect of the Czechoslovak reforms of 1968 and in the 1950s a friend of Gorbachev at Moscow State University, said in exile in 1985 that Gorbachev at first admired Khrushchev but agreed with his removal because of his hectic reorganizations and interference in local decisions. Brown, "Gorbachev," p. 5.
38. The continuing relevance for Soviet reform of NEP and its chief disciple, Nikolai Bukharin, has long been eloquently argued by Stephen F. Cohen. See especially his essay "Bukharin, NEP, and the Idea of an Alternative to Stalinism," in his collection *Rethinking the Soviet Experience: Politics and History Since 1917* (New York: Oxford University Press, 1985), pp. 71–92.

39. *Pravda*, February 26, 1986, pp. 4–5.
40. Many military officers must have resented the 1982 appointment of Vitali Fedorchuk as chief of the KGB, followed by his transfer to the Ministry of the Interior. Fedorchuk made his career in the KGB branch responsible for surveillance of the army. Peter Deriabin and T. H. Bagley, "Fedorchuk, the KGB, and the Soviet Succession," *Orbis*, 26 (Fall 1982), pp. 611–632.
41. Of the sixteen top officials of the Ministry of Defense (the minister, the fourteen first deputy and deputy ministers, and the chief of the political directorate), only three have been replaced under Gorbachev. In one case the incumbent was dying, in the other two the officer replaced was given a sinecure and re-elected to the Central Committee in 1986. The average age of the sixteen is the same today as it was in 1981—sixty-six, which makes them considerably older than civilian reference groups.
42. In addition to Gladyshev, the first deputy head of the Central Committee's administrative organs department, V. I. Drugov, was named Deputy Interior Minister in January 1986, shortly before the Vlasov appointment. Two former deputy KGB chairmen were named deputies to Fedorchuk during his time in the Interior Ministry, but one, V. Ya. Lezhepekov, had specialized in party work in the KGB. In addition, the man appointed first deputy head of the Central Committee's international information department in 1983, N. N. Chetverikov, was a former KGB official; I do not know what happened to him when this department was abolished in early 1986. A. N. Aksenov, designated head of the television and radio industry in December 1985, served as deputy chief of the Belorussian KGB for one year of the Khrushchev era.
43. The general point is stated most clearly in Archie Brown, "The Power of the General Secretary of the CPSU," in T. H. Rigby, Archie Brown, and Peter Reddaway, eds., *Authority, Power, and Policy in the USSR* (London: Macmillan, 1980), p. 136. The phrase "law of diminishing secretaries" comes from Stephen F. Cohen, *Sovieticus: American Perceptions and Soviet Realities* (New York: W. W. Norton, 1985), p. 81.
44. This point is discussed persuasively in George W. Breslauer, *Khrushchev and Brezhnev as Leaders: Building Authority in Soviet Politics* (London: George Allen & Unwin, 1982).
45. Details on promotion from within under Brezhnev are in Robert E. Blackwell, Jr., "Cadres Policy in the Brezhnev Era," *Problems of Communism*, 28 (March–April 1979), pp. 36–41; T. H. Rigby, "The Soviet Government since Khrushchev," *Politics*, 12 (May 1977), pp. 5–22; and T. H. Rigby, "The Soviet Regional Leadership: The Brezhnev Generation," *Slavic Review*, 37 (March 1978), pp. 13–14.
46. Other ex-Stavropolites now in positions of some influence include V. G. Afonin, head of the Central Committee's chemical industry depart-

ment; M. V. Gramov, head of the Soviet sport bureaucracy and newly appointed to the Council of Ministers; V. I. Kalashnikov, party first secretary in Volgograd oblast; V. A. Kaznacheyev, RSFSR Minister of Vocational Education; and S. I. Manyakin, first secretary in Omsk oblast.

47. It is probably not coincidental that one of only two 1981 Central Committee department heads (of a total of twenty-two) still to have his position today is the seventy-two-year-old head of the agriculture and food industry department, V. A. Karlov; or that the oldest person to be named to the Council of Ministers under Gorbachev is Grain Products Minister G. S. Zolotukhin, age seventy-five. Among the younger men, Razumovskii fits into the agricultural category as well as being a southerner. He was head of the agriculture department of the Council of Ministers' chancellery from 1981 to 1983, indirectly supervised by Gorbachev.

48. Aspects of these measures are discussed astutely and in more detail in Thane Gustafson and Dawn Mann, "Gorbachev's First Year: Building Power and Authority," *Problems of Communism*, 35 (May–June 1986), pp. 1–19; and also Theodore H. Friedgut, *Gorbachev and Party Reform*, Research Paper no. 62 (Jerusalem: Soviet and East European Research Centre, Hebrew University, January 1986).

49. Promotees from the Urals and western Siberia include two new Central Committee department heads (L. F. Bobykin from Sverdlovsk and L. G. Mel'nikov from Tomsk), Razumovskii's first deputy in the cadres department (Ye. P. Razumov from Kemerovo), and two of the new deputy premiers (L. A. Voronin from Sverdlovsk and G. G. Vedernikov from Chelyabinsk). As Gustafson and Mann point out (p. 8), there is no reason to overdraw the point and portray the appointees from this area as a monolithic group. Ligachev and Yel'tsin, in particular, seem to differ on broad philosophical grounds.

    Ligachev probably has more personal connections than anyone else in the group, owing to his age (sixty-six) and his service in the Central Committee apparatus in the early 1960s. For example, it was presumably his protection that saved Fedor Loshchenkov (age seventy-one) of Yaroslavl', one of the oldest regional first secretaries, from retirement in 1986. Loshchenkov, who worked closely with Ligachev in Novosibirsk and Moscow from the mid-1940s to 1961, was made Chairman of the State Committee on Material Reserves in June 1986.

50. Vadim Medvedev, recently promoted to the Secretariat, might also fit in this category, but he left Leningrad in 1970. Other ex-Leningraders who have moved up since March 1985 include V. A. Bykov, the new Minister of the Medical and Microbiological Industry and the youngest member of the Council of Ministers; A. S. Yefimov, first secretary of the Navoi oblast party committee in Uzbekistan; and V. G. Zakharov, party second secretary in the city of Moscow.

51. *Pravda*, February 2, 1986, p. 2.
52. The majority of the new ministers are technical experts who rose through the agency they now head or a closely related one, but even here there is more of a tendency for them to be recently arrived from the provinces or from a cognate party post (Gustafson and Mann, p. 8). Only one of the new deputy premiers, G.G. Vedernikov, was promoted directly from a provincial party position.
53. *Pravda*, February 28, 1986, p. 4.
54. This is based on the available biographical information on the twenty-seven individuals appointed first secretary of an RSFSR region (including Moscow city) between Chernenko's death and July 1, 1986. Twenty-one of the new secretaries came directly from a central position (twenty-two had some central experience), four from the same region (fifteen had some experience there), one from an adjacent region, defined as being within two regions of that of appointment (five had some experience in an adjacent region), and one from another region (eight had some experience in another region). Under Andropov, four first secretaries were appointed from the center, eight from the same region, two from an adjacent region, and two from another region. It is also true that many of the individuals who under Gorbachev were parachuted in from central posts, especially Central Committee inspector, were moved into those central positions when Andropov was General Secretary and Gorbachev and Ligachev between them were in charge of cadres policy. Inasmuch as full biographies are not available on all the Gorbachev appointees, information on the most recent positions held is more reliable than on previous experience.
55. *Pravda*, February 28, 1986, p. 4.
56. Rigby, "The Soviet Regional Leadership," pp. 23–24, distinguishes between patronage bonds of different intensities.
57. *Sovetskaya Rossiya*, October 10, 1967, p. 2.
58. The weakness of the wartime group is explained in Jerry F. Hough, *Soviet Leadership in Transition* (Washington, D.C.: Brookings Institution, 1980), chap. 3. The clearest discussions of what I term the Gorbachev generation are in this same book (which refers to it as the postwar generation) and in Seweryn Bialer, *Stalin's Successors: Leadership, Stability, and Change in the Soviet Union* (Cambridge: Cambridge University Press, 1980), chap. 6 (which treats the post-Stalin generation, defined slightly differently). Both scholars say more about background characteristics than about shared attitudes.
59. See, for example, the review in Burdett Loomis, "On the Knife's Edge: Public Officials and the Life Cycle," *PS*, 17 (Summer 1984), pp. 538–540.
60. The individuals referred to here are the new head of government, N. I. Ryzhkov (born 1929), and his predecessor, N. A. Tikhonov (born

1905); Ryzhkov's new deputy for defense matters, Yu. D. Maslyukov (born 1937), and his predecessor, L. V. Smirnov (born 1916); and the new Moscow mayor, V. T. Saikin (born 1937), and his predecessor, V. F. Promyslov (born 1908).

61. G. A. Korotayeva and V. P. Chichkanov, "Put' na verkhnii etazh upravleniya" (The Path to the Top Floor of Management), *Ekonomika i organizatsiya promyshlennogo proizvodstva*, no. 7 (July 1981), p. 86.
62. Ibid., pp. 86–87.
63. See the discussion in Paul Allen Beck, "Young vs. Old in 1984: Generations and Life Stages in Presidential Nomination Politics," *PS*, 17 (Summer 1984), pp. 515–524; and Samuel P. Huntington, "Generations, Cycles, and Their Role in American Development," in Richard J. Samuels, ed., *Political Generations and Political Development* (Lexington, Mass.: D. C. Heath, 1977), pp. 11–12.
64. *Moskovskaya pravda*, May 4, 1986, p. 3.
65. *Kazakhstanskaya pravda*, April 3, 1977, p. 4; this article is about generational differences in general, not specifically about politicians.
66. See, for instance, the comment by the economist Abel Aganbegyan that many of those entering high management today have excellent engineer's training "but neither a fundamental university education nor a specialized managerial education." Engineers educated even twenty years ago learned nothing about human relations, whereas now "it is inconceivable to manage a big collective without using the methods of sociology and psychology." *Izvestiya*, March 25, 1985, p. 2.
67. *Pravda*, October 2, 1985, p. 2.
68. Good examples of younger officials who have incurred Gorbachev's wrath are I. G. Ustiyan (born 1939), the Moldavian premier retired in December 1985; K. M. Aukhadiyev (born 1938), the party first secretary in Kazakhstan's Alma-Ata oblast, who was dismissed for corruption in September 1985; and R. I. Kosolapov (born 1930), relieved as editor of *Kommunist* in February 1986.
69. Two careful studies of the published articles of Soviet regional politicians find the diversity of outlook among younger officials to be as striking as the differences between them and their elders. George W. Breslauer, "Is There a Generation Gap in the Soviet Political Establishment?: Demand Articulation by RSFSR Provincial Party First Secretaries," *Soviet Studies*, 36 (January 1984), pp. 1–25; and Mark R. Beissinger, "In Search of Generations in Soviet Politics," *World Politics*, 38 (January 1986), pp. 288–314.
70. Based on analysis of the speeches as recorded in *XXVI s'ezd Kommunisticheskoi partii Sovetskogo Soyuza: stenograficheskii otchet* (The 26th Congress of the Communist Party of the Soviet Union: Stenographic Record) (Moscow: Politizdat, 1981). Thirteen secretaries

had been born in 1926 or later and eighteen before 1926. The following are the percentages of the younger secretaries who recommended or endorsed particular types of policy in their speeches, with the percentage of older secretaries doing so in parentheses: stricter ideological controls 0 (22); extensive industrial development 15 (28); intensive industrial development 69 (50); extensive agricultural development 8 (44); intensive agricultural development 38 (28); better central management 8 (17); improved consumer welfare 62 (33); regional coordination 46 (22). Compare with Breslauer, "Is There a Generation Gap in the Soviet Political Establishment?" and Beissinger, "In Search of Generations."

71. Quotations from B. P. Kurashvili, "Gosudarstvennoye upravleniye narodnym khozyaistvom: perspektivy razvitiya" (State Management of the National Economy: Development Perspectives), *Sovetskoye gosudarstvo i pravo,* no. 6 (June 1982), p. 39; L. I. Abalkin, "Perevod ekonomiki na intensivnyi put' razvitiya" (Transfer of the Economy to the Intensive Path of Development), *Voprosy ekonomiki,* no. 2 (February 1982), p. 13; *Ekonomicheskaya gazeta,* no. 21 (May 1982), p. 7; Ye. A. Lukasheva, "Sotsial'no-eticheskiye problemy sotsialisticheskoi zakonnosti" (Social-Ethical Problems of Socialist Legality), *Sovetskoye gosudarstvo i pravo,* no. 4 (April 1982), pp. 15, 17.
72. "Nastoichivo dvigat'sya vpered," p. 32.
73. See, for example, S. Kozlov, "Za chistotu i boevitost' partiinykh ryadov" (For the Purity and Militancy of Party Ranks), *Kommunist,* no. 1 (January 1986), pp. 84–85.
74. The age figure for the 1966–75 ministers is taken from Rigby, "The Soviet Government since Khrushchev," p. 7. Oddly, Gorbachev appointments to the Presidium of the Council of Ministers have averaged fifty-five years of age, whereas ordinary ministers have been two years older.
75. This is assuming that ages are distributed among the thirty-four new Central Committee members for whom date of birth is unknown in the same proportions as among the sixty-eight new members for whom the date of birth can be ascertained. All the ages will be known with certainty when the 1986 yearbook of the main Soviet encyclopedia is published in 1987.

CHAPTER 4

1. Numerous possible directions for the Soviet system are discussed in Zbigniew Brzezinski, ed., *Dilemmas of Change in Soviet Politics* (New York: Columbia University Press, 1969); George W. Breslauer, *Five Images of the Soviet Future: A Critical Review and Synthesis,* Policy Papers in International Affairs, no. 4 (Berkeley: Institute of International Studies, University of California, 1978); and William E. Odom,

"Choice and Change in Soviet Politics," *Problems of Communism*, 32 (May-June 1983), pp. 1–21.

2. Andrei Amalrik, *Will the Soviet Union Survive Until 1984?* (New York: Harper and Row, 1970).
3. *Pravda*, February 27, 1986, p. 2, and February 28, 1986, p. 4.
4. These predictions can be found in Mikhail S. Bernstam, "Demographic Depression in the USSR and the Welfare State: Their Relevance to Russian Nationalism," in Robert Conquest, ed., *The Last Empire: Nationality and the Soviet Future* (Stanford: Hoover Institution, forthcoming in 1986).
5. The political and ethical content of the reform program is emphasized in the memoir of one of its authors, Zdenek Mlynar, *Nightfrost in Prague* (New York: Karz Publishers, 1980).
6. Ludmilla Alexeyeva, *Soviet Dissent: Contemporary Movements for National, Religious, and Human Rights* (Middletown, Connecticut: Wesleyan University Press, 1985), p. 416. Roy Medvedev's program can be found in his book *On Socialist Democracy* (New York: W. W. Norton, 1977). Excerpts from the Movement for Socialist Renewal's document, which is dated November 21, 1985, are in *The Guardian*, July 22, 1986, pp. 19–20.
7. K. Chernenko, "Avangardnaya rol' partii kommunistov: vazhnoye usloviye yeye vozrastaniya" (The Avant-Garde Role of the Communist Party is an Important Condition of its Growth), *Kommunist*, no. 6 (April 1982), p. 27.
8. *Pravda*, February 26, 1986, p. 7.
9. Quotation from Alex Pravda, "Poland 1980: From 'Premature Consumerism' to Labour Solidarity," *Soviet Studies*, 34 (April 1982), p. 168.
10. In an unofficial survey in Moscow and environs in the spring of 1981, only one out of every five workers questioned, and one of four students, expressed sympathy for Solidarity. Alexeyeva, p. 415.
11. David K. Shipler, *Russia: Broken Idols, Solemn Dreams* (New York: Penguin Books, 1984), p. 207. A few members of SMOT eluded the police until 1983, and it seems to have had greater success in bringing workers and intellectuals together in tiny numbers. However, "None of the goals of SMOT were realized, with the exception of the informational bulletin." Alexeyeva, p. 410.
12. *Pravda*, July 1, 1986, p. 1.
13. Alexander Yanov, *The Russian New Right: Right-Wing Ideologies in the Contemporary USSR*, Research Series, no. 35 (Berkeley: Institute of International Studies, University of California, 1978).
14. Alexeyeva, pp. 389–390, 396–397.
15. These background features are stressed in Roger Pethybridge, *The Social Prelude to Stalinism* (New York: St. Martin's Press, 1974); and

Moshe Lewin, "The Social Background of Stalinism," in Robert C. Tucker, ed., *Stalinism: Essays in Historical Interpretation* (New York: Norton, 1977), pp. 111–136.

16. *Pravda*, April 23, 1982, p. 2.
17. Ibid., February 8, 1986, p. 2.
18. Yanov, *The Russian New Right*, p. 58.
19. The possibility of economic re-Stalinization is considered in Joseph S. Berliner, "Managing the Soviet Economy: Alternative Models," *Problems of Communism*, 32 (January–February 1983), pp. 44–47.
20. V. Kandybo, "Pravda protiv vymyslov" (The Truth versus Fabrications), *Kommunist vooruzhennykh sil*, no. 21 (November 1982), p. 81.
21. This idea was first put forward in Gertrude E. Schroeder, "The Soviet Economy on a Treadmill of 'Reforms,'" in Joint Economic Committee, U.S. Congress, *Soviet Economy in a Time of Change* (Washington, D.C.: GPO, 1979), I, 312–340.
22. S. Kozlov, "Za chistotu i boevitost' partiinykh ryadov" (For the Purity and Militancy of Party Ranks), *Kommunist*, no. 1 (January 1986), p. 85.
23. Stephen F. Cohen, *Rethinking the Soviet Experience: Politics and History Since 1917* (New York: Oxford University Press, 1985), p. 148.
24. *Izvestiya*, June 1, 1985, p. 3.
25. *Pravda*, March 2, 1986, p. 6.
26. "Conflict situations are cropping up," he has confided to leading Soviet writers about his program, "and various positions are coming to light." Ibid., June 21, 1986, p. 1.
27. Samuel P. Huntington, "Reform and Stability in South Africa," *International Security*, 6 (Spring 1982), p. 17.
28. *Pravda*, February 1, 1983, p. 2.
29. The Calvinist analogy is made in Robert Sharlet, "Soviet Legal Policy under Andropov: Law and Discipline," in Joseph L. Nogee, ed., *Soviet Politics: Russia after Brezhnev* (New York: Praeger Special Studies, 1985), p. 101.
30. *Izvestiya*, April 26, 1985, p. 2.
31. The case of the railways is analyzed in Vladimir Kontorovich, "Discipline and Growth in the Soviet Economy," *Problems of Communism*, 34 (November–December 1985), pp. 18–31.
32. Quotation from *Pravda*, August 10, 1983, p. 3.
33. Ibid., March 3, 1984, p. 2.
34. Ibid., February 2, 1986, p. 2.
35. See, for example, ibid., December 18, 1985, p. 2, and March 1, 1986, p. 5.
36. "Nastoichivo dvigat'sya vpered" (Move Urgently Forward), *Kommunist*, no. 8 (May 1985), p. 27.

37. See, for example, *Moskovskaya pravda*, December 19, 1985, p. 3, and April 16, 1986, p. 3.
38. *Pravda,* July 27, 1986, p. 2; Ye. Ligachev, "Sovetuyas' s partiyei, s narodom" (Taking Counsel with the Party and People), *Kommunist,* no. 16 (November 1985), p. 87.
39. *Pravda*, December 27, 1983, p. 2.
40. Ibid., June 12, 1985, p. 1.
41. The authoritative sources on the five-year plan are Premier Ryzhkov's report to the Twenty-seventh Congress and his subsequent report to the Supreme Soviet; in ibid., March 4, 1986, pp. 2–5, and June 19, 1986, pp. 1–5. I have benefited from the discussion of the draft plan in "Import Implications of the Dramatic Shift in Soviet Investment Strategy in 1986," *PlanEcon Report,* 2 (January 13, 1986); and also from Ed A. Hewett, "Gorbachev's Economic Strategy: A Preliminary Assessment," *Soviet Economy,* 1 (October-December 1985), pp. 285–305.
42. *Pravda*, February 26, 1986, pp. 4, 6; *Izvestiya*, April 8, 1986, p. 1.
43. *Pravda*, April 9, 1986, p. 2, and June 19, 1986, p. 4.
44. An abbreviated version is in ibid., October 9, 1985, pp. 1–3.
45. See ibid., March 4, 1986, p. 3.
46. The decision on the quality control inspectors is in ibid., July 2, 1986, pp. 1–2, and on the factory-owned stores and other changes in consumer-oriented production in ibid., May 6, 1986, pp. 1–2. Bureaucratic sabotage of the early efforts at vertical integration is described in ibid., February 28, 1986, p. 3.
47. "Nastoichivo dvigat'sya vpered," p. 31. The decision was affirmed by the Politburo, with an annual target of 1 to 1.2 million new plots, in 1986 (*Pravda*, May 16, 1986, p. 1).
48. *Pravda*, February 26, 1986, p. 5.
49. Ibid., March 3, 1986, p. 3.
50. Ibid., March 29, 1986, pp. 1–2.
51. A recent article has pointed out that local restrictions in some places, Leningrad among them, have included the setting of ceiling prices, which has restricted supply. *Sotsialisticheskaya industriya*, May 7, 1986, p. 3.
52. *Pravda*, February 1, 1986, p. 3.
53. *Izvestiya*, January 16, 1986, p. 3.
54. The Gorbachev quotations are from *Pravda*, February 26, 1986, pp. 4–5.
55. Ibid., April 24, 1985, p. 2.
56. Ibid., February 13, 1986, p. 3.
57. *Izvestiya*, April 26, 1986, p. 2.
58. Delegation to the factory level was emphasized by Gorbachev at the

Twenty-seventh Congress. But specialists spoke later of national targets for the 1986-90 plan, whereby average pay for white-collar workers would rise by 5 percent more than for blue-collar workers. *Sotsialisticheskaya industriya*, April 4, 1986, p. 3.

59. *Pravda*, March 5, 1986, p. 4.
60. *Izvestiya*, March 23, 1986, p. 2.
61. *Pravda*, February 26, 1986, p. 6, and April 24, 1986, p. 1.
62. *Izvestiya*, November 16, 1985, p. 2.
63. G. I. Shmelev, "Sotsial'no-ekonomicheskii potentsial semeinogo podryada" (The Socioeconomic Potential of Family Contracting), *Sotsiologicheskiye issledovaniya*, no. 4 (October–December 1985), p. 15.
64. *Pravda*, March 20, 1986, p. 2.
65. Quotations from ibid., February 1, 1983, p. 1; February 8, 1986, p. 1; February 26, 1986, p. 5. For a recent argument for market prices for consumer goods, see *Sotsialisticheskaya industriya*, June 5, 1986, p. 3.
66. An example of praiseful commentary on China is Fedor Burlatskii's article in *Literaturnaya gazeta*, June 11, 1986, p. 10. See also Gorbachev's warm reference in his Vladivostok speech (*Pravda*, July 29, 1986, p. 2).
67. Good descriptions of the main features of the reform are in Richard Portes, "The Tactics and Strategy of Economic Decentralization," *Soviet Studies*, 23 (April 1972), pp. 629–658; and David Granick, "The Hungarian Economic Reform," *World Politics*, 25 (April 1973), pp. 414–429.
68. *Pravda*, June 10, 1986, p. 1.
69. P. G. Hare and P. T. Wanless, "Polish and Hungarian Economic Reforms—A Comparison," *Soviet Studies*, 33 (October 1981), p. 496.
70. *Pravda*, November 23, 1982, p. 1, and December 27, 1983, p. 2.
71. The memorandum is available in Radio Liberty, *Materialy samizdata*, no. 35/83 (August 26, 1983). An English translation is "The Novosibirsk Report," *Survey*, 28 (120) (Spring 1984), pp. 80–108.
72. *Pravda*, February 27, 1986, p. 5.
73. Ibid., April 9, 1986, p. 2.
74. Ibid., February 26, 1986, p. 5.
75. G. A. Kulagin, "Nomenklatura, tsena, pribyl'" (Nomenclature, Price, Profit), *Ekonomika i organizatsiya promyshlennogo proizvodstva*, no. 11 (November 1985), p. 101.
76. *Pravda*, June 17, 1986, p. 1.
77. Ibid., June 16, 1983, pp. 1–2.
78. Ibid., March 12, 1985, p. 3.
79. Aleksandr Yakovlev, the new party secretary for propaganda and culture, was demoted in 1973 for criticizing Russian chauvinism. Yuri Voronov, the new head of the Central Committee culture department, was deposed as editor of the national youth newspaper in 1965. Ivan

Frolov, the new editor of *Kommunist,* lost a major editorial position in 1977.

80. The full text of the Yevtushenko speech, with indications of the parts excised by the censors, is printed in English translation in *The New York Times,* December 19, 1985, p. 5.
81. *Pravda,* February 27, 1986, pp. 2–3.
82. Ibid., February 28, 1986, p. 4.
83. Within his own Moscow bailiwick, Yel'tsin has kept up his campaign for frankness. In a speech shortly after the congress, he demanded that the capital city's newspapers publish more critical articles and stated that Moscow television and radio are so boring that "many of their broadcasts are watched and listened to by no one except perhaps the journalists themselves and the children who watch the program 'Good Night, Little One!'" *Moskovskaya pravda,* March 30, 1986, p. 2. Word of an exceptionally blunt Yel'tsin session with party propagandists in Moscow, said to have occurred in April, reached Western diplomats and journalists in July 1986.
84. *Pravda,* February 26, 1986, pp. 7, 9.
85. Yekaterina Sheveleva, speaking at the June congress of USSR writers; in *Literaturnaya gazeta,* July 2, 1986, p. 9.
86. Ibid., June 4, 1986, p. 10.
87. *Pravda,* June 27, 1986, p. 2; *Izvestiya,* June 29, 1986, p. 3.
88. *Pravda,* June 21, 1986, p. 1.
89. Quotations from *Literaturnaya gazeta,* July 2, 1986, pp. 6–7. Other information from *The New York Times,* June 30, 1986, pp. 1, 6; *The Observer,* June 29, 1986, p. 13.
90. Mikhail Roshchin writing about Moscow's Sovremennik Theater in *Izvestiya,* July 7, 1986, p. 3. In contrast, Vladimir Karpov at the writers' congress warned against a return to the spirit of the Khrushchev period, saying that "ignoring of the boundaries separating democracy from demagoguery sometimes leads to very unpleasant consequences." *Literaturnaya gazeta,* July 2, 1986, p. 10.
91. See Boris Rumer, "Realities of Gorbachev's Economic Program," *Problems of Communism,* 35 (May–June 1986), pp. 20–31.
92. *Izvestiya,* April 8, 1986, p. 2.
93. Huntington, "Reform and Stability in South Africa," p. 14.
94. Albert O. Hirschman, *Journeys Toward Progress: Studies of Economic Policy-Making in Latin America* (New York: Twentieth Century Fund, 1963), p. 272.
95. See, for example, *Izvestiya,* November 26, 1985, p. 3.
96. G. Kh. Shakhnazarov, "Razvitiye lichnosti i sotsialicheskii obraz zhizni" (Personal Development and the Socialist Way of Life), *Voprosy filosofii,* no.11 (November 1977), pp. 20–21.

97. *Pravda*, March 1, 1986, p. 6.
98. Ibid., November 23, 1983, p. 2.
99. Ibid., April 15, 1986, p. 2.
100. M. I. Piskotin, "Demokraticheskii tsentralizm: problemy sochetaniya tsentralizatsii i detsentralizatsii" (Democratic Centralism: Problems of Combining Centralization and Decentralization), *Sovetskoye gosudarstvo i pravo*, no. 5 (May 1981), p. 45.
101. David W. Paul and Maurice D. Simon, "Poland Today and Czechoslovakia 1968," *Problems of Communism*, 30 (September–October 1981), p. 31.
102. *Izvestiya*, April 18, 1986, p. 2.
103. Edward A. Hewett, "The Hungarian Economy: Lessons of the 1970s and Prospects for the 1980s," in Joint Economic Committee, U.S. Congress, *East European Economic Assessment, Part 1–Country Studies 1980* (Washington, D.C.: GPO, 1981), p. 522.
104. Huntington, "Reform and Stability in South Africa," p. 14.

CHAPTER 5

1. Alexander Dallin, "The Domestic Sources of Soviet Foreign Policy," in Seweryn Bialer, ed., *The Domestic Context of Soviet Foreign Policy* (Boulder, Colorado: Westview Press, 1981), p. 350. Dallin makes this point mainly about Brezhnev's policy, but it is probably best to see the Brezhnev approach as an extension of Khrushchev's.
2. Yu. V. Andropov, *Izbrannye rechi i stat'i* (Selected Speeches and Articles) (Moscow: Politizdat, 1979), p. 180.
3. *Pravda*, October 28, 1982, p. 1.
4. Quotations from "Rech' tovarishcha A. A. Gromyko na plenume TsK KPSS 11 marta 1985 goda" (Speech of Comrade A. A. Gromyko at the Plenum of the CC of the CPSU, March 11, 1985), *Kommunist*, no. 5 (March 1985), pp. 6–7.
5. The Central Committee's department of international information, created in the late 1970s, was folded into Yakovlev's propaganda department around the time of the Twenty-seventh Congress. Its head, Leonid Zamyatin, was made Soviet ambassador to Britain in late April 1986.
6. The 1980 list is in Jerry F. Hough, *Soviet Leadership in Transition* (Washington, D.C.: Brookings Institution, 1980), p. 111. Those holding the 1986 positions that most closely correspond are B. I. Aristov, I. V. Arkhipov, V. M. Chebrikov, A. S. Chernyayev, S. V. Chervonenko, P. N. Demichev, A. F. Dobrynin, M. S. Gorbachev, A. A. Gromyko, K. F. Katushev, Ye. K. Ligachev, V. A. Medvedev, N. I. Ryzhkov, E. A. Shevardnadze, S. L. Sokolov, A. N. Yakovlev, and L. N. Zaikov. Zaikov is included because his secretarial responsibilities encompass

supervision of the military and KGB and he is, I presume, a member of the Defense Council.

7. For help with information on Foreign Ministry personnel, I am indebted to Marc Greenfield of Columbia University and Claire Rosenson of Georgetown University.
8. Morton Schwartz, *Soviet Perceptions of the United States* (Berkeley: University of California Press, 1978), p. 159. See also Hough, *Soviet Leadership in Transition*, chap. 6.
9. The quotation about Dobrynin is from Arkady N. Shevchenko, *Breaking with Moscow* (New York: Ballantine, 1985), p. 259. Shevchenko, a former senior Soviet diplomat, goes on to point out that Dobrynin is a staunch supporter of the Soviet system (he could hardly be otherwise) but also that, as ambassador to Washington, Dobrynin wrote cables "unaffected by the urge of most Soviet ambassadors to tell their superiors what will agree with their preconceptions." Ibid., p. 260.
10. Quotations from *Pravda*, November 22, 1985, p. 2; October 4, 1985, p. 1; July 29, 1986, pp. 2–3.
11. Ibid., November 22, 1985, p. 2.
12. Ibid.
13. "Po-leninski zhit', po-leninski deistvovat'" (Live like Lenin, Act like Lenin), *Mirovaya ekonomika i mezhdunarodnye otnosheniya*, no. 4 (April 1986), p. 12.
14. *Pravda*, October 2, 1985, p. 2; April 19, 1986, p. 2; July 8, 1986, p. 2.
15. "Po-leninski zhit', po-leninski deistvovat'," p. 10.
16. *Pravda*, February 26, 1986, p. 2.
17. See the analysis of the original dilemma in Strobe Talbott, *Deadly Gambits: The Reagan Administration and the Stalemate in Nuclear Arms Control* (New York: Vintage Books, 1985).
18. See Dallin, pp. 344–347; and Charles Gati, "The Stalinist Legacy in Soviet Foreign Policy," reprinted in Robbin F. Laird and Erik P. Hoffmann, eds., *Soviet Foreign Policy in a Changing World* (New York: Aldine, 1986), pp. 16–28.
19. *Pravda*, October 4, 1985, p. 1, and May 24, 1986, p. 1.
20. Ibid., April 3, 1986, p. 1. For an earlier statement along these lines, see Chernenko's remarks to the Central Committee's commission on revisions to the 1961 party program: "It is understandable that the basic part of the text of the program must be devoted to problems of the country's internal development. After all, on their resolution there also depend in the final analysis our successes in foreign policy, in the struggle for peace, . . . in the competition with capitalism." Ibid., April 26, 1984, p. 1.
21. Ibid., October 4, 1985, p. 1.
22. Ibid., November 23, 1982, p. 2. Andropov's quotation (for which he did not give a source) can be identified as coming from Lenin's closing

address at the Tenth Party Conference in May 1921, which also stated that, out of international considerations, "for us questions of economic development become of absolutely exceptional importance."

23. The full history of the Soviet discussion is expertly dissected in Jerry F. Hough, *The Struggle for the Third World: Soviet Debates and American Options* (Washington, D.C.: Brookings Institution, 1986). Recent developments are summarized in Elizabeth K. Valkenier, "Revolutionary Change in the Third World: Recent Soviet Assessments," *World Politics*, 38 (April 1986), pp. 415–434; and Francis Fukuyama, "Gorbachev and the Third World," *Foreign Affairs*, 64 (Spring 1986), pp. 715–731.
24. *Pravda*, June 16, 1983, p. 2.
25. Ibid., March 28, 1986, p. 4.
26. These cost estimates are from Zalmay Khalilzad, "Moscow's Afghan War," *Problems of Communism*, 35 (January–February 1986), pp. 1–2.
27. *Pravda*, July 29, 1986, p. 3.
28. Ibid., April 9, 1986, p. 3.
29. Fedor Burlatskii, quoted in Hough, *The Struggle for the Third World*, pp. 186–187.
30. Discussion in Allen S. Whiting, *Siberian Development and East Asia: Threat or Promise?* (Stanford: Stanford University Press, 1981), especially chap. 4; and Robert W. Campbell, "Prospects for Siberian Economic Development," in Donald S. Zagoria, ed., *Soviet Policy in East Asia* (New Haven: Yale University Press, 1982), pp. 229–254.
31. See on this point V. Stanley Vardys, "Polish Echoes in the Baltic," *Problems of Communism*, 32 (July-August 1983), pp. 21–34; and Martha Brill Olcott, "Soviet Islam and World Revolution," *World Politics*, 34 (July 1982), pp. 487–504. A different reading of Soviet concerns in Afghanistan can be found in Eden Naby, "The Ethnic Factor in Soviet-Afghan Relations," *Asian Survey*, 22 (no. 3, 1980), pp. 237–256; and Alexandre Bennigsen, "Mullahs, Mujahidin, and Soviet Muslims," *Problems of Communism*, 33 (November–December 1984), pp. 28–44.
32. For the latest U.S. government efforts to measure the Soviet military burden, now using a 1982 price base, see Central Intelligence Agency and Defense Intelligence Agency, *The Soviet Economy Under a New Leader*, Paper submitted to the Subcommittee on Economic Resources, Competitiveness, and Security Economics of the Joint Economic Committee, U.S. Congress (March 19, 1986), especially pp. 35–36.
33. These changes are clearly outlined in James M. McConnell, "Shift in Soviet Views of the Proper Focus of Military Development," *World Politics*, 37 (April 1985), pp. 317–343.
34. This point is echoed in Soviet commentary about foreign powers that "want to deflect the material and intellectual resources of the countries

of the socialist fraternity away from the solution of the problems of economic and social development." A. Grabovskii, "Perspektivnyi i deistvennyi kurs" (A Far-Sighted and Effective Course), *Mirovaya ekonomika i mezhdunarodnye otnosheniya*, no. 2 (February 1986), p. 37.

35. *Pravda*, April 9, 1986, p. 3.
36. CIA/DIA, *The Soviet Economy Under a New Leader*, p. 20.
37. Gregory G. Hildebrandt, "The Dynamic Burden of Soviet Defense Spending," in Joint Economic Committee, U.S. Congress, *Soviet Economy in the 1980s: Problems and Prospects* (Washington, D.C.: GPO, 1983), I, 331–350.
38. Julian Cooper, "The Civilian Production of the Soviet Defence Industry," in Ronald Amann and Julian Cooper, eds., *Technical Progress and Soviet Economic Development* (Oxford: Basil Blackwell, 1986), pp. 31–50.
39. CIA/DIA, *The Soviet Economy Under a New Leader*, pp. 21–23.
40. See Daniel Bond and Herbert Levine, "The 11th Five-Year Plan, 1981–85," in Seweryn Bialer and Thane Gustafson, eds., *Russia at the Crossroads: The 26th Congress of the CPSU* (London: George Allen & Unwin, 1982), pp. 100–106, using figures for low productivity growth.
41. On assistance to civilian industry and the consumer, see the statement by Lev Zaikov in *Pravda*, June 28, 1986, p. 2. See also ibid., July 25, 1986, p. 1, on a Politburo decision on consumer electronics which specifically mentions, among other agencies, the Ministry of General Machine-Building, the main producer of military missiles.
42. CIA/DIA, *The Soviet Economy Under a New Leader*, pp. 21–22, 24.
43. Jan Vanous in *The Washington Post*, October 10, 1982, p. C5; *Soviet Acquisition of Militarily Significant Western Technology: An Update*, no author given but U.S. Department of Defense (September 1985), p. 12; Philip Hanson, *Trade and Technology in Soviet-Western Relations* (New York: Columbia University Press, 1981), p. 155.
44. Nikolai Smelyakov, "Na vneshnem rynke" (On the Foreign Market), *Novyi mir*, no. 3 (March 1986), pp. 197–198.
45. Ibid., p. 187.
46. See the analysis of the Soviet debates in Erik P. Hoffmann and Robbin F. Laird, *The Politics of Economic Modernization in the Soviet Union* (Ithaca: Cornell University Press, 1982), chap. 3; Bruce Parrott, *Politics and Technology in the Soviet Union* (Cambridge, Mass.: MIT Press, 1983); and Hough, *The Struggle for the Third World*, chap. 4.
47. O. Bogomolov, "Nauchno-tekhnicheskii progress v SSSR i yeye vneshnepoliticheskiye aspekty" (Scientific-Technological Progress in the USSR and its Foreign Policy Aspects), *Planovoye khozyaistvo*, no. 4 (April 1983), p. 113. Background on leadership attitudes can be found

in Bruce Parrott, "Soviet Foreign Policy, Internal Politics, and Trade with the West," in Bruce Parrott, ed., *Trade, Technology, and Soviet-American Relations* (Bloomington: Indiana University Press, 1985), pp. 46–55.

48. *Pravda*, June 12, 1985, p. 1.
49. The decree is reproduced as the centerfold in *Ekonomicheskaya gazeta*, no. 32 (August 1985).
50. *Pravda*, November 22, 1985, p. 3, and December 12, 1985, p. 2.
51. Ibid., March 4, 1986, p. 5, and June 19, 1986, p. 4.
52. Ibid., April 3, 1986, p. 1.
53. Sarah M. Terry, "Soviet Policy in Eastern Europe: The Challenge of the 1980s," in Sarah M. Terry, ed., *Soviet Policy in Eastern Europe* (New Haven: Yale University Press, 1984), pp. 351–352.
54. On the controversy over subsidization, see especially Michael Marrese and Jan Vanous, *Soviet Subsidization of Trade with Eastern Europe: A Soviet Perspective*, Policy Studies, no. 52 (Berkeley: Institute of International Affairs, University of California, 1983); Paul Marer, "The Political Economy of Soviet Relations with Eastern Europe," in Terry, *Soviet Policy in Eastern Europe*, pp. 155–188; and Josef C. Brada, "Soviet Subsidization of Eastern Europe: The Primacy of Economics over Politics," *Journal of Comparative Economics*, 9 (March 1985), pp. 80–92.
55. *Pravda*, June 16, 1983, p. 2.
56. O. Bogomolov, "SEV: ekonomicheskaya strategiya 80-kh godov" (CMEA: Economic Strategy of the 1980s), *Kommunist*, no. 7 (May 1983), p. 79.
57. *Pravda*, July 1, 1986, p. 1.
58. Ibid., April 19, 1986, p. 1.
59. O. Bogomolov, "Soglasovaniye ekonomicheskikh interesov i politiki" (The Coordination of Economic Interests and Policy), *Kommunist*, no. 10 (July 1985), pp. 91–92.
60. *Pravda*, February 26, 1986, p. 8, and July 1, 1986, p. 1.
61. Ibid., February 26, 1986, p. 8, and July 8, 1986, p. 2. In 1986 a department for "humanitarian and cultural relations" was one of several new departments created within the Foreign Ministry. Also formed were new departments for arms limitations and for international economic relations.
62. *The New York Times*, May 18, 1986, p. 13.
63. This is the conclusion of Ludmilla Alexeyeva, *Soviet Dissent: Contemporary Movements for National, Religious, and Human Rights* (Middletown, Connecticut: Wesleyan University Press, 1985).
64. U.S. Department of State, *Current Policy*, no. 399 (June 8, 1982), pp. 2–4.

65. This latter view has been put forward most strenuously in Richard Pipes, *Survival Is Not Enough* (New York: Simon and Schuster, 1984).

66. James R. Millar, "The Impact of Trade and Trade Denial on the U.S. Economy," in Parrott, *Trade, Technology, and Soviet-American Relations*, pp. 334, 342.

67. Bruce Parrott, "Conclusion," in ibid., p. 361.

68. George Kennan, "Breaking the Spell," *The New Yorker*, October 3, 1983, p. 53.

69. This point is made in Marshall D. Shulman, "An Alternative Policy for Managing U.S.-Soviet Relations," in Arnold Horelick, ed., *U.S.-Soviet Relations: The Next Phase* (Ithaca: Cornell University Press, 1986), p. 271.

Suggestions for Further Reading

Ludmilla Alexeyeva, *Soviet Dissent: Contemporary Movements for National, Religious, and Human Rights* (Middletown, Connecticut: Wesleyan University Press, 1985). The authoritative work on the dissent movement to date. Shows its tendency toward fragmentation among differing factions and currents of opinion.

Mark R. Beissinger, "In Search of Generations in Soviet Politics," *World Politics*, 38 (January 1986), pp. 288–314. A quantitative study, concluding that each Soviet political generation may be internally divided along a number of lines, and that reformist leaders thus would have to appeal to specialized subgroups.

Seweryn Bialer, *The Soviet Paradox: External Expansion, Internal Decline* (New York: Alfred A. Knopf, 1986). A panoramic view of Soviet affairs and of the interrelations among domestic legitimacy and policy, the state of the Soviet bloc, and relations with the West.

Seweryn Bialer and Joan Afferica, "The Genesis of Gorbachev's World," *Foreign Affairs*, 64 (America and the World 1985), pp. 605–644. Characterizes Gorbachev as epitomizing the best traits of his generation, but also as technocratic and authoritarian. Agnostic about his future course.

George W. Breslauer, "Is There a Generation Gap in the Soviet Political Establishment?: Demand Articulation by RSFSR Provincial Party First Secretaries," *Soviet Studies*, 36 (January 1984), pp. 1–25. Finds some differences between political generations, but also greater diversity within the emerging generation than among Brezhnev's age group.

Archie Brown, "Change in the Soviet Union," *Foreign Affairs*, 64 (Summer 1986), pp. 1048–1065. Reviews Gorbachev's performance up to the Twenty-seventh Congress. Optimistic about his reformist potential.

Archie Brown, "Gorbachev: New Man in the Kremlin," *Problems of Communism*, 34 (May-June 1985), pp. 1–24. The most useful biographical sketch.

Zbigniew Brzezinski, *Game Plan: A Geostrategic Framework for the U.S.-Soviet Contest* (Boston: Atlantic Monthly Press, 1986). Expands on Brzezinski's view of the Soviet Union as a "one-dimensional rival," strong only on the military plane, and sketches a Western strategy for neutralizing the Soviet threat.

Stephen F. Cohen, *Rethinking the Soviet Experience* (New York: Oxford University Press, 1985). Polished essays on Soviet political history and its relevance for present choices. Sees conservatism and reformism as tendencies present in the Soviet system since the Revolution.

Thane Gustafson, *Reform in Soviet Politics: Lessons of Recent Policies on Land and Water* (Cambridge: Cambridge University Press, 1981). How policy innovation occurred under Brezhnev, from the germination of new ideas to attempts to implement them.

Thane Gustafson and Dawn Mann, "Gorbachev's First Year: Building Power and Authority," Problems of Communism, 35 (May-June 1986), pp. 1–19. Especially informative on Gorbachev's personnel policy.

Ed A. Hewett, "Gorbachev's Economic Strategy: A Preliminary Assessment," *Soviet Economy,* 1 (October-December 1985), pp. 285–305, with commentary by Philip Hanson pp. 305–312. Focuses on Gorbachev's investment and spending priorities and on the postponement of decisions on major economic reform.

Erik P. Hoffmann and Robbin F. Laird, eds., *The Soviet Polity in the Modern Era* (New York: Aldine, 1984). A compendium of many of the best articles on the Brezhnev era.

Jerry F. Hough, "Gorbachev's Strategy," *Foreign Affairs,* 64 (Fall 1985), pp. 33–54. Appeals for avoidance of simple dichotomies between reform and discipline, and between détente and anti-Westernism, in evaluating Gorbachev's options.

Jerry F. Hough, *The Struggle for the Third World: Soviet Debates and American Options* (Washington, D.C.: Brookings Institution, 1986). A revealing study of disparate Soviet views of the Third World and of the general trend toward realism in Soviet assessments.

Joint Economic Committee, U.S. Congress, *Soviet Economy in the 1980s: Problems and Prospects* (Washington, D.C.: GPO, 1983). The latest of the Joint Economic Committee's "green books" on the Soviet economy, with detailed information on nearly every aspect of economic performance.

Ellen Jones and Fred W. Grupp, "Infant Mortality Trends in the Soviet Union," *Population and Development Review,* 9 (June 1983), pp. 213–246. Marshaling statistical evidence, explains some of the upturn in infant mortality in the 1970s as an artifact of changes in Soviet definitions and reporting techniques.

Nancy Lubin, *Labour and Nationality in Soviet Central Asia* (Princeton, N.J.: Princeton University Press, 1984). Shows how ethnic frictions in Central Asia have been mitigated by the growth of the second economy, in which non-Russians are disproportionately active.

Zhores A. Medvedev, *Gorbachev* (New York: W. W. Norton, 1986). A hastily done but interesting biography, valuable mostly for information and speculation about Gorbachev's early career.

James R. Millar, "The Little Deal: Brezhnev's Contribution to Acquisitive Socialism," *Slavic Review,* 44 (Winter 1985), pp. 694–706. Predicts that new leaders could not easily undo the Brezhnev regime's contract with the population, tolerating the pursuit of individual and family gain through petty enterprise and exchange relationships.

Martha Brill Olcott, "Soviet Islam and World Revolution," *World Politics,* 34 (July 1982), pp. 487–504. Argues that the Islamic revival does not threaten

Soviet ethnic stability and that the country's large Moslem population may be something of an asset to Soviet foreign policy.

Bruce Parrott, ed., *Trade, Technology, and Soviet-American Relations* (Bloomington: Indiana University Press, 1985). Essays analyzing Soviet failures and successes in foreign trade. Generally pessimistic about Western and American use of trade incentives and sanctions to serve other objectives.

Richard Pipes, *Survival Is Not Enough* (New York: Simon and Schuster, 1984). Maintains that severe application of Western economic and other pressures can induce the Soviets to mount major internal reforms and adopt a more conciliatory foreign policy.

Boris Rumer, "Realities of Gorbachev's Economic Program," *Problems of Communism*, 35 (May-June 1986), pp. 20–31. Argues that Gorbachev has not yet confronted the difficult conceptual and political problems bound up with significant economic reform.

S. Frederick Starr, *Red and Hot: The Fate of Jazz in the Soviet Union 1917–1980* (New York: Oxford University Press, 1983). Demonstrates through the history of Soviet jazz that the regime, unable to develop a fully effective official culture, has slowly had to cede ground to popular tastes and Western influences. Excellent background for cultural politics after Brezhnev.

Index

About the Author

Timothy J. Colton was educated at the University of Toronto and Harvard University. Since 1974 he has taught Soviet affairs and comparative government at the University of Toronto, where he is now Professor of Political Science and Director of the Centre for Russian and East European Studies. His publications include a book on Canadian politics and *Commissars, Commanders, and Civilian Authority: The Structure of Soviet Military Politics* (Harvard University Press, 1979). He is currently writing a book on the government and politics of the city of Moscow.